AN ORAL|VISUAL HISTORY BY
THE RED HOT CHILI PEPPERS

with Brendan Mullen

I FIRST ENCOUNTERED FLEA AND ANTHONY ONE AFTERNOON IN EARLY SUMMER '83 WHEN THEY WHIRLED UNANNOUNCED INTO MY OFFICE AT CLUB LINGERIE IN HOLLYWOOD, WAVING AN AUDIO CASSETTE TAPE IN MY FACE AND INSISTING I LISTEN TO IT ON THE SPOT.

CUTE. VERY TOUCHING. I TOLD THEM THERE'S NO TAPE PLAYER HERE, AND I ONLY LISTENED TO UNSOLICITED CASSETTES AT HOME SINCE I'D AVERAGE TWENTY TO THIRTY OF THOSE DAMNED THINGS A WEEK FROM ALL OVER THE U.S. — FREQUENTLY OVERSEAS, TOO.

I HAD A LOT OF CALLS TO TAKE AND MAKE BETWEEN NOON AND SIX. I WAS THE LINGERIE'S BOOKER AND RESIDENT SATURDAY NIGHT DEEJAY AT THE TIME. BEFORE ME THESE TWO HIGH-ENERGY YOUNG PUPS WHO FINISHED EACH OTHER'S SENTENCES JUST WEREN'T HAVING IT. THEY WEREN'T GOING TILL I'D HEARD THIS TAPE. NO LEAVING IT IN AN ENVELOPE, LIKE EVERYONE ELSE. IT WAS THE ONLY COPY. WHAT FOOL-ASS CLUB PROMOTER LISTENS TO UNSOLICITED TAPES IN FRONT OF SOME SORRY BAND? WHAT IF THEY TOTALLY SUCK? YOU'RE STUCK LYING OR TELLING 'EM SO TO THEIR FACES, WHEREUPON THEY EITHER DECK YOU — OR HATE YOU FOR LIFE.

C'MON, MAN . . . TWO SONGS . . . THAT'S ALL . . . YOU GOT TIME FOR THAT . . .

WE HAD NO SECURITY SETUP LIKE THE WHISKY A GO-GO ON THE STRIP. DURING THE DAY ANY OLD BUGGER OFF THE STREET COULD GLIDE FREELY THROUGH THE CLUB'S FRONT ENTRANCE AND ON UP TO THE OFFICE: SUDDENLY ONE OF MY TWO INVADERS NOTICED JIMMY, THE JANITOR DOWNSTAIRS CLEANING UP THE BAR AREA AND THE DANCE FLOOR — A CHEERY, WHISTLE-WHILE-YOU-WORK KIND OF GUY WHO TOILED TO THE CRACKLED SOUNDS OF A BEAT-UP, PAINT-SPLATTERED FM-AM/CASSETTE PLAYER.

"WHAT ABOUT THAT TAPE PLAYER DOWN THERE?" SAID ONE OF THE DYNAMIC DUO POINTING DOWN OVER THE BALCONY.

DAMN. CORNERED. WHAT COULD I DO? FORBID JIMMY TO LEND THEM THE TAPE PLAYER AND DEMAND THEY LEAVE THE PREMISES AT ONCE? CALL THE COPS? ABSURD. TRAPPED. **THEY LOOKED BARELY OLD ENOUGH TO GET IN THE JOINT AT NIGHT — THE TWO PRANCING AROUND ME, AS IF THEY WERE ALREADY ONSTAGE MUGGING FOR A ROCK VID.**

"OKAY, OKAY," I SUBMITTED. "BUT TWO SONGS, THAT'S IT. THEN I HAFTA GET BACK ON THE PHONES HERE."

ONE OF THE PAIR SCAMPERED DOWNSTAIRS TO BORROW THE PLAYER WHILE THE OTHER TOLD ME THE TAPE WAS A FOUR-TRACK PRODUCED AND ENGINEERED IN A GARAGE THAT SAME AFTERNOON BY FEAR DRUMMER EXTRAORDINAIRE SPIT STIX, WHOM THEY SEEMED TO KNOW I HELD IN HIGH REGARD. I HAD BEEN BOOKING FEAR INTO NUMEROUS PUNK ROCK SHOWS AT VARIOUS VENUES AROUND LOS ANGELES SINCE THE LATE 1970s.

MY INITIAL TESTINESS WAS GIVING WAY TO CURIOSITY, ESPECIALLY AFTER THEY SAID THEY ALSO IDOLIZED GEORGE CLINTON AND THE METERS — HUGE PLUSES IN MY MUSICAL OMNIVERSE SINCE I'D BEEN SPINNING ALL THE USUAL SUSPECTS FROM CLINTON'S P-FUNK EMPIRE, AS WELL AS THE METERS, JAMES BROWN, OHIO PLAYERS, FATBACK, DEFUNKT, BLOOD ULMER, KONK, FELA, MATERIAL, SUGARHILL GANG, TOMMY BOY, AND A FEW 99 RECORDS TRACKS DURING MY SATURDAY NIGHT SETS FOR THE PAST TWO YEARS.

"THAT'S WHY WE'RE HERE," SAID ONE. AHA.

I WAS SKEPTICAL ABOUT SKINNY WHITE RUG RATS PLAYING FUNK (INWARDLY I WAS WINCING, "YEAH, RIGHT, SURE YOU DO, KIDDO").

BUT IT DIDN'T HURT THEIR CASE THAT THE BAND HAD ALREADY PLAYED DOWN THE STREET A WEEK OR SO AGO AT THE RHYTHM LOUNGE, A THURSDAY NIGHT PROMOTION BY SALOMON EMQUIES AND DEEJAY MATT DIKE, WHO LATER COFOUNDED DELICIOUS VINYL.

THE MUSIC — RAW, SPED-UP FUNK-ROCK — WAS IMMEDIATELY CAPTIVATING.

I ASKED FLEA AND ANTHONY IF THEY KNEW OF THIS HARD-CORE TRASH-GOES-RASTA BAND FROM WASHINGTON, D.C., NOW GETTING BACK TOGETHER AFTER A FEW YEARS LAYOFF — HOW ABOUT OPENING FOR BAD BRAINS? THEY LOOKED AT EACH OTHER AND ME LIKE I WAS CRAZY.

They danced out of the club all the way up the street, as if I'd just told them they'd won the lottery.

The Chili Peppers sounded even better live than I could ever have hoped for — scarily tight. Speed funk with cranked guitar and speed raps. Why not? **JACK IRONS AND FLEA TOGETHER FRIGHTENED THE BEJESUS OUT OF ME. HILLEL SLOVAK WAS SPINNING HIS GUITAR AROUND WHILE HE WAS PLAYING IT** like Andy Gill from Gang of Four goes Hendrix goes Catfish Collins. Anthony Kiedis was a can't-take-your-eyes-off rapping, bouncing ball of energy. Both bands crushed it that night.

I needn't have worried about covering the guarantees. A steady beat of expectation had been building on the Red Hot Chili Peppers. Flea and Anthony promised to help me drum up some support — and they turned in a huge guest list of the movers 'n' groovers. In the end everyone got paid and laid.

Much like the Rolling Stones, who began in the early 1960s as serious-minded blues missionaries, so the Chili Peppers originally took it to the stage as exuberant funk evangelicals. The Peps also came from a musical lineage that traced back to the Germs, X and, of course, Fear, in which Flea played for a short while. The Peppers fused it all into a cheeky vaudeville of punk and funk and rap.

RHCP (and Bad Brains and Fishbone, too) totally reset the bar for stop-on-a-dime, metal-punk-dub-whatever musicianship. Even in thrash — punk or metal — you now had to be able to really play. Endless touring opened the door for everything. The Chili Peppers are relentless international road dawgs, must-go-on musician-showdudes. The madcap jump-around intensity of the Peppers' live shows got them through the lean times until "Higher Ground," a Stevie Wonder cover from their *Mother's Milk* album, broke out on MTV in 1989.

The Chili Peppers anticipated and helped pave the superhighway for the eventual crossover of the new-reality hip hop emanating from the South Bronx to traditionally suburban hard rock/metal audiences — a mixed crowd of frat boys, punkers, surfers, and alterna-kids, many of whom were first led at least to the idea of "urban" music during the early 1980s. The Peppers introduced rap music to the chain-wallet, skate-bro crowd, and tapped into the national nerve of teens estranged from corporate "hair band" rock as disseminated by FM radio and MTV. They made it possible for the Beasties to get airplay when *Licensed to Ill* came out and for Faith No More to have their fifteen mins — and they helped introduce George Clinton to a generation of white kids. The Peppers were one of the first bands to be featured on *120 Minutes*, which helped to prime the pump for rock-crit darlings Nirvana and the subsequent "alternative" boom.

IN SHORT, THE RED HOT CHILI PEPPERS HELPED SHAPE THE DIRECTION FUTURE MODERN ROCK WOULD TAKE WORLDWIDE.

Although it might not have seemed like it would turn out that way. Despite grueling odds at the beginning — changing personnel, drug problems, disappointing sales, lack of widespread FM radio airplay — the Peps prevailed.

But that's their tale to tell. So jump on in.

Brendan Mullen, Los Angeles, September 2009

(Brendan Mullen passed away in October 2009; writer Kateri Butler, his longtime companion, helped finish this book.)

LOOKING THROUGH ALL THESE PICTURES TRIGGERS A MULTITUDE OF EMOTIONS FOR ME.

THE FIRST AND MOST SHALLOW ONE IS VANITY, WONDERING IF I LOOK GOOD. HAHAHAHAHA. BUT THAT PASSES PRETTY QUICKLY AND I AM STRUCK BY THE MOMENT OF THE PHOTO, THE FEELING OF THE TIME IT WAS TAKEN, AND WHERE WE WERE AT ON OUR BEAUTIFUL AND HAPPYSAD JOURNEY. IT'S PRETTY FUCKING HEAVY ACTUALLY, LIKE THINKING HOW MUCH WE HAVE CHANGED OVER THE YEARS, AND ALL THE DIFFERENT DYNAMICS OF OUR LIVES THAT SHAPED US, AND ALSO REALIZING SO CLEARLY THAT NOTHING HAS CHANGED AT ALL — WE'RE ALL STILL JUST TRYING TO GET IT ON, MAKE SOMETHING GREAT.

I AM OVERPOWERED BY THE LOVE THAT IS INSIDE ME. I ALWAYS HAVE BEEN. SOMETIMES I HAVE BEEN ABLE TO USE IT TO GREAT EFFECT, AND OTHER TIMES I HAVE BEEN TERRIFIED BY IT TO THE POINT OF TOTAL PARALYSIS. LOOKING AT THESE PHOTOGRAPHS THOUGH, THE LOVE THAT I FEEL FOR MY BANDMATES IS COMPLETE. THE TEARS THAT WELL UP IN MY EYES AS I TYPE RIGHT NOW COME FROM MY MOST PROFOUND AND HIGHEST SELF. HILLEL SLOVAK, THE GREAT ARTIST AND FRIEND, WITHOUT WHOM I NEVER WOULD HAVE PLAYED THE BASS GUITAR AND WHOSE EARTHLY PRESENCE I MISS EVERY DAY. JOHN FRUSCIANTE, THE MASTER MUSICIAN WHO I AM SO FORTUNATE TO HAVE CONNECTED WITH IN THE DEEPEST MIND-MELDING KIND OF WAY, WHO TAUGHT US HOW TO TAKE OUR BAND TO A HIGHER LEVEL. CHAD SMITH, THE LOVABLE BEHEMOTH OF THE DRUM CRUSHING WHO IS MY TRUE PARTNER IN RHYTHM,

WHO GROUNDS US FROM FLOATING OFF INTO THE SISSY-BOY ETHER. AND ANTHONY KIEDIS, MY BROTHER FROM ANOTHER MOTHER, THE DYNAMIC WHIRLWIND FROM WHOM THE ENERGY FROM THE CENTER OF THE EARTH FLOWS LIKE A FUCKING TORNADO, AND WITHOUT WHOSE PERSISTENCE AND POIGNANT LOYALTY THE RED HOT CHILI PEPPERS WOULD HAVE DISSOLVED LONG AGO. JACK IRONS, THE ORIGINAL FUNKY BEAT WE HUNG OUR HATS ON, I LOVE YOU. THESE GUYS ARE MY TRUEST AND MOST REAL FAMILY . . . OH, AND I LOVE MYSELF, TOO.

WHEN WE FIRST DECIDED THAT WE WOULD MAKE A PICTURE BOOK I IMAGINED A NICE THING FOR PEOPLE TO FLIP THROUGH, JUST A PICTURE BOOK, NOTHING SERIOUS OR IN-DEPTH LIKE A REAL BOOK OF LITERATURE. BUT LOOKING AT THIS THING, I REALIZE THESE PICTURES TELL MORE THAN WORDS EVER COULD. I CAN'T SPEAK FOR THE OTHERS, BUT — THOUGH I TRY MY BEST TO EXPRESS MYSELF — WHEN I LOOK AT MY QUOTES, I ALWAYS FEEL THAT MY WORDS FALL SHORT. I CAN NEVER REALLY GET TO THE HEART OF THE MATTER, BUT WHEN I LOOK AT THE PHOTOGRAPHS, IT IS ALL THERE, NOTHING CAN HIDE. ALL THE HONESTY, THE PRETENSE, THE COURAGE AND ONE-OF-A-KINDNESS, THE UNBRIDLED JOY, THE MELANCHOLY, AND THE SHIELDS WE PUT UP TO SHELTER OUR SCARED, VULNERABLE LITTLE SELVES, IT'S ALL THERE. WHOA.

I WANT, ON BEHALF OF MY BANDMATES, TO THANK OUR FRIEND, THE LATE GREAT BRENDAN MULLEN, WHOSE SPIRIT PERMEATES EVERY BIT OF PULP AND INK THAT MAKE THIS BOOK. WE LOVE YOU, BRENDAN.

—FLEA

CONTENTS

CHILI PEPPERS

003

ME AND MY FRIENDS

A WHEN WE BEGAN A HUGE PART OF WHO WE WERE WAS IN THE SPIRIT OF JEST.

F I NEVER CONSIDERED A LONG CAREER — ANTHONY WAS THE ONE WITH CAREER GOALS. **I MIGHT HAVE HAD SOME CRAZY ROCK STAR FANTASY OF BEING IN A LIMOUSINE, BUT I NEVER IMAGINED DOING ANYTHING ELSE BUT THIS AND MAKING AN OKAY LIVING.**

J I CAME INTO THE RED HOT CHILI PEPPERS AS A GREENHORN TEENAGER NOT CLEAR AS TO WHAT I HAD INSIDE OF ME. ANTHONY, FLEA, CHAD, [PRODUCER] RICK [RUBIN], [ENGINEER] BRENDAN [O'BRIEN] AND THE SPIRIT OF HILLEL SLOVAK HELPED ME FIND MY VOICE AS AN ARTIST AND GUITAR PLAYER. THEY ENABLED ME TO MAKE MUSIC THAT REACHED A MUCH LARGER AMOUNT OF PEOPLE THAN I EVER IMAGINED AND I REALLY VALUE THEIR PLACE IN MY LIFE.

C IN THIS DAY AND AGE THE CHILI PEPPERS WOULD HAVE GOTTEN DROPPED AFTER THE FIRST RECORD. THERE'S NO TIME FOR DEVELOPMENT ON A LABEL ANYMORE. IT'S FUCKING SAD.

ENTERTAINMENT

F I ALWAYS WANTED TO BE THE BEST I COULD AT WHAT I WAS DOING. BUT THEN, ANYTIME THERE WAS AN OPPORTUNITY TO BE IN FRONT OF A CAMERA I WAS RIGHT THERE AND TURNING IT ON! LIKE BAM. DOING WHATEVER WE COULD WITH FACES OR CRACKING JOKES, ME AND ANTHONY. WE ARE DEFINITELY ENTERTAINERS. I WANTED TO BE A PAID ENTERTAINER LIKE SAMMY DAVIS. **I'VE ALWAYS BEEN A SHOWMAN.** IT IS WANTING VALIDATION BUT ALSO TO BE GREAT AT IT. I REMEMBER SEEING ROCK BANDS BEFORE I WAS EVER IN ONE — THE WHOLE THING IS CRAZY. YOU HAVE TO GO CRAZY.

LA WEEKLY

SONS ★ OF ★ THE ★ CITY

THE RED HOT CHILI PEPPERS' SONGS OF SALVATION

BY JOHN ALB...

reverb   MUSIC WINTER 2002   PETER GABRIEL ★ FATSO JETSON ★

WEST COAST HOUSE ★ PATRICK PARK

EMIT REMMUS

 I STARTED DRUMMING WHEN I WAS SEVEN. I WAS REALLY LUCKY TO DO WHAT I LOVE AT SUCH AN EARLY AGE. DON'T KNOW WHY I GRAVITATED TOWARD DRUMS — MY BROTHER PLAYED GUITAR, MY SISTER PIANO, MUSIC WAS ALWAYS AROUND. BUT I NEVER HAD THAT, "OH, I WANT TO PLAY BECAUSE OF THIS GUY OR THAT BAND OR WHATEVER." **PARENTS GENERALLY DON'T FORCE THEIR KIDS TO PLAY DRUMS OR LOUD INSTRUMENTS, LIKE THEY WOULD PIANO OR FLUTE LESSONS. I JUST GRAVITATED TOWARD HITTING THINGS.** MY FIRST DRUMS WERE BASKIN-ROBBINS ICE CREAM TUBS UPTURNED. THERE WAS A KID'S TOY AT THE TIME CALLED LINCOLN LOGS, WOODEN LOGS LIKE FROM A LOG CABIN — I USED THOSE FOR STICKS. BETTER THAN NOTHING! THEN I GOT THIS DIMESTORE KIT THAT QUICKLY GOT TOTALLY TRASHED. THE ICE CREAM TUBS ACTUALLY HELD UP BETTER THAN THIS SHITTY LITTLE CHEAPO KIT. MY PARENTS WERE LIKE, "OKAY, HE LIKES THIS AND IS STICKING WITH IT." I WASN'T PUSHED INTO IT. MY BROTHER, TWO YEARS OLDER, WAS VERY INFLUENTIAL. I LOOKED UP TO HIM. WHEN I WAS ABOUT SEVEN OR EIGHT, AROUND '68 OR '69, HE WAS REALLY INTO ENGLISH HARD ROCK. LUCKILY, BOTH MY PARENTS WERE VERY SUPPORTIVE WITH THE MUSIC. WE HAD A BASEMENT WHERE I PLAYED MY DRUMS LOUD. THEY PREFERRED IT WHEN THEY WERE OUT OF THE HOUSE. MY MOM WOULD BE LIKE, "GO, GO, I'M GOING OUT SHOPPING NOW — GOOD TIME FOR YOU TO PRACTICE."

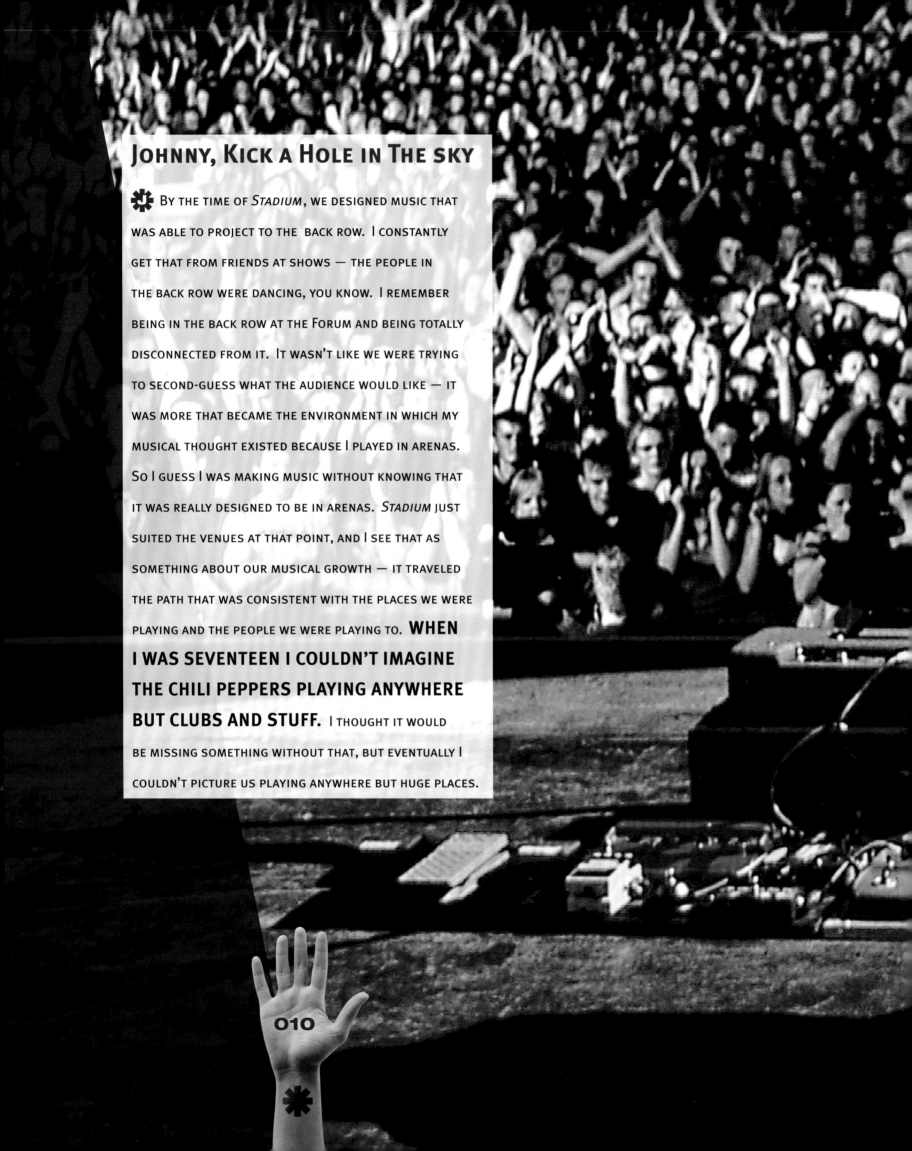

Johnny, Kick a Hole in The sky

❋ By the time of *Stadium*, we designed music that was able to project to the back row. I constantly get that from friends at shows — the people in the back row were dancing, you know. I remember being in the back row at the Forum and being totally disconnected from it. It wasn't like we were trying to second-guess what the audience would like — it was more that became the environment in which my musical thought existed because I played in arenas. So I guess I was making music without knowing that it was really designed to be in arenas. *Stadium* just suited the venues at that point, and I see that as something about our musical growth — it traveled the path that was consistent with the places we were playing and the people we were playing to. **When I was seventeen I couldn't imagine the Chili Peppers playing anywhere but clubs and stuff.** I thought it would be missing something without that, but eventually I couldn't picture us playing anywhere but huge places.

010

Don't Forget Me

✱ Once I left the nest with my dad, we went back and forth between being close and not-so-close. Then when I was able to make a really good living in music, **I WENT BACK AND STARTED SHARING THE REWARDS OF OUR GOOD FORTUNE WITH FAMILY, BUT SPECIFICALLY WITH MY FATHER.** Because I had watched him from — as soon as I moved in, there was always a bit of a financial dilemma. There were times when he had a pocket full of $100 bills but a month later there would be nothing. As smart as my father was — and he was creative more so than myself — he never had the knack for making a living. When he became an actor even — he just wasn't a good businessman. He was creative and had a great outlook on life, but didn't have the golden thumb. So when I just kind of stumbled into money being in a band, it never looked like it would lead to financial success — we did have financial success despite ourselves — I was able to go back and share that with my dad.

013

MUSICAL CHAIRS

THE MAKING OF

015

THE *BAND

Out in L.A.

✳ We started the Red Hot Chili Peppers after I'd reconciled with Hillel and he forgave me for quitting What is This?

Salomon Emquies (deejay and promoter): Flea was playing with my friend Gary Allen and he said, **"CAN I DO ONE SONG WITH ANTHONY BEFORE GARY STARTS HIS SET? LIKE A FUNKY RAP KIND OF THING?"** "Sure," I said.

Gary Allen: I was still the singer in Neighbors' Voices – this exotic bunch of way-out French Moroccan dope fiends from Paris who played great music — when I got a call from Michael Balzary, who wasn't Flea yet. He wanted us and his band to play together. When I left Neighbors' Voices in late '82 I formed my own band. It was Michael, Jack, and Hillel. Everybody except for Anthony, who introduced the idea of opening up for me, like he did with What is This? It was a great idea. I loved it. Anthony was crashing with Flea at Hillel's, off Western and Hollywood.

✳ We did our first show [as Tony Flow and the Miraculously Majestic Masters of Mayhem] in the middle of shooting Suburbia, and everyone came — Maggie Ehrig, Christina Beck, Chris Pedersen, all my friends from the cast and crew — like a big to-do. Even if it wasn't something they liked, they still came out and it meant a lot to me to have their approval.

Gary: [On the night of the Rhythm Lounge show] Anthony did his one-song intro first and then I played. I was wearing a wedding dress and Anthony forced me to come in and sit in the front row to watch him! The Rhythm Lounge, near Larchmont Village in Los Angeles, was packed on Thursday nights.

✳ We'd hang out at the Rhythm Lounge every Thursday. Get fucked-up and hit on chicks. Matt Dike was deejay there — he played funk and hip-hop and he dug '70s stoner rock party music, too.

✳ Rhythm Lounge was the trendy, cool haps, count on it.

Gary: Gorgeous young Euro thangs diggin' la musique Afrique, the sounds of my peoples, as played by Matt Dike. It was *the* It Place at that time. Very fashion-influenced, I thought, as much as it was about the music.

Jack Irons (original RHCP drummer): "Out in L.A." was the first piece — you couldn't really call it a song. It was just a guitar riff that Hillel and I had jammed on for hours for fun, but it wasn't a real song — it was never intended to be anything. We just played the riff and Anthony did one of his wacky speed raps over it.

✳ I had a bass line and had Hillel do guitar to it, and then we went to the show and played and people loved it. We had a whole choreographed dance thing. We did our dance and then played "Out In L.A." and it was pretty fucking explosive. We did it and it was just BAM! From the first note. A five-minute set. Anthony came with a boom box and the dance, and then the song — it was like two minutes. **SOMETIMES BANDS JUST SORT OF CREEP INTO IT AND FIND THEIR WAY, AND BAM — FOR US IT WAS FROM THE GET-GO.**

Salomon: It went over really well! So well, that when they were done I said to come back in a couple of weeks and maybe do three or four songs. ➤

The RHYTHM LOUNGE

the RED HOT CHILI PEPPER

next week 3/31 at midnight

017

MATT DIKE (DEEJAY AND PROMOTER): THEY COULDN'T DECIDE BETWEEN THE [NAMES] THE FLOW AND RED HOT CHILI PEPPERS. I TOLD 'EM, "DUDE, THE FLOW IS LAME . . . TONY FLOW? NO WAY! DUDE, RED HOT CHILI PEPPERS ROCKS SO MUCH MORE."

KEITH "TREE" BARRY (FRIEND AND MUSICIAN): NO MATTER WHAT THEY'LL TELL YOU, NO MATTER HOW MY GOOD FRIENDS RE-SPIN IT, I WILL ALWAYS TAKE CREDIT FOR THE NAME — I'M PRETTY DARN SURE OF THAT SHORT OF INVENTING A TIME MACHINE! THEY WERE ALWAYS REAL PROPONENTS OF GETTING TOGETHER AND REHEARSING. THEY DIDN'T GO INTO ANY OF THESE THINGS POORLY PREPARED. THEY WERE WELL PREPARED — CHILI PEPPERS MUSICALLY AND CONCEPTUALLY TIGHT, ALWAYS A CLEAR CONCEPT.

GARY: THEY WOULD REHEARSE EVERY DAY IN THE APARTMENT. ANTHONY STARTED RAPPING WHILE THEY CAME UP WITH SOME REALLY FUNKY THINGS. THEY'D TAKEN ON THESE WEIRD NAMES. KEITH BARRY WAS TREE, MICHAEL BECAME FLEA, HILLEL WAS SLIM AND ANTHONY WAS SWAN. **MICHAEL WAS ALL, "I'M GOING TO BE FLEA" AND I SAID, "WHY YOU WANNA CALL YOURSELF SOMETHING THAT GETS UNDER THE SKIN AND SUCKS BLOOD?!"**

HILLEL GOT NICKNAMED PICK HANDLE SLIM — WHICH HE LIKED — BY PINETOP PERKINS WHEN WE OPENED UP FOR HIM AT OUR FIRST SHOW IN LONDON AT DINGWALLS. HE HAD ALL SORTS OF NICKNAMES. WE USED TO CALL HIM THE ISRAELI COWBOY — HE WAS SO FUNNY. A REAL ARTIST, ROMANTIC AND SENSITIVE. A GREAT PAINTER.

SALOMON: AFTER ABOUT A MONTH OR SO THEY WERE BACK AS THE RED HOT CHILI PEPPERS. THEY WALK INTO THE CLUB WITH A BIG BOOM BOX AND THEY GOT ONSTAGE AND STUFF — IT WAS WILD. IT FILLED THIS VOID. THIS WHITE BOY FUNK THING. IT JUST WORKED AND IT WAS PERFECT TIMING. EVERYONE PRESENT LOVED IT.

No Chump Love Sucker

✳ HILLEL SLOVAK WAS A HARD ROCK MUSICIAN THROUGH AND THROUGH, WHOSE PRIME MUSICAL INFLUENCES WERE HENDRIX, SANTANA, ZEPPELIN, '60S AND '70S HARD ROCK. **THIS AMAZINGLY TALENTED ISRAELI KID OPENED UP AVENUES OF EXPRESSION FOR ME I DIDN'T KNOW I HAD.** NOT ONLY THAT, HE WAS A BEACON, A TOUCHSTONE OF SANITY. HILLEL WAS A TRUE ARTIST IN MORE THAN ONE MEDIUM. UP UNTIL MEETING HIM I LOOKED DOWN ON BASIC ROCK MUSIC. I WAS RAISED IN A JAZZ HOUSEHOLD.

MY STEPFATHER AND HIS CIRCLE HAD INGRAINED IN ME THAT ROCK WAS FOR DUMBOS WHO TOOK WHAT MUSIC WAS FORCED DOWN THEIR THROATS BY CORPORATIONS AND DIDN'T THINK FOR THEMSELVES. I THOUGHT ROCK MUSIC WAS ALL ABOUT HAIRCUTS AND FASHION AND NOTHING TO DO WITH TRUE EXPRESSION. I STILL LOVE JAZZ WHEN IT'S DONE RIGHT, BUT IT WAS HILLEL WHO FIRST GOT ME INTO HARD ROCKIN'. NOT ONLY WAS IT REAL FUN TO PLAY, PLAYING IT GOT YOU LAID — EASY! HE'S LIKE, "OUR BAND JUST ISN'T HAPPY WITH OUR BASS PLAYER — WOULD YOU LIKE TO PLAY BASS WITH US?" TWO WEEKS LATER I'M UP ONSTAGE WITH ANTHYM, HILLEL'S BAND, WITH JACK IRONS ON DRUMS AND ALAIN JOHANNES SINGING LEAD, PLAYING GUITAR. I ALSO BECAME THE BAND'S BOOKING AGENT. THE CARD I GAVE EVERYONE SAID "MIKE B.: BOOKING INFO." I WORKED HARD TO GET GIGS, ANY GIG, NO MATTER HOW SMALL, ANYWHERE THEY'D TAKE US. WE'D DO BATTLE OF THE BANDS OR PLAY THE ICE HOUSE IN PASADENA, LIKE FOURTH BAND ON A TUESDAY NIGHT WHERE WE HAD TO WAIT OUTSIDE BECAUSE WE'RE TOO YOUNG TO GO IN. OR WE'D PLAY SOME MEXICAN RESTAURANT DOWNTOWN. WE WANTED TO BE MORE ARTY. AND SO ANTHYM EVENTUALLY BECAME WHAT IS THIS?

021

CLUB Lingerie

FULL BAR • MUST BE 21 W/ VALID I.D. • LARGE DA
6507 SUNSET BL. HOLLYWOOD 46

Saturday, June 2
Kick Summer Off With a Bang!

RED HOT CHILI PEPPERS

FEAR

Circle Jerks

022

No More Nothing

⬡ One night I went to the Lingerie blazing on acid and saw Fear play undercover, billed as the North Van Nuys Gay Men's String Quartet. It was so great! Fear blew my mind. They were all really good players playing their butts off. Awesomely tight musicians. Philo [Cramer, Fear's guitarist] was really cool and knowledgeable. And then a few days later I look in the newspaper — Fear is auditioning bass players. I was like, "Oh, wow! Coming down!" The audition went good and I was in right away.

⬡ Lee Ving, the leader and front guy and Derf Scratch, the bass player, had been tight with John Belushi who'd just recently OD'd at the Chateau Marmont from speedballing. Belushi had sought out and befriended Lee and Derf, tried real hard to get Fear on *SNL*. It's well documented, I'm sure, in the annals of East Coast punk rock and *SNL* history about the set getting trashed by rabid punk rockers in the studio audience. Fear's shtick was out-punking the punks by being comic — it was a send-up by older chops dudes. Fear was no kiddie punk rock band — it was a cartoon of what some heavyweight musician dudes thought the most ridiculous punk rock band could be.

⬡ I quit What is This? to join Fear, and they were pretty angry at me.

⬡ Flea was really on a different track than the rest of that band. I remember seeing a show and he was finding his voice in a very cool way. When he first learned bass guitar it was just Hillel teaching him some Led Zeppelin and whatever songs — AC/DC. He was just mimicking. His background was as a trumpet player. He started taking these more creative-sounding solos. He had this one wonderful solo — he seemed so out of context and was just on his own trip. The most exciting part of the show was the bass solo, and he was all, "Yeah, yeah, I just learned how to do that and want to learn more!" Jack and Hillel grew up idolizing the classic rock bands of the '70s. They didn't understand it was their job to take it to a new place. Flea clearly understood, **"IT'S MY JOB TO MAKE MUSIC FOR PEOPLE OF THIS GENERATION." I WAS SO PROUD OF HIM FOR THAT, AS A MUSICIAN, AND OF COURSE IT CAME TO A CRASHING HEAD WHEN HE GOT AN AUDITION FOR FEAR.** He was confiding to friends, "I dunno what the fuck to do. Do I leave my blood brothers?"

⬡ Everyone said, "You gotta follow your heart . . . " ➤

➤ ✱ FEAR'S MUSICIAN CHOPS BLEW US ALL AWAY. UNFORTUNATELY, THEIR ONSTAGE PATTER WASN'T VERY PC FOR MOST PEOPLE, BUT WE JUST DIDN'T TAKE ANY OF THEIR CROWD-BAITING SHIT SO SERIOUSLY. IT WAS FUN. THEY TRIED TO UPSET EVERYONE IN THE ROOM. BAR OWNERS LOVED THEM BECAUSE THEIR AUDIENCE WOULD DRINK THE BAR DRY, BUT WAITRESSES AND BARTENDERS HATED THEM BECAUSE THEIR CROWD WAS PUNK LOWLIFES LIKE US, ALWAYS TOO BROKE OR TOO CHEAP TO TIP!

✱ **WHEN I FIRST SAW LEE VING I JUST THOUGHT HE WAS A SUPERSTAR — HE WAS THE GREATEST.** SO ALIVE AND TENSE AND THE SONGS WERE SO GOOD AND HE SANG SO GOOD. I THOUGHT IT WAS JUST THIS PERFECT, TIGHT, MUSCULAR PUNK, PACKAGED SO VICIOUSLY.

✱ WE THOUGHT LEE VING WAS THIS WONDERFULLY ENTERTAINING HELLION KIND OF GUY, THE BADASS OUTLAW BIKER IMAGE AND ALL, LIKE SOME TOUGH OLD BLUES SINGER DUDE IN THIS MAXED-OUT PSYCHO PUNK BAND WITH A KILLER GUITAR PLAYER AND DRUMMER WHO CRUSHED IT LIVE! WHEN FLEA REPLACED DERF AS FEAR'S BASS PLAYER IT CREATED A PROFOUND SHIFT IN OUR LITTLE SCENE. WE WERE MOVIN' ON UP FROM GAWKERS IN THE PIT TO WHERE ONE OF OUR VERY OWN WAS NOW UP THERE IN ONE OF THE GREATEST L.A. BANDS EVER TO COME OUT OF THAT TIME.

✱ A FEW WEEKS AFTER I FIRST GOT IN FEAR I'M OVER AT LEE VING'S HOUSE FOR A SPAGHETTI DINNER, OR LIKE PIZZA OR SOMETHING ON A SUNDAY, AND PENELOPE SPHEERIS IS THERE. LEE INTRODUCED ME AS HIS NEW BASS PLAYER, SHE'S LIKE, "OH WHOA, THERE'S THIS MOVIE I'M MAKING" AND I SOON GOT IN THAT, TOO.

PETE WEISS (FRIEND AND MUSICIAN): JON HUCK, WHO BECAME THE BASS PLAYER IN THELONIOUS MONSTER, GOT ME THE BOOM GUY GIG ON *SUBURBIA*. FLEA PLAYS RAZZLE. HIS GIMMICK IS MAKING FUNNY FACES, BEING SPONTANEOUS — HE HAD A PET RAT WHICH HE PUTS IN HIS MOUTH. HE'S LIKE THE MAIN SIDEKICK. LOTS OF MUGGING AND CUTAWAYS TO HIM MAKING FACES AFTER A LOT OF DIALOGUE. FLEA GOT PLENTY OF PRACTICE IN FOR A MILLION PHOTO SHOOTS IN THE FUTURE OF FACIAL MUGGINGS WITH THE RED HOT CHILI PEPPERS. PENELOPE JUST TAPPED INTO SOME OF FLEA'S NATURAL CHARACTERISTICS. DURING THE FILMING, THEY WERE SHOOTING ONE OF THE PUNK GIGS OVER AT A THEATER ON SUNSET. FLEA HAD NEVER DONE A STAGE DIVE BEFORE. I WAS LIKE, "LISTEN MAN, IF YOU ARE EVER GOING TO DO A STAGE DIVE, DO IT ON CAMERA, BECAUSE THEN YOU WILL NEVER HAVE TO DO IT AGAIN." HE'S DONE A MILLION SINCE, I'M SURE, BUT YEAH, HE WAS ALL SCARED, AND, LIKE, "I DUNNO-O-O-O ABOUT THIS."

✱ *SUBURBIA* WAS A GREAT EXPERIENCE. I DIDN'T KNOW ANYONE IN THE PUNK ROCK SCENE. I ALSO MET NEW PEOPLE THAT WAY — PETE WEISS, MAGGIE EHRIG, CHRISTINA BECK, ANDRE PEG LEG, CHRIS PEDERSEN FROM THE PATRIOTS, AND A BUNCH OF OTHER PUNK KIDS THAT YOU SEE IN THE MOVIE. THE MOVIE'S PLOT, SUCH AS IT WAS, WAS ABOUT AN OLD ABANDONED HOUSE IN SUBURBAN LOS ANGELES, LIKE DOWNEY — KINDA A WASTELAND, FLAT, BORING, VAPID, VACUUM OF HUMANITY IN CALIFORNIA. KIDS ARE LIVING IN THIS REPO'D HOUSE. CARRYING ON IN A PUNK ROCK KIDS WAY. **I WAS A REALLY FUCKED-UP KID MYSELF, BUT I WAS MAKING SOME MONEY, $100 A DAY — A FORTUNE FOR THE TIME.**

025

Lovin' and Touchin'

✳ I met a guy at the Lingerie from Atlanta. This tall rocker-looking bass player dude came up asking who manages me. I said, "You are looking at him." He said, "Well, you need a professional," and I was like, "Who?" He said this friend of mine, go see him, Lindy Goetz on Ventura Boulevard. Next day we show up, knock on the door, "We're The Red Hot Chili Peppers. We hear you're a manager. Wanna manage us?" He'd seen us at the Kit Kat and I think he'd been there at Lingerie. We played him a tape and he was so good-natured, cheerful, and funny. What's not to love? He had records of the Ohio Players up on his wall — we loved those guys. "If you are in any way affiliated with them, that's good enough for us." And, he's like "Well, I like your music and you seem cool. What do you wanna do here?" We said, "Well, you buy us lunch and you can be our manager." His first stroke of genius was buying us lunch. That's how he got his foot in the door and we were forever grateful. He continued to buy us lunch and that was very meaningful for us at that point because we were hungry.

Lindy Goetz (manager): I was a musician, a drummer, prior to working for record companies where I was a promotions director at MCA and Mercury Records working for classic rock and pop acts like the Who, Neil Diamond, Sonny and Cher, Lynyrd Skynrd. I had a production company before that. I was never officially the Ohio Players' manager. I was working at the label they were on. They were in-between — a short period where I tried to help move them to a different label because I personally liked their music so much.

✳ **I'M NOT SURE IF LINDY WAS REALLY A MASTERFUL BUSINESS FELLOW — MORE A FATHER FIGURE AND A LOVING, FUNNY GUY. SOMEHOW HE WAS ABLE TO PUT HIMSELF AT OUR LEVEL — TO EXIST FREELY AND HAPPILY AMONGST OUR CHAOS.** He loved us and we loved him. He had record company experience working for Mercury during the heyday of the payola thing. He was involved in promotion. Lindy was good friends with Davy Jones. His brother Stuart was a child actor who'd starred in *Flipper*

AND *OLIVER* ON BROADWAY WITH DAVY, AND SO THEY BECAME LIKE FAMILY MEMBERS, DAVY JONES AND THE GOETZ BROTHERS. LINDY ACTUALLY WENT ON TOUR WITH THE MONKEES — HE WAS A DRUMMER. HE MAY HAVE DONE SOME DRUMMING WITH THEM. MOST VALUABLE TO US IN 1983 — HE KNEW THE RECORD COMPANY DESIGN.

LINDY: IT ALL HAPPENED PRETTY QUICK DURING MOST OF '83. I HAD NEVER MANAGED ANYONE BEFORE. IT WAS ALL NEW TO ME. THE BAND WAS SO FAR TO THE LEFT AT THE TIME THAT THE MOST IMPORTANT THING WAS TO GET A DEAL — GET THEM OUT THERE TOURING.

BOB FORREST (FRIEND AND MUSICIAN): ALREADY THEY'RE THE MOST TALKED-ABOUT BAND ON THE L.A. CLUB SCENE. IT JUST EXPLODED REALLY FAST — ORGANICALLY, NATURALLY — THE CHARGE THRIVED ON MOMENTARY CHAOS. IT WAS SO DIFFERENT A MUSIC THAN WHAT WAS BEING PLAYED. TIMING WAS IMPECCABLE. FUNK WAS COMING IN, WAS EXTREMELY TRENDY WITH YOUNG WHITE CLUB GOERS OF OUR AGE GROUP, BUT NOBODY DID IT WITH PUNK ROCK ENERGY LIKE THE CHILI PEPPERS DID. FLEA WAS LIKE, "MAN, I WANNA MAKE BASS THE LEAD INSTRUMENT IN THIS FUCKIN' BAND."

LINDY: WE DID WELL IN CLUBS — THE QUESTION EVERY NIGHT WAS, DID WE HIT PERCENTAGE? THEIR NEW BOOKING AGENT, TRIP BROWN, WAS GREAT. I LEARNED HOW TO DO CLOSE-OUTS AND EVERYTHING ELSE FROM HIM. FROM THE GET-GO WE WERE ATTRACTING A CROWD. WE WERE GETTING OFFERS FOR $50 TO $100 GUARANTEE A NIGHT PLUS PERCENTAGE! IF HE ASKED FOR $300 THEY'D GET JITTERY AND HOLD THE PERCENTAGE. WE LEARNED QUICKLY TO GO IN LOW, PROMOTE IT AS STRONG AS WE COULD OURSELVES, AND COLLECT A BIGGER BACKEND PERCENTAGE. WE WERE MAKING MONEY FROM JUMP STREET — NOT A FORTUNE, BUT WE WERE LIVING. EVERYBODY HAD THEIR OWN APARTMENT. NO DAY JOBS.

LINDY BECAME A TRUE FRIEND AND STUCK WITH ME THROUGH THE DARKEST, UGLIEST AND LOWLIEST HOURS AND NEVER SHOWED ME ANYTHING BUT LOVE. EVEN WHEN IT LOOKED LIKE I WAS PURE LIABILITY — NO ASSET, NO MONEY GENERATION, NO FUN — JUST A GUY SLEEPING IN HIS OFFICE, HIS HOME OFFICE IN A TWO-BEDROOM APARTMENT IN STUDIO CITY NEAR THE *BRADY BUNCH* HOUSE. I SLEPT IN HIS OFFICE FOR AT LEAST A MONTH ON THE FLOOR. **I WAS A DIRTY, DISHEVELED GUY WHO WOULD STEAL THE CHANGE OUT OF HIS DRAWER AND BORROW HIS CAR TO GO DOWNTOWN IN THE MIDDLE OF THE NIGHT. HE PUT UP WITH ALL OF THAT.** HE ALSO DROVE THE VAN ON OUR VERY FIRST TOUR EVER. HE WAS IN THE TRENCHES FOR YEARS. I'M SO GLAD HE DIDN'T LEAVE TOO EARLY, THAT HE STUCK AROUND AT LEAST THROUGH THE *BLOOD SUGAR* ERA. I ALWAYS FELT A LITTLE WEIRD HE LEFT RIGHT BEFORE OUR POWERFUL RUN OF '99 THROUGH NOW — SO MUCH OF THE FOOTWORK IN THE EARLY YEARS HE DID.

BUCKLE DOWN

🅐 FEAR WERE OLDER, MORE ACCOMPLISHED MUSICIANS HOPING TO KEEP MAKING A LIVING FROM IT. ONCE THE RED HOT CHILI PEPPERS STARTED GETTING SOME CLUB DATES, LEE VING PUT PRESSURE ON FLEA, LIKE, "HELLO, SO, DUDE, YOU'RE IN ANOTHER BAND NOW? WHAT'S IT GONNA BE?"

🅕 I HAD FALLEN IN LOVE WITH THE RED HOT CHILI PEPPERS. I WAS PLAYING WITH MY BROTHERS AND WE WERE A FAMILY. FEAR WAS BEGINNING TO GO IN A HEAVY-METAL DIRECTION, WHICH I THOUGHT WAS BORING. I WAS SITTING BY THE TELEPHONE TRYING TO BUILD UP THE NERVE TO CALL LEE AND QUIT FEAR. **I WAS KIND OF INTIMIDATED BY LEE. AT THAT EXACT MOMENT THE PHONE RANG AND IT WAS LEE TELLING ME I WAS FIRED FROM FEAR.**

LINDY GOETZ (MANAGER): WHEN I TOLD THEM, "WE JUST GOT OFFERED A RECORD DEAL WITH EMI/ENIGMA," HILLEL AND JACK TOLD ME THEY COULDN'T DO IT, BECAUSE THEY WERE IN ANOTHER BAND. I'M LIKE, "WHAT ARE YOU TALKING ABOUT? WHAT OTHER FUCKING BAND? WHOA . . . NOW YOU'RE TELLING ME THIS?

DAMN!" THEY SAID THEY HAD A DEAL WITH MCA FOR WHAT IS THIS? AND THEY COULDN'T DO IT. NOT GOOD. THINGS WERE SHAKY ENOUGH AS IT WAS GETTING THE DEAL WE GOT, SO I TOLD THE GUYS NOT TO SAY ANYTHING TO ANYBODY.

🅐 WE JUST QUIETLY GOT CLIFF MARTINEZ AND JACK SHERMAN TO REPLACE IRONS AND HILLEL, AND PROCEEDED FORWARD AS IF EVERYTHING WAS PEACHES 'N' CREAM. SO LONG AS FLEA AND I WERE CONSTANTLY JUMPING UP AND DOWN IN THEIR FACES LIKE BOUNCING BEANS, THAT WAS MORE THAN ENOUGH RED HOT CHILI PEPPER FOR THEM TO BEAR.

🅕 WHAT IS THIS? WAS HILLEL AND JACK'S BAND, AND THEY TOOK THAT WAY MORE SERIOUSLY THAN THE CHILI PEPPERS. IT

WAS DEFINITELY LIKE A SIDE, JOKE, FUN THING TO DO OUTSIDE OF REGULAR BANDS. AS SOON AS THEY GOT A RECORD DEAL THEY QUIT THE CHILI PEPPERS, AND WE HAD TO GET TWO OTHER GUYS.

CLIFF MARTINEZ (RHCP DRUMMER 1983–86): I PLAYED DRUMS WITH THE CHILI PEPPERS FROM 1983 TO 1986. GETTING IN THE BAND WAS EASY. FLEA HAD ALREADY SEEN ME PLAY IN THE WEIRDOS AND LYDIA LUNCH'S 13-13. HE'D SEEN ME AT THE KIT KAT WITH ROID ROGERS. I THINK I'D EVEN PLAYED WITH HIM ONCE OR TWICE IN TWO BALLS AND A BAT, AND SO I JUST SAID, "YEAH, COURSE I WOULD, I'D LOVE TO." I'D SEEN THE CHILI PEPPERS SEVERAL TIMES AND KNEW WHAT WAS EXPECTED. FLEA OFFERED ME THE SPOT WITH NO AUDITION. ANTHONY ONLY ASKED ME ONE THING, "SO CLIFF, HOW OLD ARE YOU?" I SAID, "TWENTY-NINE," AND HE SAID, "OH, WOW, TWENTY-NINE! YOU EVER HAVE A DOCTOR LAY A HEAVY TRIP ON YOU?" I

SAID, "NO, I DON'T HAVE ANY HEALTH PROBLEMS AT THE RIPE OLD AGE OF TWENTY-NINE!" THAT WAS IT. THINGS WERE KIND OF BORING ON THE LOCAL CLUB SCENE — THE CHILI PEPPERS WERE ONE OF THE FEW INTERESTING THINGS GOING ON.

LINDY: CLIFF WAS OLDER, A MUCH MORE EXPERIENCED MUSICIAN, BUT A FRIEND, WHO JUST SEEMED TO FIT. BUT JACK WAS JACK. HE WAS GREAT, BUT THERE WAS A LOVE/HATE RELATIONSHIP FROM DAY ONE. THEY ONLY HAD FIVE OR SIX SONGS, SO JACK WAS DEFINITELY INVOLVED

IN COMPLETING THE REST OF THE FIRST ALBUM. JACK WAS AN AMAZING GUITAR PLAYER, ONE OF THOSE WHO WENT TO THAT SCHOOL [MUSICIANS INSTITUTE] IN HOLLYWOOD. HOWEVER, THERE WAS NOTHING ABOUT HIM WHATSOEVER THAT FIT WITH BEING A CHILI PEPPER. EVEN THOUGH THEY BROUGHT HIM IN, THEY NEVER REALLY WELCOMED HIM INTO THE BAND. THEY HAD TO ACT QUICK BEFORE EMI FOUND OUT ABOUT THE HUSH-HUSH PERSONNEL SWITCH, SOMETHING I WAS BANKING ON THEM NOT REALLY GIVING A SHIT ABOUT EVEN IF THEY DID KNOW. I JUST DIDN'T WANT THEM GETTING WIND OF ANY INSTABILITY OR SHAKINESS.

✳ WE HIRED JACK SHERMAN BECAUSE HE WAS A REALLY GOOD PLAYER AND HE KNEW ABOUT FUNK MUSIC — WAY MORE THAN WE DID. I DIDN'T KNOW VERY MUCH ABOUT THAT STUFF YET, MAYBE "TEAR THE ROOF OFF" AND "ONE NATION" BUT I DIDN'T KNOW "COSMIC SLOP," "STANDING ON THE VERGE." JACK TURNED ME ON TO A MUCH WIDER SCOPE OF GEORGE CLINTON AND HIS MUSIC. AND HE HAD SOME REALLY GOOD FUNKY RHYTHMS HIMSELF. FOR SURE JACK'S INFLUENCE SEEDED THE IDEA OF HOOKING UP WITH GEORGE CLINTON TO PRODUCE.

BUT JACK SHERMAN JUST WASN'T QUITE RIGHT FOR US. WE WERE ALWAYS MAKING FUN OF HIM. HE WAS FUNNY AND QUIRKY AND A REAL SMART GUY. WE MUST HAVE DRIVEN HIM CRAZY. **HE WAS SO INTO OVER-CONTROL AND KEEPING THINGS IN PROPER PARAMETERS — AND WE'RE JUST CRAZED LOONS OUT OF OUR MINDS, FUCKING SHOOTING COKE INTO OUR EYEBALLS, TAKING ACID AND SHIT.** BLOWING IT EVERY WHICH WAY WE TURNED. IT MUST HAVE BEEN SO HARD FOR HIM BECAUSE HE NEVER KNEW WHAT WE WERE GONNA DO NEXT.

029

GRAND PAPPY DU PLENTY

✱ WHEN I WAS THIRTEEN OR FOURTEEN I HAD A GUITAR
TEACHER WHO ALSO PLAYED BASS, WHO WAS AUDITIONING FOR
THE CHILI PEPPERS AROUND THE TIME OF JACK SHERMAN. I HEARD
ABOUT THEM FIRST FROM HIM. HE SAID THERE WAS THIS BAND HE WAS WAITING TO
FIND OUT IF HE WAS IN. FOR SOME REASON I'D ASSUMED HE WAS TRYING OUT FOR
BASS. SOON AFTER THAT I SAW THE "TRUE MEN DON'T KILL COYOTES" VIDEO ON
MTV. MY FIRST IMPRESSION OF FLEA WAS LIKE, **"DOESN'T MAKE ANY
SENSE THEY COULD DO THIS BAND WITHOUT THIS GUY!"**
FROM THE FIRST SECOND OF SEEING THEM IT WAS OBVIOUS FLEA WAS NOT A
REPLACEABLE MEMBER.

I QUICKLY FOUND OUT MY GUY WAS UP FOR THE GUITAR SPOT.

030

The Red Hot Chili Peppers

"you are invited to celebrate the new record of (the Hot Chili Peppers) (One Hot Minute)

R.S.V.P. (818)

→ on Map →

WANTS TO GET FUNKED UP

In '82 I joined a new group. This guy owned a big venue, Pine Knob Music. He had this crazy idea of putting together a supergroup of the best Detroit musicians. It was ridiculous, but great for me. I got to play with people much better than me. What good luck! Who better to learn from? Some had been to music school, whereas I'd come from this white-ass Anglo blues-rock background. My initiation into the Funk was playing with Larry Fratangelo, a percussionist with George Clinton's P-Funk, an Italian guy. Anyone who ever recorded in Detroit, he did their sessions. Larry showed me about dynamics, how to build a song, how to play with a percussionist. He taught me about time and about just listening — drumming for him wasn't just keeping a good beat and doing a fill and crash on the chorus. He took me under his wing and coached me with dope funk beats and gave me all this music to listen to — James Brown, George Clinton, Sly Stone, Graham Central, Rufus. I was still bashing away up to this point, not much finesse, but I hung in there and played with him for a year straight until I finally felt like I could call myself a real musician with versatility. I ran into Larry a few years later, and he told me, **"I JUST DID THIS SESSION FOR GEORGE — THESE CRAZY KIDS FROM CALIFORNIA CALLED RED HOT CHILI PEPPERS,"** **AND I ASKED HOW IT WAS AND HE SAID GOOD,** **AND THAT WAS IT.** To him it was just another session, but enough to where he mentioned that I might check it out.

Organic Anti–Beat Box Band

Jack Irons (original RHCP drummer): I rejoined the band in summer of '86.

✳ Jack came back and there was a fantastic feeling to have him back. It led to a lot of the inspiration for *Uplift Mofo* — a lot of the jubiliation that can be heard in the lyrics of that record were behind being reunited. Also, I was still struggling with addiction but I started getting glimpses of this new ball of light called sobriety, which was completely new to me. But I found a lot of the power and love in the transformation aspect of going completely confused and dependent to the rush of sobriety. Jack Irons had his signature drum style, real simple and steady, and above all, funky. I remember some great moments in the studio with Hillel where we were dancing and hugging and celebrating the magical process that is recording. Cliff was an incredible part of the Red Hot Chili Peppers and a huge, creative catalyst for all kinds of music that we made. It made us part of who we were — he was great. Unique and spontaneous, and we had so much fun writing and touring with Cliff. But we were also very destructive individuals, and I think we wore pretty badly on Cliff's patience and nerves. As humble and patient a fellow as he is, he was like, "Jeez, if it isn't one thing it's another with these loonies!" Both sides knew it was a matter of time before we needed to part ways — him leaving was mutual. The *Uplift* sessions were testament to our dysfunction. EMI gave us five grand to make demos and we just spent it all on drugs. We go into the studio and all this coke was around. I was like, "Where did all this coke come from?" and they were like, "Oh, part of the budget." I was delighted. What a wonderful surprise treat! I was like, "Wow, I didn't know we could do that. Let's get more!" We just spent days on end being high and well . . .

Cliff Martinez (RHCP drummer 1983–86): I had done demos for what would become the *Uplift* record, but I was really losing interest. They sensed it. I HAD FALLEN OUT OF LOVE WITH THE MUSIC, TOO. I JUST DIDN'T LIKE THE CONSTANT TRAVEL, THE GRIND OF TOURING. CREATIVELY IT WAS A LOW POINT IN THE BAND. WAY TOO DRUGGED-UP. IT WAS TIME TO GO.

✳ Cliff was the only one hard at work during the sessions, always with a look of intense dissatisfaction like, "Come on guys — let's not waste time." Maybe that was the beginning of the end of Cliff. He even started programming drum machines, which we had always been opposed to. We were into waving the flag of the real drummer — we were the Organic Anti–Beat Box Band — although Hillel would later try to teach us the drum machine and showed us it could, in fact, be used as an artistic instrument. Cliff was a little ahead of his time, that was the beginning of his movie scoring career. Like he had to teach himself how to work machines to make music without having to be dependent on flaky, fucked-up punks on dope who take forever to get anything done.

Cliff: Probably what drove me out of the band more than anything was having to sit shoulder-to-shoulder in a smoke-filled van, day in, day out, on eight-to-ten-hour drives.

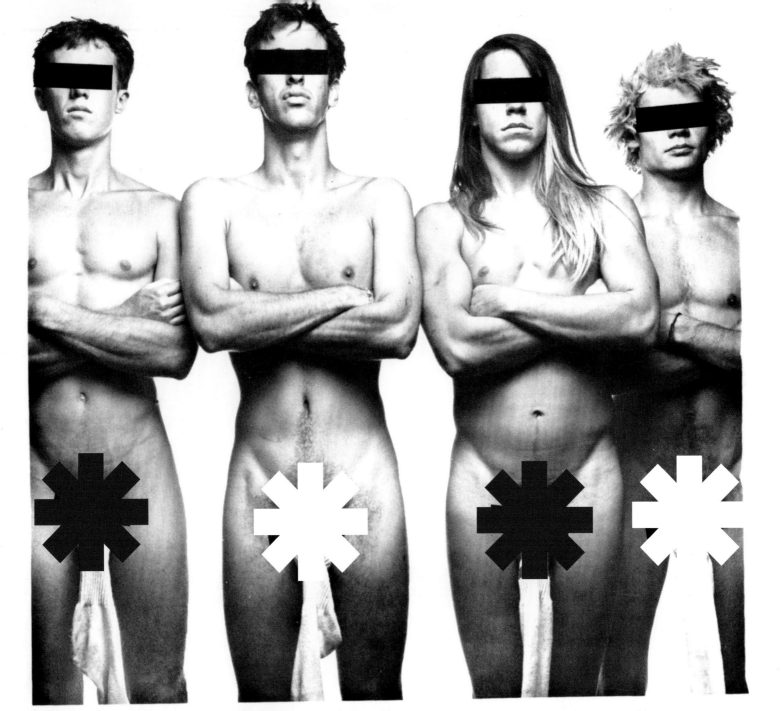

IF YOU'RE SICK AND SICK AND TIRED, OF BEING SICK AND TIRED

FIGHT LIKE A BRAVE

The new Red Hot Chili Peppers single
from the forthcoming album
THE UPLIFT MOFO PARTY PLAN

Subterranean Homesick Blues

F I can't remember who actually fired Anthony, probably me. He was so strung-out he wouldn't even show up. It went on for months and months and months.

A Okay, so I'm out of the band, deservedly so. I was pretty pissed off at them, but clearly I offered them no choice with my erratic, selfish behavior. This calamity, this personal catastrophe of being booted from the Red Hot Chili Peppers was all of my own doing. I had become an absentee junkie singer — they had no option and every right to dismiss me. I put up no fight. I was running on empty and I knew it.

Lindy Goetz (manager): We were trying to teach him a lesson so we "fired" him. Auditioning all these singers, my god. I remember they brought in this tattooed guy. He was a great singer — I mean he wasn't a Pepper, but he was great.

A I slunk back to Grand Rapids, tail between my legs, to get off drugs and to learn to accept my fate — that it was all over. I had totally blown it with the Red Hot Chili Peppers. I was really no longer in the band, the greatest thing in my life so far.

Jack Irons (original RHCP drummer): But it worked, temporarily, at least. It got him to go live with his mom in Michigan and get clean — do whatever he had to do. We did some auditioning, but no Red Hot Chili Peppers without Anthony, no way. But we were committed to trying, one way or another.

F **FINALLY, WE GOT SOMEONE ELSE — RIDICULOUS BECAUSE ANTHONY IS IRREPLACEABLE. WE TRIED A COUPLE GUYS AND IT WAS STUPID. FINALLY, OF COURSE, HE CAME BACK.**

Jack: In the end I said, "Look, we just gotta get Anthony back. This just isn't gonna work without him." We look at each other, what we all already knew, unspoken — it's the truth. Accept it, deal with it.

A I called Flea a month or so later to wish him well since they were evidently going on without me, and he offered me the job back.

Jack: I think it was me who called Anthony in Michigan. He said, "I'm doing good, I'm clean and I want to do it. I want to come and write." He came back ready to go. We finished the record [*The Uplift Mofo Party Plan*]. It was pretty straightforward from that point. He was clean, sharp and had written more lyrics. Michael [Beinhorn] was very happy to see him — we all were relieved and happy to see him alive, of course. We had a lot of tracks prerecorded with me, Flea and Hillel. Anthony went immediately to work and finished up a bunch of demos, then we went to Capitol and cut everything.

LICENSED TO ILL

☀ WE FIRST MET RICK RUBIN WHEN WE WERE STILL REHEARSING IN THE BACK ROOM OF EMI RECORDS — THE BACK STUDIO, OUR REGULAR LAIR FOR THE FIRST THREE OR FOUR YEARS. HE BROUGHT TWO MEMBERS OF THE BEASTIE BOYS WITH HIM. THEY WERE HIGH ON THE SUCCESS OF *LICENSE TO ILL* AND WE WERE ON OUR ASSES ONCE AGAIN, GUTTED, TITS UP FROM THE FLOOR FOR THE UMPTEENTH TIME.

✺ I MET RICK FIRST TIME AT THE CATHAY DE GRANDE. SOMEONE INTRODUCED US. MAYBE THE BEASTIE BOYS, OR CHRIS [DOWD] FROM FISHBONE — "HEY THIS IS RICK RUBIN, YOU HAVE TO MEET HIM." HE HAD PRODUCED *LICENSE TO ILL*. AND THEN WE WERE REHEARSING ONE DAY AND HE CAME BY WITH THE BEASTIE BOYS TO TALK TO US ABOUT MAYBE WORKING TOGETHER. WE WERE JUST A MESS. ANTHONY AND HILLEL WERE ALL STRUNG OUT, AND THERE'S A DISMAL GRAY CLOUD OF PARANOIA ALL OVER OUR ROOM. RICK TOLD ME YEARS LATER, "MAN, IT WAS DEPRESSING WALKING IN THERE — THE VIBE WAS SO DARK AND WEIRD, SO NEGATIVE." I'M LIKE, "DUDE, SAY HELLO TO PATHETIC JUNKIEDOM."

☀ SO THEY CAME, AND WE HAD ACTUALLY PLAYED SOME WEIRD SHOWS WITH THE BEASTIE BOYS BEFORE THEY WERE HUGE. THEY SAT DOWN IN OUR TATTY LITTLE DEN SPACE AND WE PLAYED SONGS FOR THEM. I WAS HIGH AS A KITE AND WE WERE ARGUING, BANTERING AND WHATNOT. RICK WAS A SMART, SHELTERED KID FROM LONG ISLAND WITHOUT A LOT OF EXPOSURE TO DRUG ADDICTS, HOLLYWOOD OUTLAWS, THE BURGLARS, URCHINS, DEALERS, AND HUSTLERS AND THE OTHER LOWLIFES AMONG OUR CIRCLE OF SICK PUPS STARRING IN *OUR OWN PRIVATE HOLLYWOOD*. TURNS OUT HE WAS, IN FACT, SCARED TO DEATH OF US.

✺ THE BEASTIES ARE A GOOD GROUP. THEY GRABBED OUR INSTRUMENTS AND STARTED JAMMING AND BROKE STRINGS.

039

It was different cultures — like they're so alive, so much fun, healthy, exuberant young males, nice upper-middle-class Jewish boys from New York who loved punk rock and rap as much as we did.

Rick Rubin (producer): **The scene was really dark. I didn't know what to make of it, but I knew I didn't want to be in that room.** We hadn't really been around hard drugs before. The way the guys were looking at each other was like they didn't trust each other. I remember thinking, "I want nothing to do with this." It felt especially odd because I had met Flea several times and he was always really excited and energetic like, "Come see our band — it's really cool" and then I come by and it's like this totally weirded-out scene.

Rick is pretty straight-edge, no dope or alcohol in his life. He's not a man in recovery, just one never interested in libertinage like us and our ilk. Then our paths went far away for a long time. It wasn't until I got sober in the late '80s that we came back to talking. That would have been late '89 or early '90, and we became fast friends at that time and it was just a no-brainer — it was time to work together. And to his credit, he really did for the first time in our career figure out how to get us on tape, how to let us be us, and capture it with the help of [engineer] Brendan O'Brien. It was the thing eluding producers up to that time — just capturing our magic and putting it on vinyl.

THEY'RE RED HOT

HILLEL — ANIMATED, INTELLIGENT, HANDSOME — THIS DUDE REALLY HAD IT GOING ON. HIS SLOVAKIAN LENGTH SERVED HIM WELL BOTH IN LIMB AND FACE. HE LOOKS LIKE HE'S STILL HAVING FUN — HASN'T REACHED THAT POINT OF "OH PLEASE, NOT ANOTHER PICTURE." YOU KNOW WHEN WE STARTED TAKING PICTURES IT WAS SO FUN AND CREATIVE — AFTER ABOUT 20,000 PHOTO SESSIONS IT IS VERY DIFFICULT TO MAINTAIN ENTHUSIASM. I THINK A BIG REASON WE STARTED GETTING SO HEAVY INTO CONTORTING AND DISTORTING OURSELVES IS THAT IT WAS A REACTION TO THESE PRETTY BOYS IN THE MUSIC SCENE — THESE GUYS WEARING MAKEUP AND TRYING TO LOOK AS HANDSOME AND BEAUTIFUL AS POSSIBLE. **I THINK WE WERE REACTING AGAINST THAT SORT OF PRETTY-BOY METAL LOOK. WE ALWAYS WERE TRYING TO LOOK LIKE A COVER OF *MAD* MAGAZINE.**

SKINNY SWEATY MAN

A WHEN WE MADE OUR FIRST RECORD WITH CLIFF [MARTINEZ] — *FREAKY STYLEY* IN THE BURNT-OUT GHETTO LAND OF DETROIT — HE WOULD WEAR THIS COLORFUL MOOSE HAT INSPIRED BY GEORGE CLINTON. THIS WAS CLIFF'S ODE TO GEORGE. HILLEL HAD RETURNED AFTER THAT, AFTER QUITTING. HE HAD A GREEN HAT WHICH IS REFERRED TO IN THE SONG "SKINNY SWEATY MAN." **HILLEL EITHER IS KEEPING COINS IN THE HAT OR COCAINE,** WHICH IS PART OF THE NATURE OF THE "SKINNY SWEATY MAN." WEIRD THING IS, THE LESS MONEY WE HAD, THE MORE STYLISH WE WERE. WE NEVER EVER REACHED THE PINNACLES OF STYLE THAT WE HAD REACHED WHEN WE WERE BROKE WITH NO PLACE TO LIVE. WE JUST MANAGED TO COME UP WITH THE COOLEST CLOTHES EVER. ONCE WE GOT PAID OUR SENSE OF ORIGINAL STYLE REALLY WENT OUT THE WINDOW. WEIRD THING.

Taste the Pain

✻ As soon as we landed at LAX we both made beelines for our dealers. Instead of going, "Oh okay, let's go work on music," we both hit the streets running — Hillel in one direction and me the other. It wasn't two days later that he died. That was the end of the *Uplift Mofo Party Plan*.

✻ It was the day of the Tyson-Spinks fight, and I went and picked up Perry Farrell and [his girlfriend] Casey Niccoli to go watch it at [Goldenvoice promoter] Rick Van Santen's house. Jane's had just wrapped *Nothing's Shocking*, and Perry's like "My new record — listen to it," so we listen in the car on the drive down, and I was amazed. I realized that they were a great, great band. Then Tyson knocked Spinks out in five seconds, and then I went home. It was just a big, weird day. Tyson knocked him down in the first round, and I heard Jane's Addiction, a band that would change my life and influence our musical direction, **AND THEN I CAME HOME LITERALLY LIKE A HALF HOUR LATER, AND GOT THE PHONE CALL THAT HILLEL WAS DEAD. I WENT INTO MAJOR SHOCK.**

✻ Hillel was showing signs of wear and tear from his use. We played the festival [in Finland] with the Ramones, and we came back from that, and we'd already had lengthy discussions about quitting drugs. Mainly because you couldn't get it out there in Finland — and because they'd stopped working. Things seemed to be better without them. But we weren't quite able with conviction to make it to that.

Lindy Goetz (manager): Tried calling Hillel — no luck getting through. Went to his apartment, no one answers. Then a neighbor, the manager or whoever, called saying she smelled something, and the cops opened the door. It was a matter of him being nearly clean and then suddenly scoring, and whatever he scored was too powerful or he did too much.

Bob Forrest (friend and musician): Texas Terri, who lived in the apartment next to Hillel's, was hysterical when she called. She said, "You need to get a hold of Flea and Anthony." I said, "Call 9-1-1" because it had been happening frequently with our circle of friends. She said it was too late, where were Flea and Anthony? I was like, "Oh, my God, no, please, no." I just knew it was about Hillel and drugs. I knew they were at Rick Van Santen's house watching the Tyson-Spinks fight. I'm trying to call and the answering machine keeps coming on and I'm leaving messages like, "Stop watching the fucking fight — Hillel is dead, and within an hour they're gonna call his mom." So I go running over there. And I looked in the doorway — it smelled awful. Cops are questioning me about phone numbers on the nightstand. I'm so trying not to totally freak out. I'm like, "Listen, his mother just had a heart attack — call her and she could die. I don't know his brother's number, but I know where he lives. I'll go there, and I'll tell him." Jamie Slovak lived right by me on Fountain, and Tree [Keith Barry] is at

Hillel
1963

MY HOUSE. I TOLD HIM "HILLEL IS DEAD AND THEY'RE GOING TO CALL ESTHER AND TELL HER — WE NEED TO GET JAMIE." SO TREE IS CRYING AND FREAKING OUT. WE PULL UP. TREE STARTS LAUGHING, AND THEN I START, HYSTERICAL PANIC LAUGHTER. SITTING IN FRONT OF JAMIE'S HOUSE **LAUGHING, CRYING, BAWLING, WAILING** — TRYING TO STOP LONG ENOUGH TO WALK UP THE DRIVEWAY TO TELL HIM HIS BROTHER IS DEAD, THAT HE NEEDS TO GO AND IDENTIFY THE BODY.

I WENT MISSING IN ACTION AND EVENTUALLY CALLED MY GIRLFRIEND IONE [SKYE] TO LET HER KNOW I WASN'T DEAD, BECAUSE I'D VANISHED FOR TWO DAYS. SHE WAS SOBBING OVER THE PHONE. I'M LIKE, "OH, I'M SORRY, DON'T HATE ME, PLEASE FORGIVE ME. I'M COMING HOME AS SOON AS I GET THIS NEXT BATCH." I THOUGHT SHE WAS SOBBING BECAUSE IT WAS ONE MORE TIME I'D DISAPPEARED ON HER. WHEN SHE STAMMERED OUT THAT HILLEL WAS DEAD, I SAID, "NO, HE'S NOT, THAT'S MISINFORMATION. WHOEVER IS SAYING THAT IS WRONG — IMPOSSIBLE." I DENIED IT AND DIDN'T ALLOW MYSELF TO FEEL THE TRUE NATURE OF GRIEF AND LOSS UNTIL I GOT OUT OF REHAB. I WENT TO VISIT HIS GRAVESITE, AND STARTED SPEAKING TO HIS GHOST, AND THEN I REALIZED, "OH SHIT, MY PARTNER IS GONE." THAT WAS VERY PAINFUL. JACK DEALT WITH IT IN A DIFFERENT WAY. HE DECIDED HE DIDN'T WANT TO DO THIS ANYMORE — TOO MUCH OF A REMINDER BEING PART OF A GROUP WHERE YOUR FRIEND ENDS UP DYING. HILLEL'S DEATH TRAUMATIZED EVERYBODY, IT REALLY DID. WE ALL HANDLED IT DIFFERENT WAYS. I WENT INTO DENIAL FOR TWO MONTHS — IT DIDN'T HIT ME. I DID SOB, BUT I WAS AT A COMPLETE LOSS AND CONTINUED TO GET HIGH

EVEN AFTER HILLEL DIED — BUT I COULDN'T REALLY GET HIGH AT THE SAME TIME. I WAS PUTTING ALL THESE DRUGS IN ME, BUT I WAS STILL FEELING EVERYTHING. WHEN WE GOT HOME AND DIVIDED MONEY FROM THE TOUR, AGAIN I WAS SHOCKED BECAUSE I GOT $10,000. I WAS LIKE, "WHAT?! HOW IS THAT EVEN POSSIBLE? TEN GRAND!" MOST I'D EVER BEEN UP IN MY LIFE SO FAR. I CALLED A FRIEND. I'M LIKE, "I DON'T KNOW WHAT TO DO. I CAN'T GET HIGH ANYMORE — IT ISN'T WORKING." HE'S LIKE, "WELL, YOU SHOULD GO TO REHAB." AND I'M LIKE, "WHAT THE FUCK IS REHAB? HOW MUCH IS IT?" HE SAYS, "LIKE $10,000. HOW MUCH DO YOU HAVE?" AND I SAID "I HAVE $10,000." HE SAID, "WELL, IF I WERE YOU, I'D SPEND IT ON THAT."

LINDY: **WHEN HILLEL PASSED AWAY, THE BAND WAS READY TO FALL APART. WE WAITED A BIT. I HAD A BOAT IN THE MARINA, WHERE ANTHONY, FLEA AND JACK ALL WENT FOR A MEETING, AND I SAID "WHAT DO YOU WANT TO DO?"** I MEAN, WE ALL FELT TERRIBLE — MY GOD, HE WAS OUR BROTHER AND PAL — BUT ARE WE GOING ON OR ARE YOU GOING TO CALL IT QUITS? JACK DIDN'T WANT TO STAY, BUT FLEA AND ANTHONY WANTED TO KEEP IT TOGETHER IN HIS HONOR.

AFTER JACK QUIT, FLEA AND I WERE LEFT WITH EACH OTHER ONE MORE TIME. ALTHOUGH WE BOTH LOVED HILLEL TO THE ENDS OF THE EARTH — JACK, TOO — IN THE END IT DIDN'T SEEM LIKE A REASON TO STOP PLAYING MUSIC.

045

Stone Cold Bush

✳ When the Chili Peppers hired [Funkadelic guitarist] DeWayne "Blackbyrd" McKnight, Robert Hayes and I started playing with [former Dead Kennedys drummer] D. H. Peligro. "Stone Cold Bush" on the *Mother's Milk* album was something the three of us recorded, with D. H. singing. But Robert wasn't so into playing with D. H. after he sussed he could have a drug problem. Robert was picking up on it even though D. H. was hiding it from us. Robert was trying to steer me away from what we were doing with D. H. When D. H. got hired for the Chili Peppers, that band stopped. Then me and Robert were playing, and then I joined the Chili Peppers and Robert moved back to Atlanta.

✳ Blackbyrd's songs didn't seem like Red Hot Chili Pepper songs. They were solo project songs, which turned out to be an issue with him. He was so used to being a guy that wrote music by himself that I guess it would be difficult for someone to then try and go write music with all these other people, which is what we were used to. We grew up together. We have developed telepathy. Guys jamming and vibing off each other and writing about shared experiences. So plugging a human being into that unique songwriting format is a little awkward. And it was awkward for Blackbyrd and for us. But he was a bitchin' guitar player. His ideas were all very cool, they just didn't work for us. He was also put off by our madness and intensity. I remember the first show we played with him on Sunset Boulevard at some club. Beforehand, he was terrified — he was like, "I feel like someone is going to break my guitar by accident or something." I'm like "No, no, it'll be fine." **AND THEN I ENDED UP KICKING HIM IN THE HEAD THE VERY FIRST SONG. I GOT OVEREXCITED, JUMPED UP IN THE AIR, AND ACCIDENTALLY WHOMPED HIM UPSIDE THE HEAD.** He had fun, but he was also very much, "Man, I don't know about this."

✳ Flea and I had already jammed together a few times. Flea told Bob [Forrest] about my guitar playing. The guitar player in Thelonious Monster had just quit, so Bob asked Flea for my number, and Flea was like, "All right, I'll give you his number, but I have first dibs." So Bob called me. I had seen them a bunch. I liked them a lot. They were fun. So I auditioned and they accepted me, but Anthony was there during the audition and he called Flea afterward and said, "He's got to be in the Chili Peppers." One of them called asking if I wanted to be in the band. I said, "More than anything." Anthony fired Blackbyrd, and I called Bob and told him, and he was like, "I figured that was gonna happen." ➤

▶ 🅐 I MET JOHN AT A BACKYARD BBQ. D. H. INTRODUCED US. HE'S LIKE, **"YOU HAVE TO HEAR THIS KID. HE'S A TEENAGER, AND A PRODIGY, LOVES RED HOT CHILI PEPPERS LIKE CRAZY, AND CAN PLAY ALL YOUR SONGS ON ALL DIFFERENT INSTRUMENTS."** I REMEMBER GOING, "WOW, THAT'S AMAZING SOMEONE IS CAPABLE AND LIKES US ENOUGH TO LEARN AND DO THAT." I MET HIM AT THE PARTY, AND WE HAD A NICE TALK — I THOUGHT HE WAS A COOL YOUNG DUDE, BUT I HADN'T HEARD HIM PLAY. SOMEHOW HE AND FLEA HAD A JAM SESSION IN FLEA'S APARTMENT — JUST THE TWO OF THEM. THEY HAD RECORDED SOME OF IT — AND I THINK THIS WAS EVEN PRIOR TO BLACKBYRD. FLEA SAID, "THIS IS KIND OF WEIRD BECAUSE I KNOW WE HAVE A GUITAR PLAYER ALREADY, BUT THIS KID IS MORE UP OUR ALLEY." HE PLAYED ME HIM RIFFING WITH JOHN AND I WAS LIKE "WHOA, LET'S DO WHAT WE HAVE TO DO." WE STILL HADN'T HIRED HIM, AND THEN I STARTED HANGING OUT WITH JOHN A LITTLE, AND HE SAID, "I'VE GOT TO GO AUDITION FOR THELONIOUS MONSTER." I'M LIKE "COOL, I'LL DRIVE YOU TO BOB'S GARAGE." SO, I DROVE HIM TO THE AUDITION. HE GOT UP THERE AND KILLED IT WITH THE MONSTER. I'M LIKE, "I CAN'T LET HIM JOIN THE MONSTER. HE'S OUR GUITAR PLAYER — I'VE GOT TO INTERVENE NOW!" IT WAS LIKE, "WE HAVE TO GET THIS KID. I HATE TO DO THIS TO BOB, BUT WE CAN'T LET HIM SLIP AWAY." IN SOME WAYS BOB KNEW JOHN WAS MEANT TO BE WITH THE CHILI PEPPERS. BOB WAS PROBABLY PISSED OFF AND FRUSTRATED THAT WE WERE SOMEHOW STEALING WHAT COULD HAVE BEEN THEIR GREAT GUITAR PLAYER, BUT AT THE SAME TIME, I FELT LIKE THERE WAS AN UNSPOKEN UNDERSTANDING OF "I GET IT — THIS IS YOUR GUY." BOB IS GENEROUS IN THAT WAY WHEN HE KNOWS SOMETHING IS MEANT TO BE — HE WON'T FIGHT IT. HE'S ALWAYS BEEN COMPETITIVE, BUT ALWAYS BEEN VERY SUPPORTIVE. WHEN IT CAME TIME FOR BLACKBYRD TO GO — FLEA AND I HAD BEEN THROUGH SO MANY HIRINGS AND FIRINGS WITH JACK SHERMAN

AND SO ON — THAT IT WAS MY TURN TO DO THE FIRING ON THIS ONE. I CALLED BLACKBYRD AND VERY EARNESTLY EXPLAINED WHY IT WASN'T PANNING OUT, BUT HE TOOK IT OUT ON ME PERSONALLY. HE'S LIKE, "MOTHERFUCKER, ANTHONY, I AM GOING TO BURN YOUR MOTHERFUCKIN' HOUSE DOWN." I'M LIKE, "WHOA! I'M JUST THE MESSENGER HERE." LUCKILY, I DIDN'T HAVE A HOUSE TO TORCH, BUT THE MENACE OF IT WAS DISTURBING NEVERTHELESS. I ALSO SAW D. H.'S DRUG USE AS DERAILING AND DETRIMENTAL TO OUR WORKING. HE'S A GREAT DRUMMER AND A BEAUTIFUL PERSONALITY AND COOL-LOOKING, BUT HIS SPECIALTY DIDN'T FIT WITH THE TYPE OF DRUMMER THAT FLEA NEEDED FOR HIS BASS PLAYING. D. H. IS A GREAT PUNK DRUMMER, BUT THESE OTHER FUNKIFIED THINGS WE DO WEREN'T HIS FORTE. IT WAS ALSO TAKING LONGER AND BECOMING MORE OF A STRUGGLE THAN WE NEEDED OR COULD AFFORD IT TO BE. ADD TO THAT MY CONTROL FREAK NATURE — NOT HELPFUL.

✱ **WE NEEDED A DRUMMER THAT WAS MORE VERSATILE AS A MUSICIAN AND LESS ON THE PATH OF SELF-DESTRUCTION THAT WE'RE TRYING TO STAY OFF OF AFTER LOSING HILLEL.** IT WAS THE SADDEST FIRING TO TAKE PLACE IN THE HISTORY OF OUR BAND.

✱ WE REALLY LOVED HIM. I REMEMBER FLEA MANNING UP AND TAKING HIS TURN WITH THESE GOD-AWFUL FIRINGS, BUT WHEN HE CALLED D. H., IT WAS A SAD, SAD THING. HE BECAME SO DISTRAUGHT OVER HAVING TO RELEASE A FRIEND — HE ENDED UP THROWING UP, OUT OF ANXIETY AND SADNESS. I REMEMBER GOING, "OH JEEZ, THAT'S WORSE THAN GETTING A THREAT TO BURN DOWN MY HOUSE." SO NOW WE HAVE JOHN AND NO DRUMMER. WE HOLED UP IN ATWATER IN SOME LITTLE SPACE THERE, AND STARTED AUDITIONING DRUMMERS. IT IS SO HARD. WE DIDN'T REALIZE HOW LUCKY WE WERE WHEN WE FORMED THAT THERE WAS NO AUDITION. IT WAS JUST FOUR FRIENDS PLAYING MUSIC TOGETHER IN A BAND.

The Greeting Song

✳ My first show with the Chili Peppers was in Phoenix, Arizona, the second was the John Anson Ford Theater — first L.A. one. I was real nervous. The first year or so I wanted to be in the band so bad, I wanted to do a good job so much. **I WAS TRYING TOO HARD TO BE LIKE WHAT I THOUGHT A CHILI PEPPER SHOULD BE RATHER THAN JUST BEING MYSELF . . . MUSICALLY ON GUITAR AND IN MY PERSONAL LIFE.**

Bob Forrest (friend and musician): John Frusciante, he is what Anthony needed.

✳ Most people are accustomed to more or less remaining the same. I would always lose friends for this reason or that reason. I didn't have many good friends until I was in the band. Friends just weren't as giving or as loyal as I was until I met the group of people around the time of being in the band. I was alone and sad a lot, but always happy and feeling good about myself. I felt my life was going to go somewhere good — I could feel good things happening

✳ When John joined the band, he and Anthony were inseparable twin pussy hounds, dressing the same, hanging out together. John was Anthony's sidekick — his own Mini-me buddy. Socially at least.

✳ John idolized Anthony, they were rooming together on the road. I saw his immaturity in different ways, but his playing was untouchable. At first he would do whatever they said, he was following Anthony around like his shadow. Whatever they did they were together. Anthony was sober. We started to rehearse, and to make money on weekends we'd play at colleges. Vassar, whatever, whoever had the moolah to get us for the weekend.

✳ Whatever Anthony wanted to do, John did it, until eventually John realized he needed to declare who he was away from Anthony, and so he started going the complete opposite against him. John was drinking and getting high and stuff which newly-sober Anthony wasn't very happy about.

✳ Nowadays, John won't listen to old stuff because I don't think he was being true to himself, he was more emulating what he thought the Chili Peppers needed and playing like Hillel.

✳ At first it was a real strain for me to attempt to step into Hillel Slovak's shoes, but I began to discover my own path after I started identifying more with the simplicity

OF HIS PLAYING — ORIGINALLY I WAS THINKING OF BEING MORE BUSY THAN HIM. I OWE A LOT TO HILLEL FOR WHERE I WENT WITH MY PLAYING, LIKE IF I TRIED TO COMPETE WITH FLEA'S BASS PLAYING AT ITS BUSIEST, IT WAS SCREWING UP THE CHEMISTRY. SO I STARTED SIMPLIFYING EVERYTHING TO SUIT THE LIMITATIONS HILLEL'S PLAYING IS BASED AROUND. BY RESTRICTING MYSELF, LIKE, "I'M NOT GOING TO USE MY PINKY AS MUCH BECAUSE HILLEL DIDN'T USE IT MUCH, AND STOP PLAYING SUPER FAST, STOP DRAWING ATTENTION TO YOURSELF SO MUCH WITH YOUR PLAYING," IT TAUGHT ME TO LET THE MUSIC BREATHE MORE SO THE OTHER INSTRUMENTS COULD BREATHE MORE, SO THAT WHEN FLEA DOES HIS BUSY THINGS IT REALLY MEANS SOMETHING. THE MORE I SAID, "OKAY, I'M NOT GONNA DO THIS TECHNIQUE OR THIS AND THAT," THE MORE ORIGINALITY FLOURISHED. BY REMOVING THE PRESSURE OF TRYING TO DO SOMETHING IMPRESSIVE, I STARTED TO GET MORE ORIGINAL. I WANTED TO PLAY LIKE A BAND MEMBER INSTEAD OF SHOWING OFF. I THOUGHT I COULD BRING SOMETHING WITH MY TECHNIQUES — THAT VAN HALEN TECHNIQUE AND CERTAIN TYPES OF HARMONICS — BUT I JUST DROPPED ALL THAT STUFF AND STARTED PLAYING MORE LIKE SOMEONE FROM THE '70S.

BOB: JOHN HAS THAT SAME THING FLEA AND ANTHONY HAVE, VERY SPECIAL AND DIFFERENT. WHEN I MET JOHN, THERE WAS NO WAY HE KNEW HOW TO WRITE SONGS. HE WAS ALREADY LIKE A GUITAR PLAYER'S GUITAR PLAYER, SCARY FOR ONE SO YOUNG! JOHN WAS A VIRTUOSO MUSICIAN OBSESSED WITH WEIRD THINGS. CAPTAIN BEEFHEART, FRANK ZAPPA, HE WAS EVEN GOING TO BE IN ZAPPA'S BAND AT SOME POINT.

JOHN WAS THIS STRANGE LITTLE TEENAGE SKATEPUNK KID WHO ALSO DIGS THIS WHOLE OTHER SIDE OF SUPERCOMPLEX MUSIC, BUT WITH THE CHOPS TO ACTUALLY PULL IT OFF.

FLEA LIKES DEVO, FEAR, THE CIRCLE JERKS, JAMES BROWN AND FUNK, BUT THEN JOHN LOVES THE GERMS AND BLACK FLAG AS MUCH AS BEEFHEART AND ZAPPA. TWO STALWART MUSICIANS IN THE CHILI PEPPERS LOVE WEIRD, OBSCURE THINGS, AND TOGETHER THEY MAKE MUSIC THAT BECOMES UNIVERSALLY HUGE AND POPULAR.

⁜ I WAS WANTING TO BE DIFFERENT AND ORIGINAL AND BRING A NEW ELEMENT, BUT I WAS GOING ABOUT IT THE WRONG WAY. I WAS STILL THINKING IN TERMS OF BEING A WILD, WACKY CHILI PEPPER AND NOT IN TERMS OF ALL THE MUSIC I LIKED AND HOW IT COULD HAVE BEEN APPLIED TO THEIR SPECIAL ELEMENTS. IT WAS A REAL CONFUSING TIME — THERE WAS A LOT OF PRESSURE FOR SOMEONE TO COME INTO A BAND WITH A BUILT-IN AUDIENCE THAT REALLY LOVES THEM. MY THINKING WAS BASICALLY, "THE OBJECTIVE HERE IS TO BE LIKED BY THE PEOPLE IN THE BAND, AND BE LIKED BY THEIR AUDIENCE." I CAN'T WORK THAT WAY, AND I TRIED FOR YEARS TO BE THAT WAY.

LINDY GOETZ (MANAGER): JOHN WAS A REAL ASSET — AS GREAT AS HILLEL WAS. JOHN BROUGHT MELODY THAT THE BAND REALLY DIDN'T HAVE. JOHN WRITES KIND OF HOOK-Y — NOT SOLO-Y STUFF. HE HELPED ANTHONY START TO SING, COACHING HIM ONE ON ONE, JOHN WOULD SQUAT THERE WITH HIS GUITAR AND GO THROUGH A MELODY FOR ANTHONY TO SING ALONG TO. THAT NEVER HAPPENED WITH HILLEL. AS CLOSE AS THEY ALL WERE, JOHN HELPED THEM BECOME A COMMERCIAL BAND SUCCESSFUL BEYOND THEIR DREAMS. JOHN STILL DOES BACKGROUND VOCALS TO THIS DAY, BUT HE GOT ANTHONY TO WHERE HE FELT COMFORTABLE WORKING WITH HIM, IT WASN'T FORCED.

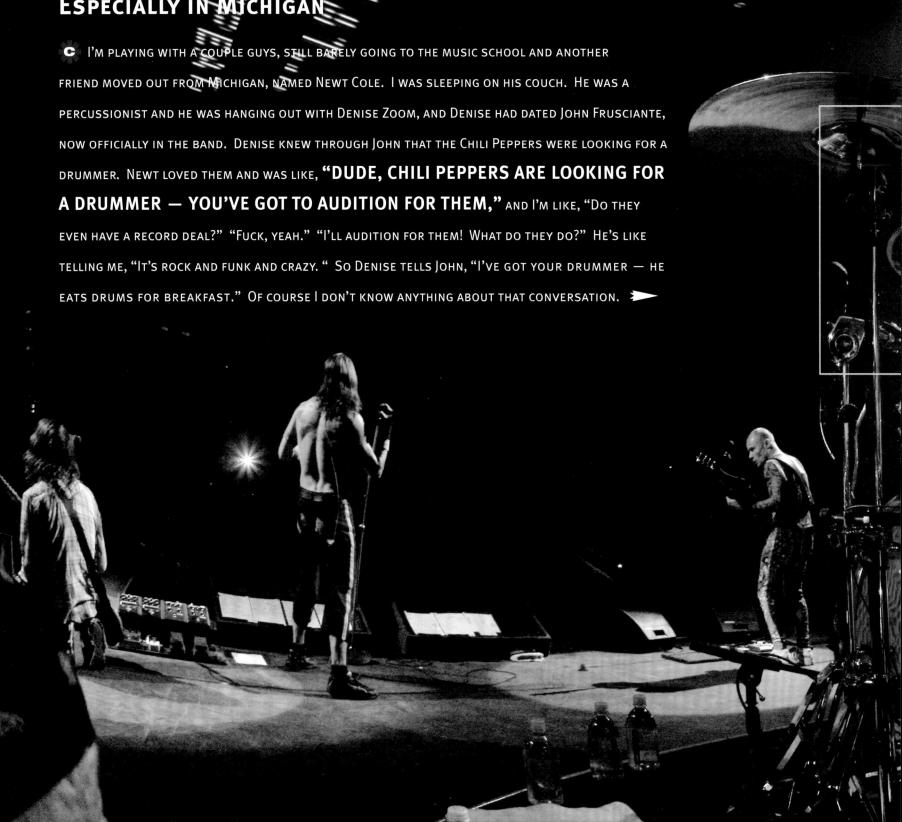

ESPECIALLY IN MICHIGAN

C   I'M PLAYING WITH A COUPLE GUYS, STILL BARELY GOING TO THE MUSIC SCHOOL AND ANOTHER FRIEND MOVED OUT FROM MICHIGAN, NAMED NEWT COLE. I WAS SLEEPING ON HIS COUCH. HE WAS A PERCUSSIONIST AND HE WAS HANGING OUT WITH DENISE ZOOM, AND DENISE HAD DATED JOHN FRUSCIANTE, NOW OFFICIALLY IN THE BAND. DENISE KNEW THROUGH JOHN THAT THE CHILI PEPPERS WERE LOOKING FOR A DRUMMER. NEWT LOVED THEM AND WAS LIKE, **"DUDE, CHILI PEPPERS ARE LOOKING FOR A DRUMMER — YOU'VE GOT TO AUDITION FOR THEM,"** AND I'M LIKE, "DO THEY EVEN HAVE A RECORD DEAL?" "FUCK, YEAH." "I'LL AUDITION FOR THEM! WHAT DO THEY DO?" HE'S LIKE TELLING ME, "IT'S ROCK AND FUNK AND CRAZY. " SO DENISE TELLS JOHN, "I'VE GOT YOUR DRUMMER — HE EATS DRUMS FOR BREAKFAST." OF COURSE I DON'T KNOW ANYTHING ABOUT THAT CONVERSATION. ➤

▶ ✸ Chad's audition was funny as hell. We'd probably checked out twenty drummers already, some were bad and good and okay. One guy I really liked from Chicago, a sort of Jack Irons type. **Then we heard this Chad guy "ate drums for breakfast."**

✿ On the phone I was faking my way through like, "Yeah, I know you guys" and they're like, "What kind of punk rock do you listen to?" and I'm all, "Oh yeah, I like Sex Pistols, Ramones, Clash" — all the name-check punk rockers. So I fly down to Hully Gully [rehearsal studios] and I go buy the *Abbey Road* cassette tape on the way and listen to it in the car — "Fight Like a Brave" and "Fire" and more. I got my drums, it was a short drive and the cassette hadn't finished so I sat in the parking lot until I'd heard it all. That was my real introduction to Red Hot Chili Peppers, the actual music, so I waddle in there bow-leg cocky like, "Hey, I can do this — woo-hoo." The Chili Peppers weren't a big band to me. I wasn't nervous — it wasn't like I was trying out for Guns N' Roses. What else did I have going? RHCP was a band that was still kind of underground, but like maybe something is gonna happen soon with them. Inside I wanted the gig real bad, of course, but gave off the impression I really didn't give a shit either way. You wanna jam, man? Let's fuckin' jam.

✸ He had the headband and the long hair and the heavy metal guy jacket, and I was like I hate heavy metal guys. We were underground punk rockers. We were like, those are the enemy, the hair metal guys, the pay-to-play clowns that hate punk rockers.

✿ Flea was the first smartass to come up to me, "Hey, so is that your breakfast!? Ha-ha." John had a red Mohican do. It was a lot about how they looked, almost as much as the music, and now these guys are looking at me like this clueless rock bozo from Detroit — this big jock, no-punk hairy asshole in a bandana, long hair, shorts, in a worn-out torn Metallica T-shirt heisted from Goodwill, or something. I looked way too Gazzarri's on the Strip to them for sure, and there wasn't jack I could do about it. I just wasn't cool or punk hip, whichever way you cut it. Even worse for the Chili Peppers' image, I'm like way taller, like a big hairy-assed teddy fucker, and they were cute 'n' cuddly, cheeky rug cubs, now rollin' their eyes, like, "Check out the dumb metal freak guy (wink-wink) straight outta

pay-to-play at the Troubadour and Gazzarri's (wink-wink), haha." Luckily my playing overshadowed all that — and who the fuck can tell how tall a drummer really is sitting down behind a trap kit? I just shrugged at their attitude. Who gave a shit anyway? Not me. Weren't the original punk rockers always basically saying, "FTW, I Gotta Be Me?"

✸ **I thought he's so goofy, like this guy will never do, but then we started playing and he was so fucking on fire.**

I was laughing so hard while we were playing going, "Oh my god, he's so good!" I just remember him screaming and destroying the drums.

✿ [Producer] Michael Beinhorn was on the couch with Anthony as I set up. They had these amused looks on

THEIR FACES. WE START JAMMING AND FLEA DOES THE SAME THING WE DO TO THIS DAY — HARD FAST, WE START GOING FOR IT, THE OVERDRIVE SPEED FUNK THINGIE. ANTHONY GETS UP OFF THE COUCH AND HE'S DIGGING IT. I'M LIKE, "THIS IS GOOD, MAN!" LOUD, PROGRESSIVE AND FUN. WE JAM FOR A WHILE UNTIL JOHN BROKE A STRING. I'VE NEVER SEEN ANYONE CHANGE A STRING FASTER! WE'RE STILL JAMMING LIKE OUR FUCKING MINDS ARE GONE, AND I DIDN'T EVEN NOTICE.

LINDY GOETZ (MANAGER): WE HAD AUDITIONS FOR DRUMMERS — AND THERE WAS ONE THEY REALLY LIKED. THEN CHAD COMES IN AND SETS UP. HE'S A BIG-BONED IN-YOUR-FACE GUY'S GUY — I LIKED HIM THE SECOND I SAW HIM. HE WAS AS VISUAL AND AS

MUCH OF A SHOWMAN BEHIND THE DRUMS AS FLEA WAS BEHIND THE BASS. BUT, HE WAS THE HEAVY METAL GUY — HE HAD THAT MIDWEST HEAVY METAL ATTITUDE THAT FLEA AND ANTHONY WERE SO NOT INTO. CHAD'S POUNDING AWAY, AND I'M SITTING THERE GOING, "THIS IS THE COOLEST FUCKING DRUMMER I'VE EVER SEEN IN MY LIFE." THE GUY'S INSANE — HE'S JUMPING IN THE AIR, SMACKING CYMBALS, FUCKING HOGWILD.

WE DID FAST, CRAZY SHIT AND THEN FLEA WANTED TO SEE ME KEEP A STRAIGHT BEAT. I HAD JUST HEARD THEIR SHIT FIFTEEN MINUTES AGO, SO I WAS LIKE OKAY, STRAIGHT FUNK. TO ME IT WAS LIKE JAMES BROWN ON SPEED. NO FUCKIN' PROBLEM. I'M LOVIN' IT. FLEA'S ALL YELLIN', "COME ON, MOTHERFUCKER . . . FASTER,

HARDER" AND I'M LIKE RAGIN' AND ROARIN', SPITTIN' AND CUSSIN' AND HOLLERIN' FULL ON. **I'M LIKE A CRAZED GORILLA — I WENT INSANE, "BRING IT ON, FOOL — YOU WANT HARD AND FAST, MOTHERFUCKER? I'LL SHOW YOU FUCKIN' HARDER AND FASTER . . . GAAAAR-GAAAAR . . .** HEY PUNK ROCKER, YOU WANNA BE FUNKY? LICK ME! SUCK ON THIS, SUCK ON THAT! BON APPETIT! GAAAAAR — GAAAR."

I WAS LAUGHING MY ASS OFF. IT WAS JUST ONE OF THOSE MOMENTS WHEN YOU GET SOMETHING IN A ROOM AND JUST TAP IT, YOU KNOW?

FLEA AND JOHN WERE ENTHUSIASTIC, ANTHONY I COULDN'T TELL, BEINHORN NOT SO MUCH — I THOUGHT HE WAS A ROADIE AT FIRST. HE'S LIKE, "OKAY, THAT'S IT. COOL, WE'LL CALL YOU, LET YOU KNOW." IT WASN'T LIKE YOU'RE IN, YOU'RE THE GUY! I DIDN'T KNOW WHAT TO THINK. I THOUGHT IT WENT WELL, AND I'D ENJOYED THE HELL OUT OF IT, THAT'S FOR SURE. FLEA SAID, "YOU ARE THE FIRST THAT EVER LED ME — I BROUGHT IT IN AND THEN YOU DOUBLE-TIMED IT."

AFTERWARD — WE DIDN'T WANT TO SAY IT THEN — WHEN HE LEFT WE WERE LIKE, NO ONE COULD EVER BE THAT GOOD, IT WAS AMAZING. I WAS WORRIED HE WOULDN'T UNDERSTAND OUR SCENE, AND I WAS STILL CONCERNED ABOUT THE IMAGE BECAUSE HE LOOKED LIKE SOME GnR GUY! IN THE END, ANTHONY GOES, "OH, WELL, HE HAS TO SHAVE HIS HEAD."

THEY CALLED ME AND SAID, **"OKAY, YOU'RE IN THE BAND, BUT YOU'VE GOT TO SHAVE YOUR HEAD!"** I DON'T REMEMBER WHO WAS TALKING. PROBABLY ANTHONY. I WAS LIKE, "DUDE, I'M NOT SHAVING MY FUCKING HEAD — **FUCK THAT SHIT."** LATER, THEY WERE LIKE, "WE RESPECTED THAT YOU DIDN'T BUCKLE."

I Could Have Lied

✳ I was eighteen when I joined the band. I was totally off balance. When I quit I was twenty-two and I just thought everything's over. I needed time to do absolutely nothing — time to have no responsibilities other than to experience life. The resentment I built up against Anthony is real personal stuff. Honestly, I think in his soul he really wanted me to be exactly what I am, but he has certain needs from people that even he has no explanation for.

✳ There were a few things John was really mad at me about, too. We talked. I had offended him over a bunch of things. He's anti-everything to the point where we're flying to Japan and he's really upset when we get there. **SUDDENLY HE ANNOUNCES HE CAN'T GO ON AND WANTS TO QUIT. "WOW! GREAT TIMING, DUDE!"** I was going through my own personal shit and was real unhappy myself. I was recovering from divorce, having a hard time dealing with it, and couldn't sleep. I didn't think I could make it. Literally it felt like the walls were closing in. I was stressed, in a near-panic state all the time, miserable beyond human endurance, ready to collapse. Probably one of the worst times in my life, for sure.

✳ John just isolated himself. It was just so important for the four of us to connect while we play — we're not the fucking Eagles who don't talk to each other at all, not even onstage. This is a gang, a tribe, a big family, a brotherhood. Maybe it's dysfunctional, maybe we differ on things, of course we sometimes get on each other's nerves, but it's still a fuckin' family at the end of it with a whole ➤

LOTTA LOVE AND RESPECT FOR EACH OTHER. NAME ONE FAMILY THAT DOESN'T GET INSANE BEHIND CLOSED DOORS AND DRAWN BLINDS.

ME AND ROBERT HAYES, MY FRIEND FROM MUSICIANS INSTITUTE, WERE ALWAYS THINKING OF DOING SOMETHING TOGETHER. HE WAS ALWAYS TRYING TO TALK ME INTO QUITTING THE BAND AND HIM QUITTING THIS INTERESTING KIND OF JAZZ BAND HE WAS IN. AND THEN HE DIED — HIS BAND VAN CRASHED TWO DAYS BEFORE MY LAST JAUNT WITH THE CHILI PEPPERS. I WAS JUST THINKING AND CRYING ABOUT HIM ALL THE TIME. I QUIT THE BAND IN THE MIDST OF THAT. WE WENT TO HAWAII AND THEN JAPAN, AND JAPAN WAS JUST . . .

I KEPT THINKING HE'LL COME AROUND, IT'S JUST A PHASE. AND THOUGH THERE WERE SOME GOOD NIGHTS, FOR SURE, BY THE TIME WE GOT TO JAPAN, JOHN THOUGHT PEOPLE WERE TRYING TO KILL HIM. LIKE LITERALLY TWO HOURS BEFORE WE'RE GOING ON, JOHN TELLS OUR TOUR MANAGER, TONY SELINGER, "I CAN'T TAKE IT ANYMORE, I HAVE TO GO HOME RIGHT NOW."

I WAS ALREADY SO MAD AT MYSELF FOR NOT QUITTING MONTHS BEFORE. I KNEW I WASN'T GOING TO BE HAPPY ON TOUR BUT I WENT ANYWAY. IT HAS ALWAYS BEEN AN UNBEARABLE THOUGHT WHAT ME AND ROBERT COULD HAVE DONE AND THAT I COULD HAVE TAKEN A MORE EXPLORATORY DIRECTION WITH HIM RATHER THAN LIMITING MY OUTLET TO MAKING POP MUSIC. WE COULD HAVE APPLIED ELEMENTS OF THE MORE EXPERIMENTAL AND JAZZ THINGS. THERE WERE THINGS POINTING TOWARD WHAT WE MIGHT HAVE DONE ON MY FIRST SOLO RECORD. I'VE ALWAYS REGRETTED I DIDN'T QUIT RIGHT WHEN WE FINISHED RECORDING *BLOOD SUGAR* BECAUSE I COULD FEEL INSIDE ME I HAD OTHER DIFFERENT MUSICAL THINGS TO EXPLORE. I WAS SO FULL OF REGRET FOR NOT HAVING DONE IT

WHEN THERE WAS THE CHANCE TO PLAY MUSIC WITH ROBERT THAT WHEN HE DIED ALL THE WIND WAS OUT OF MY SAILS AND I JUST WANTED TO PAINT AND DRAW AND STUFF. I DIDN'T EVEN REALLY WANT TO PRACTICE OR PLAY MUSIC ANYMORE.

LINDY GOETZ (MANAGER): THEY FLEW TO JAPAN TWO DAYS BEFORE ME. THE MINUTE I LANDED AT THE HOTEL THE TOUR MANAGER CALLS AND SAYS, "YOU GOTTA GET OVER HERE!" I WAS LIKE, "WHAT'S THE PROBLEM?" HE'S LIKE, "SO, DUDE, YOU SITTIN' DOWN? JOHN QUIT!!" I GO, "ARE YOU CRAZY? WHAT THE FUCK ARE YOU TALKING ABOUT?" I GET RIGHT OVER TO THE VENUE AND JOHN DOESN'T WANNA PLAY. I GO, "GET THE FUCK ONSTAGE AND PLAY." HE PLAYED THAT SHOW, AND WE PUT HIM ON A PLANE HOME AFTERWARD.

RICK RUBIN (PRODUCER): **WHEN I HEARD THE NEWS I WAS ASTOUNDED. IT COMPLETELY BLEW MY MIND. I HADN'T SEEN ANY SIGN OF A RIFT BUILDING.** I JUST COULDN'T PROCESS IT, COULDN'T TAKE IT IN. FOR ME IT WAS LIKE THIS ALL CAME FROM OUT OF NOWHERE. JOHN HAD JUST CONTRIBUTED EVERYTHING HE HAD TO MAKING THIS WONDERFUL MASTERPIECE RECORD THAT EVERYONE LOVED, AND NOW THIS? WHY? HOW? EVERYONE WAS IN SHOCK. IT WAS A MASSIVE TRAUMA FOR THE BAND AND THOSE WHO LOVED THEM.

WHEN HE LEFT THE BAND, HE HAD NO CONTACT WITH ANTHONY. THESE GUYS WERE THICK AS THIEVES WHEN HE FIRST JOINED — NOW IT WAS THE OPPOSITE. JOHN BASICALLY IGNORED ANTHONY ONSTAGE.

MY RESENTMENT TOWARD ANTHONY WAS PROBABLY MORE RESENTMENT TOWARD MYSELF FOR NOT QUITTING SOONER THAN I DID. THAT'S NO FAULT OF HIS OWN — WHAT HE WANTED TO BE AND WAS DESTINED TO BE WAS A STAR. MAYBE WHAT I DO ISN'T GOING TO BE ACKNOWLEDGED BY PEOPLE, BUT THAT'S ME. IT'S MY NATURE TO DO THINGS THAT ARE WEIRDER AND LESS UNDERSTOOD, AND THAT WAS A PATH I NEEDED TO TAKE.

REPLACING JOHN WAS A HARD THING. ARIK MARSHALL WAS A GREAT PLAYER — PROBABLY COULD HAVE BEEN A GREAT GUITAR PLAYER FOR US, BUT CERTAIN THINGS JUST DIDN'T WORK. THE [BLOOD SUGAR] TOUR WENT WELL — AUSTRALIA, EUROPE — BUT WHEN WE GOT BACK AND IT WAS TIME TO START REHEARSALS FOR THE NEW RECORD, ARIK SEEMED REALLY ALOOF AND REMOVED, NOT REALLY INTO IT. SHOWING UP LATE AND STUFF. HE COULD JAM, BUT WHEN WE STARTED WRITING, FOR WHATEVER REASON, HE DIDN'T REALLY FLOW. ANTHONY WAS LIKE, "WOW, SOMETHING IS WEIRD." SO ONE DAY WE SAT DOWN WITH HIM AND SAID, "ARIK, ARE YOU IN AND COMMITTED TO THIS BAND, OR ARE YOU FEELING LIKE NEITHER HERE OR THERE ABOUT IT?" WE GOT A LUKEWARM HERE-AND-THERE HAND WIGGLE IN HIS REPLY. WE WERE LIKE, "OKAY, WE'LL GET A NEW GUITAR PLAYER." AFTERWARD HE WAS REALLY BUMMED — HE SAID HE JUST MEANT HE WASN'T HAPPY ABOUT SOME THINGS, BUT IF THEY GOT BETTER HE'D BE SO INTO IT. BUT WE'D ALREADY DECIDED AT THAT POINT, HE WASN'T THE GUY. IT WASN'T REALLY GOING ANYWHERE WITH US ANYWAY. NO ONE'S FAULT — JUST THE SITUATION. ARIK IS A GREAT GUITAR PLAYER. WE SURE WERE LUCKY TO HAVE PLAYED WITH SOMEONE OF HIS STATURE AS MUSICIAN.

WE HIRED DAVE NAVARRO AFTER A LONG, TORTUOUS PERIOD TRYING TO FIND A REPLACEMENT FOR JOHN. **THAT GUITAR PLAYER THING WAS TOTAL SPINAL TAP.** WE HAD A TECH THAT WOULD JAM IN ONE ROOM TO SEE IF THEY COULD PLAY AT ALL, AND THEN IF THEY WERE GOOD ENOUGH ROBBIE WOULD SEND THEM IN TO US. DUDES PAINTED UP YELLOW — EVERY FREAK EVER. IT WAS SO DEPRESSING. NOBODY HAD AN ORIGINAL BONE IN THEIR BODY. I GOT WORSE AS A DRUMMER PLAYING WITH THESE PEOPLE! FLEA WAS SICK AT THE TIME SO HE WASN'T THERE FOR A LOT — IT WAS TORTURE.

DAVE NAVARRO (RHCP GUITARIST 1993–98): I'VE BEEN PLAYING AND TOURING IN ROCK BANDS SINCE '85. THOUGH WE WERE IN SIMILAR SOCIAL CIRCLES, I DIDN'T REALLY CROSS PATHS WITH THE CHILI PEPPERS UNTIL LIKE 1989. I LOVED TO GO WATCH THEM, THEY WERE SUCH AN ENTERTAINING ACT, BUT I DON'T REMEMBER LIKING THEIR RECORDS SO MUCH. ALWAYS AMAZING LIVE. THAT'S HOW THEY'D BUILT UP THEIR REP. I WAS THE GUITAR PLAYER IN JANE'S ADDICTION, WHO'D DONE TWO WONDERFUL ALBUMS FOR WARNER BROS. THAT WEREN'T REALLY HUGE MEGASELLERS, BUT WE HAD A STRONG FOLLOWING IN SOUTHERN CALIFORNIA AND THE MIDWEST. AFTER JANE'S BROKE UP ERIC AVERY AND I MADE THE DECONSTRUCTION ALBUM. AT THE END OF THAT, I JOINED THE CHILI PEPPERS.

JOHNNY NAVARRO (DAVE'S COUSIN): WE WERE DRIVING AROUND ONE DAY AND MY COUSIN DAVE GOES, "DUDE, I HATE TO SAY THIS, BUT I WANT TO BE A FUCKING ROCK STAR. I WANT ALL THAT THAT ENTAILS." THE PEPPERS HAD ALREADY ASKED HIM ONCE TO COME DOWN AND PLAY. THEY JAMMED AND PLAYED COVERS AND HE TOLD ME AFTER THAT "I HAVE A SENSE THEY'RE GOING TO ASK ME TO JOIN THE BAND." I WAS LIKE, "FUCKING DO IT, MAN — IF YOU FEEL GOOD ABOUT SAYING IT, THEN GO FOR IT." HE SAID, "ALL RIGHT, I'M SUPPOSED TO JAM WITH THEM AGAIN. IF THEY ASK ME, I'M GONNA DO IT."

DAVE: THE CALL WAS PRETTY MUCH OUT OF THE BLUE. FLEA ASKED IF I WANTED TO TRY OUT FOR THE BAND AND I INITIALLY DECLINED BECAUSE I WAS STILL RECORDING WITH ERIC. BUT WHEN THE RECORD WAS DONE, IT TURNED OUT I WANTED TO TOUR BEHIND IT MORE THAN ERIC DID AT THE TIME, SO WHEN FLEA CALLED AGAIN TO SEE IF I WANTED TO JAM, I WAS MORE OPEN TO IT.

WE HAD THIS MASSIVE AUDITION THING, AND WE AUDITIONED PEOPLE, AND WE HIRED THIS GUY, BUT IT DIDN'T WORK OUT. AND THEN DAVE MADE HIMSELF AVAILABLE. HE WAS READY TO GO. HE WAS READY TO BE IN A BIG ROCK BAND AND PLAY. HE COULD DO IT, AND HE COULD PLAY ALL THE OLD SONGS.

PEACH

Marshall

061

WE'D BEEN JAMMING WITH JESSE TOBIAS, AND IT WAS GREAT — ONE TIME IT WAS SO GOOD IT ACTUALLY WENT SOMEWHERE. REAL FIRE AND IT FELT GOOD, AND HE'S IN. *ROLLING STONE* WRITES AN ARTICLE ABOUT HIM, AND HE QUITS HIS BAND AND THEY'RE PISSED. IT WAS HORRIBLE TO HAVE TO TELL HIM THAT WE HAD ASKED DAVE NAVARRO BEFORE AND HE'D SAID NO, BUT NOW HE'S SAYING YES — OH, MAN. SHIT WAS GOING ON WITH JESSE AND HIS GIRLFRIEND, IT DIDN'T FEEL GOOD.

RICK RUBIN (PRODUCER): **NAVARRO WAS NOT REALLY A BIG FAN OF THE HILLEL SLOVAK BLUEPRINT. HE HAD A WHOLE DIFFERENT STYLE — MORE ORCHESTRAL.** HE'LL PLAY TWENTY TRACKS TO MAKE THIS BIG SYMPHONIC SOUND AS OPPOSED TO MINIMALIST FUNK GUITAR. A WHOLE DIFFERENT ANIMAL, BECAUSE THE BASS TAKES UP MORE SPACE IN FUNK. DAVE IS SO NOT THAT.

LEAP FOR ME, SUCH AN ENORMOUS SEA CHANGE IN MY LIFE THAT IT WAS VERY UNCOMFORTABLE. I TRIED TO MAKE THAT CLEAR TO THEM, AND THEY TRIED TO UNDERSTAND, BUT IT WASN'T UNTIL FLEA JOINED JANE'S ADDICTION DURING THE 1997 RELAPSE TOUR THAT HE TOOK ME ASIDE AND SAID, "HOW ON EARTH DID YOU HANDLE JOINING THE CHILI PEPPERS? THIS IS SO STRESSFUL!"

RICK: DAVE IS HIS OWN KIND OF PRIVATE PERSON WHO DOES WHAT HE DOES. NOT TO TAKE ANYTHING AWAY FROM HIM, BUT THE EXPECTATION WAS OVER HOW THEY WERE GOING TO DO IT, AND IT WAS VERY DIFFERENT IN HOW HE DID IT. **THEIR NOT STAYING TOGETHER HAD MUCH MORE TO DO WITH PERSONALITIES THAN MUSICAL STYLE** — ALL THAT COULD'VE BEEN WORKED OUT SOMEHOW OVER TIME. WHILE THE DIFFERENCES WERE HUGE, I THINK THEY COULD HAVE MANAGED THOSE HURDLES IF THEY LIKED BEING WITH EACH OTHER. THE OTHER DIFFERENCE IS BOTH FLEA AND ANTHONY ARE VERY UPBEAT. THE BAND IS POSITIVE, EVEN IN THE SAD SONGS THERE IS AN UPLIFTING FEELING. DAVE IS A DARK CHARACTER, PERIOD — WITH VERY DARK HUMOR TO GO WITH IT.

✿ THERE'S HUGE PRESSURE ON HIM BECAUSE WE'RE A BIG ROCK BAND AND EVERYONE'S SAYING, "OH THE BEST OF JANE'S AND THE BEST OF CHILI PEPPERS — WHAT'S IT GONNA BE LIKE?" IT CREPT ALONG, REAL TENTATIVE, BUT THERE'S NO, "THIS IS THE SHIT!" MOMENTS. AND I REALLY LIKED DAVE — WE HIT IT OFF WITH GOOD TIMES. I HAD A BUDDY, SOMEONE IN THE BAND TO BE SOCIAL WITH.

✿ WE WERE ADEQUATE. WE WERE DOING THE JOB, BUT WE DIDN'T REALLY CONNECT A LOT.

DAVE: IT WAS REALLY AWKWARD AT FIRST TO JOIN A PRE-EXISTING BAND. I CAME FROM JANE'S ADDICTION, HAD A LITTLE HISTORY. SOME PEOPLE HAD HEARD OF ME, HAD HEARD OUR MUSIC, BUT **THE CHILI PEPPERS WERE SUCH AN ENORMOUS WELL-TUNED MACHINE** TO STEP INTO, LIKE THIS INTERNATIONAL RECORDING AND TOURING JUGGERNAUT. THEY HAD ALREADY RELEASED *BLOOD SUGAR* — IT WAS SUCH AN ENORMOUS

063

Naked in the Rain

✳ Right when I quit the band — and once Jane's Addiction stopped — it seemed I was around Perry Farrell a lot in partying-type situations. Perry said, "I understand where you're coming from, because I did the same thing with Jane's Addiction. You can't just do something because you're successful at it. You have to go the next step and make it part of yourself." I can't remember exactly what he said. I still don't know how to explain it, but I still think I was right. I think Perry felt the same way then, and I hope he still does.

I had lots of empathy with Perry for resisting success in his behavior, which I feel is an important thing for people to do. Like when **I SEE THESE BANDS TODAY AND THEY'RE JUST CHASING SUCCESS AND THEY'LL DO ANYTHING FOR IT, IT'S REALLY SO UNEXCITING, SO BORING, SO TRANSPARENT.** I saw Perry resisting success, not so much spitting in its face, just not jumping right into it because **IF YOU GO JUMP INTO THE ARMS OF SUCCESS IT WILL CRUSH YOU.** The way he dealt with that — even if he regrets it now — was really inspiring to me. I would have never been able to do all the shit I had to do to get to where I am now at this point in my life where I'm pretty much set with everything. In my own way I also resisted success, and I'm glad I did. In the short run it made my life hard, and it made a lot of people really confused, but in the long run I feel good about it.

Johnny Depp and Gibby Haynes did a movie at my house. I'd made this decision that I was going to be a drug addict. I was already taking drugs recreationally — had been for about a year, but there was a point when I was so depressed after I quit the band and I had so many things on my mind, things I couldn't resolve with things I'd figured out about my own life and human nature. As I was figuring them out they were really exciting, but once I'd figured them, the world just seemed like this ugly place. My perception of things flipped — everything once beautiful was now ugly.

I used to go up on my roof that was a couple of hundred feet in the air because it was on a hill on stilts. My outfit for going up on the roof to wage war against the ghosts — goggles that Perry gave me and my ski mask with every part of my body covered. No holes. Sweatpants tucked into socks. You couldn't get into me on any level. It made a lot of sense at the time!

Rick Rubin (producer): I visited John when he was at a low point several times. It was shocking — everyone thought he was clearly going to be dead soon. He was on this path. Completely unapologetic that he was on a path that was final. Not a thought of getting clean — he wanted to be a drug addict. He ended up nearly killing himself several times and burning his house down.

Kim White (EMI promotion): John didn't really live anywhere, and all his checks were coming to Flea's house. One day Flea's daughter Clara started drawing on the back of a $600,000 royalty check with a crayon. Another one was in the backyard blowing around in the weeds! Flea said, "I tell him they're here but he doesn't ever wanna pick them up."

✳ I was painting all the time, my life was painting and these four-track home recordings would become my second solo record. Since I had quit the band I just didn't care that much about my music anymore. Painting made me happy. Maybe I didn't want to see myself so clearly because in my music you could hear exactly what was going on inside of me. ➤

BOB FORREST (friend and musician): JOHN WAS DOWN AND OUT. HE SAID THE IRS WAS HOLDING HIS MONEY. AND SO, I GAVE HIM LIKE $40, AND HE GOES "NO," AND I SAID IT WAS FINE, AND I WAS LIKE, "JOHN, I OWE YOU THOUSANDS OF DOLLARS." AND HE GOES, "$12,500, ACTUALLY!"

COCAINE PSYCHOSIS WE USED TO CALL IT. EXAMPLES OF IT — "WHAT ARE THEY WHISPERING ABOUT ME BEHIND THIS WALL?" "SOMEBODY WANTS TO KILL ME." THOSE ARE THE MOST NORMAL ONES. I NEVER HAD ANY OF THAT. I GOT IT EVEN WORSE. ONCE I CALLED PERRY FARRELL AT LIKE 7:00 IN THE MORNING AND SAID, "HOW DO YOU GET SNAKES OUT OF YOUR EYES?" HE SAID, "WHAT?" I SAID, "THERE'S SNAKES IN MY EYES — HOW DO I GET RID OF THEM?" PERRY TOLD ME I WAS OFF BALANCE — TOO MUCH YIN, NOT ENOUGH YANG OR SOMETHING. I COULDN'T GET ANY ENJOYMENT FROM BEING ALIVE ANYMORE. BEING ON HEROIN AND COCAINE ALL THE TIME, I FELT LIKE MYSELF AGAIN. **EVERYBODY WAS TRYING TO CONVINCE ME TO STOP. I'D SAY, "GIVE ME ONE GOOD REASON." NOBODY COULD.** PERRY, WHO I RESPECTED SO MUCH, WAS THE ONLY ONE. ONE NIGHT HE DROVE BY MY HOUSE IN THE MIDDLE OF ONE OF HIS FAMOUS CRACK BINGES THAT WENT ON FOR DAYS. HE SAT IN HIS CAR AND EXPLAINED, "YOU GOT TO TAKE DRUGS AND NOT TAKE DRUGS. ONCE YOU DO IT FOR A WHILE IT'S THAT MUCH HARDER TO STOP — LIKE IF YOU STOP NOW YOU SHOULD BE ABLE TO DO IT IN A FEW DAYS, BUT IF YOU STOP IN FOUR YEARS OR SOMETHING, IT'S GONNA TAKE MUCH LONGER, BUT FOR NOW, LET'S GET YOU TO THE HOSPITAL." WE PULL INTO THE PARKING LOT. I HAD ABOUT AN OUNCE OF PERSIAN AND ABOUT THE SAME OF COKE. PERRY SAID HE WAS GOING TO TOSS IT TO THE BUMS IN VENICE OR SOMETHING — YEAH, RIGHT. I JUST KEPT ON DOING AS MUCH AS I

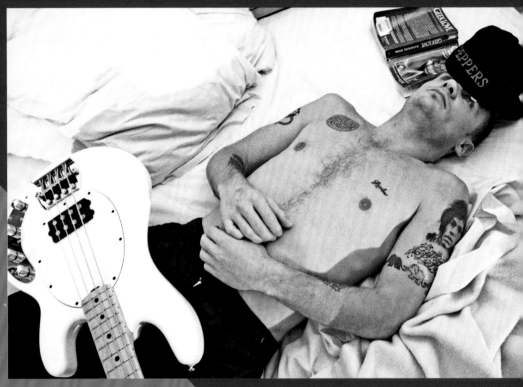

COULD BEFORE WE WENT INSIDE. SO WE GET TO THE EMERGENCY ROOM AND PERRY SAYS TO THE NURSES, "LISTEN, I'M GOING TO BE REALLY HONEST WITH YOU. HE'S REALLY ON A LOT OF DRUGS RIGHT NOW, SO WHY DON'T YOU WAIT ON GIVING HIM ANY MEDICATION." WHAT HAPPENS AS SOON AS PERRY'S GONE AND I'M MOVED INTO A BED? ANOTHER NURSE BRINGS ME ALL THESE PILLS AND SAYS, "TAKE THESE." I SAID, "DO I HAVE TO?" SHE SAID, "YES." I SAID, "I JUST DID A LOT OF DRUGS" — AND SHE SAID, "TAKE THEM." **SO I TOOK 'EM AND WOKE UP WITH A CATHETER IN MY DICK IN A WHITE ROOM WITH NO DOCTORS OR NURSES AROUND ME. I HAD OVERDOSED — DIED FOR A SECOND.** THEY WERE WORRIED ABOUT GETTING SUED. THEY PUT ME IN THE LOCK-DOWN AREA. I WAS ON SO MUCH MEDICATION I DIDN'T REMEMBER WHAT HAPPENED UNTIL I'D BEEN OUT OF THE HOSPITAL FOR LIKE FOUR DAYS. AS SOON AS THEY LET ME OUT OF THE LOCK-DOWN SECTION I HAD FRIENDS COME GET ME. NOBODY HELD IT AGAINST ME. THAT WAS WHAT I NEEDED TO DO AT THAT PERIOD OF TIME. IT TOOK A COUPLE OF YEARS OF NOT BEING A DRUG ADDICT TO FEEL LIKE A NORMAL PERSON.

067

Can't Stop

🔆 After Dave left, things were really up in the air with nothing going on. The year of nothing. Lindy had gotten remarried to a nice lady — she wanted to move to Ojai. Lindy had been through everything with us, and it was looking pretty bleak — could have broken up for sure. That was the only time I really thought, "Oh, this might be it." Lindy said, "I think it is time. I just want to move up to Ojai." He said he was thinking of retiring, and we were like, "Okay, fine. That's great," but he had this puppy dog look on his face like he kind of wanted us to talk him out of it.

Dave Navarro (RHCP guitarist 1993–98): We had finished an album, finished the '97 touring cycle, and had just finished a Jane's Addiction tour with Flea. If there was ever a time to part ways, that was the perfect time. The '97 Relapse tour wasn't kiddin' about going all the way out — it was pretty chaotic. Flea had never seen that kind of chaos coming from me. I was in such disarray I was in no position to go back, and I don't think they were in any position to have me back.

🔆 **DAVE SAID AFTER WE ASKED HIM TO LEAVE THE BAND, "THE ONLY GUY YOU SHOULD GET FOR THIS BAND IS JOHN FRUSCIANTE."**

🔆 Flea came to me one day and said, "I don't think our band is working anymore." It was the tail end of the Navarro era, and Dave had gone off the deep end getting high, and wasn't really feeling what we were doing anymore anyway. It was okay, it just wasn't meant to be — love the guy — but if it's not working, it's not working. I agreed. But then Flea says, "I don't think it would work with another guitar player, either." I was like "I can't think of anybody, either." And then he throws me for a loop, "The only person I would want to do this band with any longer is John Frusciante." John Frusciante? My first thought was, "Oh, no — this is Flea's way of saying it's over" because working again with John seemed such an impossibility. I sit on that comment for a bit and I'm like, "Seriously, he's not saying that as a metaphor for Goodnight Irene?"

Get On Top

C Sometime in early '98 Flea called me up asking if I wanna come over and watch the Lakers game. Though we share season tickets this wasn't like a regular thing. We don't watch games on TV together — we go to the court. So I go over there and I walk in, and there's Anthony sitting next to Flea. I'm like, "I knew it! Something is up." Anthony goes, **"WHAT DO YOU THINK ABOUT JOHN REJOINING?" AND I WAS JUST LIKE, "JOHN. JOHN FRUSCIANTE? THAT JOHN?" I SERIOUSLY THOUGHT I'D HEAR ABOUT HIM BEING DEAD OR OD'ING.** I saw him play the Viper Room one time — he had two teeth left, really puffy-eyed, looking and sounding really bad. Royalty checks were still coming in, but somehow John lost everything. He was selling stuff — platinum records — and cashing royalty checks at the check-cashing place on Hollywood Boulevard. It wasn't good. I guess he'd run out and one day I saw him at a bus stop — it was an extremely weird, disturbing feeling. There I am with Dave Navarro, the new guitar player, and there's John standing at a fucking bus stop. The guy who wrote all these great songs — my buddy and someone I cared about. He really looked like a different guy, and it freaked me out.

A John coming back was as divine a moment as our band has ever experienced. We've had a bunch of divine occurrences insisting something beautiful take place despite our individual screw-ups. Something greater takes place. I hadn't spoken to John in about six years, no communication at all. I bumped into him a couple times — awkward moments. I'm like, "Well, John doesn't like me, and this and that and why would you even say John? He's off in his own weird world." Flea says, "I have a feeling." I had to sit on that one — "like a feeling?" John was still deep into narcotics at that point, but Flea thinks he'd be willing to change his ways and come play with us. I'm like, "You have to be kidding? Like, how is he going to accept being in a band with me? Let alone give up drugs and somehow come back to his senses."

Next thing you know, John puts down the narcotics and comes around. I still wasn't sure he still wanted to be in the band, but I went to visit him, and he was a bit crazy but in this beautiful way. John has a unique outlook on life and nature. We started connecting and it wasn't ugly or painful — not nearly as awkward as it should have been after eight years of being foes.

C I didn't know that Anthony had gone and visited him in hospital or any of that stuff. He said John was doing a lot better and in rehab. Like last time I heard, you guys wouldn't talk to each other, and he's all, "No, no, we've buried the hatchet." I was still skeptical — that's a lot of years, six already. I didn't even know if he could play or had been playing. You have to remember this guy was in bad shape. I think Dave [Navarro] gave John a guitar —

MAYBE WHEN HE WAS IN THE HOSPITAL, AND I KNOW SINCE THEN JOHN GAVE IT BACK. LIKE, A LES PAUL OR SOMETHING. **EVEN THOUGH JOHN'S A HUGE JANE'S ADDICTION FAN, HE REFUSED TO LISTEN TO ANYTHING OFF *ONE HOT MINUTE*. HE SAID IT WAS LIKE SOMEBODY ELSE IS FUCKING YOUR GIRLFRIEND.** WE'VE NEVER DONE ANYTHING OFF THAT — JOHN'S NOT INTO IT AND HASN'T LISTENED TO IT.

WE DECIDED TO PLAY MUSIC TOGETHER. IT WAS SO NATURAL, AND IT REALLY WAS THE TRUE DEFINITION OF THE REBIRTH — OLD ENERGY WENT AWAY AND ALL THIS NEW ENERGY AROSE. IT WAS SO INNOCENT AND SO PURE. FLEA HAD A LITTLE GARAGE — WE SET UP THE DRUMS AND BASS AND GUITAR AND MIC, BARELY ROOM TO MOVE, BUT WE STARTED SHOWING UP TO THIS GARAGE AND PLAYING. JOHN HAD SORT OF FORGOTTEN HOW TO PLAY GUITAR. IT WAS GOOD BECAUSE HE WAS COMPELLED TO RELEARN THIS INSTRUMENT THAT HE'D ONCE HAD MASTERY OVER. IT HAPPENED REAL NATURALLY, AND THOSE WERE THE SONGS FOR *CALIFORNICATION*.

WE DECIDE TO JAM IN FLEA'S GARAGE. THERE'S JOHN, LOOKING GOOD, LOTS OF HUGS, AND I'M LIKE, "WOW." I SHOULDN'T SAY IT WAS LIKE WE NEVER STOPPED PLAYING, BUT IT WAS GETTING BACK TO JAMMING. WE CAME UP WITH A LOT OF STUFF RIGHT AWAY. IT REALLY FELT GOOD. HE WAS STILL GETTING HIS CHOPS BACK AND HE WAS STILL THE CONCEPT DUDE, BUT YOU COULD TELL HE WAS HAPPY TO BE THERE. WE JUST HAVE THAT CHEMISTRY — FOR SOME REASON THE FOUR OF US WERE PUT ON THIS EARTH TO PLAY MUSIC TOGETHER, AND IT REALLY IS A FORCE OF NATURE YOU CAN'T DENY. WE WERE SO LUCKY, SO BLESSED FOR IT TO HAPPEN AGAIN — ANOTHER CHANCE. I WAS HAPPY FOR HIM, HAPPY FOR US, HAPPY FOR EVERYONE. IT WAS JUST A REALLY POSITIVE EXPERIENCE. AND SO WE JUST REHEARSED IN FLEA'S GARAGE WITH HIS DOG MARTIAN HANGING OUT. IT WAS LIKE WE WERE A GARAGE BAND. NO ONE WAS EXPECTING ANYTHING OUT OF US — A LOT OF TIME HAD GONE BY, WE WERE MAKING SONGS JUST FOR US. I REMEMBER COMING UP WITH THREE OR FOUR GOOD ONES, LIKE "SCAR TISSUE," "PARALLEL UNIVERSE," "DIRT," AND THEN WE WENT ON A LITTLE TOUR — JUST TO GO OUT AND PLAY. PLACES LIKE STOCKTON AND MODESTO, WEIRD CALIFORNIA TOWNS.

THAT'S WHEN PETER [MENSCH] AND CLIFF [BURNSTEIN] FROM Q PRIME STEPPED IN. AT THAT POINT IT LOOKED KIND OF LIKE THE CHILI PEPPERS WERE DEAD IN THEIR TRACKS — SEEMED ODD TO HAVE ONE OF THE BIGGEST MANAGEMENT TEAMS IN THE BUSINESS COME SPEAK TO US. BUT THEY DID, AND SAID THEY WERE INTERESTED IN MANAGING US, BUT, "WE TAKE CARE OF OUR BUSINESS. DON'T CALL US BECAUSE YOU ARE ON TOUR AND FORGOT A JACKET — DON'T PICK UP THE PHONE. WE'RE NOT GOING TO BABYSIT, BUT IF YOU WANT TO MAKE A RECORD WE'LL MANAGE YOU." WE WERE LIKE "WELL, WE ARE GOING TO MAKE A RECORD, AND JOHN FRUSCIANTE IS BACK IN THE BAND."

071

Higher Ground

✳ Flea and I are disturbingly linked on some weird astral plane. He once went to see a psychic or past life reader type. She said, do you have a best friend blah blah blah, and she describes me. And she's like, Well, **YOU GUYS HAVE BEEN SLOGGING THROUGH LIFE FOR CENTURIES TOGETHER,** and in the last century or two, I saved him in Italy. There was a war and he was dying in the streets and I saved him and we went on to build ourselves up during this time of strife. Whether it is true or not — that certainly describes how we can be connected at certain times. When we are writing a record together, at least two times a week we'll show up wearing identical clothing, obscure identical clothing — it is the weirdest thing ever.

✳ When I first met Anthony at Fairfax High, right away, I thought he was a unique human with heaps of style and charisma. Back in '76, everyone had long poodle hair and bell bottoms, lotsa mullets, but here's this stand-out guy with a '50s crew cut looking weird. Bonding was easy. He told me he'd been in a movie — Sylvester Stallone's son for ten seconds in *F.I.S.T.* I was a shy, weird kid, not antisocial, more like nonsocial. My mom tells me when I met Anthony, I came home from school and was all, **"MOM, MOM, I FOUND SOMEONE I CAN TALK TO"** and it was the first time I had said that in a long while. We just became best friends.

075

F ANTHONY AND I WOULD JUMP OFF BUILDINGS INTO SWIMMING POOLS FOR KICKS. AND THERE WOULD BE OLD LADIES SUNNING THEMSELVES AND WE'RE FLYING OUT INTO THE SKY ALL, "AHHH!" AND THEY'RE LIKE, "OH, MY GOODNESS!" WE'D JUMP OUT WAVING OUR DICKS IN THE AIR. WE DID IT ALL THE TIME — "OH, THERE'S A POOL, WONDER HOW HIGH THAT ROOF IS?" ONE DAY ANTHONY MISSED THE POOL AND BROKE HIS BACK — THAT WAS FUCKING BAD. WE CLIMBED UP AND JUMPED OFF, I WENT FIRST. IT WAS A TEENY-TINY KIDNEY-SHAPED POOL. I HEARD BEHIND ME A CRACK, LIKE SPLAT! I LOOKED BACK AND SEE ANTHONY IN THE POOL WAVING HIS BODY AROUND. AT FIRST I THOUGHT HE'S JUST CLOWNIN', BUT WHEN HE PULLED HIMSELF OUT, HIS BODY WAS GREEN AND SHAKIN'. FUCK, I'M LIKE KNOCKING ON DOORS, "PLEASE CALL 9-1-1." SOMEBODY CALLED AN AMBULANCE. I'M PANICKY, LIKE, "DUDE, I'M OUTTA HERE IF CQPS ARE COMING — I HAVE AN OUTSTANDING WARRANT." ANTHONY AND I DID THINGS LIKE THAT CONSTANTLY. IT WAS JUST WHAT WE DID. IT WAS ALWAYS LIKE, WHAT CAN WE DO THAT'S RIDICULOUS? **WE WERE ALWAYS LOOKING FOR SOMETHING TO DO THAT WAS FUCKED-UP AND CRAZY TO MAKE OUR NIGHT.** AT WESTWOOD AND WILSHIRE THERE WAS A HUGE BIG BILLBOARD AND SOMEONE SAID IT WAS THE BUSIEST INTERSECTION IN THE WORLD. WE TOOK QUAALUDES ON A SATURDAY NIGHT AND CLIMBED UP ON THAT BILLBOARD — WE WERE JUST YANKING OUT OUR DICKS AND TWIRLING THEM AROUND.

077

ETHER

✳ I HAD MADE A FRIEND AT FAIRFAX HIGH WHOSE FATHER RAN THE HOLLYWOOD ACTORS THEATER. MY FATHER HAD BEEN IN A NUMBER OF PLAYS THERE WITH THE DIRECTOR OF THIS THEATER WHOSE SON, DONDI BASTONE, HAD COME IN AND OUT OF FAIRFAX HIGH FOR A SECOND. DONDI WAS LIKE SIXTEEN, HAD HIS OWN PAD NEAR WILCOX AND SANTA MONICA BOULEVARD, A QUITE GNARLY PART OF HOLLYWOOD. THIS GUY WAS A GROWN-UP KID. DONDI WAS WAY AHEAD OF THE CURVE WHEN IT CAME TO ADULT LIFESTYLE. LIVING ON HIS OWN, SUPPORTING HIMSELF — HE EVEN HAD A CAR.

KEITH "TREE" BARRY (FRIEND AND MUSICIAN): ANTHONY HUNG OUT WITH US IN HIGH SCHOOL. HE WAS THESPIAN IN HIS LEANINGS, A DRAMA DWEEB. NOT AT ALL LIKE JACK, FLEA AND HILLEL. NOT A MEMBER OF THE MUSIC DEPARTMENT — HE WAS JUST THE COOL DUDE WHO HUNG OUT WITH THE BAND.

I REMEMBER TWO THINGS HAVING A TREMENDOUS INFLUENCE ON HIM — "RAPPER'S DELIGHT" BY SUGARHILL GANG HIT WHEN WE WERE STILL IN HIGH SCHOOL AND THE OTHER THING WAS THE IN-YOUR-FACE SEXUAL LYRICS OF PRINCE'S "DIRTY MIND."

➤

A DONDI HAD AN AMAZING AWARENESS OF MUSIC AND THE RECORD COMPANY BUSINESS. HIS PARENTS WERE SOMEHOW CONNECTED. WHEREAS I LISTENED TO WHATEVER I STUMBLED INTO THROUGH MY DAD, OR THE RADIO, THIS GUY ACTIVELY PURSUED IT AND WAS A REAL CONNOISSEUR. ALL WE EVER DID WAS STAY HOME, GET HIGH, AND LISTEN TO MUSIC — WALLS FULL OF RECORDS. OUR LIFESTYLE BECAME LISTENING TO THEM. I WOULD COME HOME FROM SCHOOL AND HE WOULD'VE GONE TO DIFFERENT RECORD COMPANIES AND GOTTEN NEW STUFF. WE'D LAUGH AND FIGHT AND DANCE AND TRY TO GET CHICKS UNTIL WE PASSED OUT.

F DONDI AND ANTHONY WERE BOTH INTO ACTING AND BECAME CLOSE AND LIVED TOGETHER. HE WAS A HUGE MUSICAL INFLUENCE IN OUR CIRCLE — HE TURNED US ON TO MUSIC THAT WAS SO MUCH HIPPER THAN REGULAR RADIO SHIT OR ANYTHING WE WERE USED TO. DONDI WAS A RECORD JUNKIE, ALWAYS PLAYING US SOMETHING

NEW AND EXCITING LIKE TALKING HEADS, DEFUNKT, PRINCE, LOTS OF GREAT JAZZ AND CLASSIC HOMEGROWN U.S. '80S PUNK ROCK — LIKE X, FEAR, BLACK FLAG, ADOLESCENTS, DEAD KENNEDYS, BAD BRAINS, AND ALL THE REST OF 'EM. WHAT AN ERA!

TREE: DONDI GOT ANTHONY INTO PRINCE AND FUNK AND RAP ALL AT THE SAME TIME, AND I THINK ANTHONY EVENTUALLY STARTED SEEING HIS WAY FROM THESPIAN TO FRONT MAN FOR A FUNK-DRIVEN ENSEMBLE OF SOME SORT.

A DONDI GOT ME INTO THE CLASH, TALKING HEADS, GANG OF FOUR, PRINCE — HE'D ALSO PLAY JAZZ ALL DAY LONG, AS MUCH JAZZ AS STRAIGHT ROCK 'N' ROLL, NEW WAVE AND PUNK. WE GRADUALLY BECAME WIDE OPEN TO ANYTHING BECAUSE OF DONDI.

F I WAS REALLY INTO "VIRTUOSO ROCK" LIKE FUSION AND PROG AND SHIT — AND I STILL CAN DIG ON SOME OF THAT STUFF — BUT NOW IT WAS PUNK ROCK, RAP, AND GANG OF FOUR. THAT WAS THE BIG ONE, THE BIG BANG, THE ONE THAT GOT US ALL TO HANG A SHARP MUSICAL LEFT. HILLEL LOVED GANG OF FOUR, LOVED THIS ANDY GILL BIZARRE GUITAR STYLE. WE ALSO REALLY DUG ARTSY INTELLECTUAL POST-PUNK LIKE ECHO AND THE BUNNYMEN AS MUCH AS WE LOVED THE FURTHER-OUT NEW YORK BANDS LIKE MATERIAL, FRED FRITH, LOUNGE LIZARDS, JAMES "BLOOD" ULMER — THE DARING, TAKE-CHANCES EXPERIMENTAL SHIT.

A I LIKED EVERYTHING — LINDA RONSTADT AND TOM WAITS AND PUNK ROCK AND DISCO. VILLAGE PEOPLE NEVER GOT THROUGH TO ME, BUT MORODER SEQUENCER DISCO AND THE FUNKY SHIT DID.

F WE WENT TO SEE FRED [FRITH] WITH BILL LASWELL FROM MATERIAL AT THE WHISKY — THEIR GROUP WAS MASSACRE. THAT SHOW REALLY BLEW MY MIND. I DIDN'T KNOW ABOUT A CERTAIN RATIO OR JAMES WHITE AND THE BLACKS TILL LATER. ALAIN [JOHANNES] AND JACK [IRONS] NEVER REALLY GOT INTO THE PUNK ROCK THING.

A WHEN DONDI BROUGHT HOME THE FIRST GANG OF FOUR RECORD, I WAS LIKE, "OKAY, LET'S HEAR IT," AND I WAS LIKE, "OMIGOD, THAT'S THE GREATEST THING I'VE EVER FUCKING HEARD." WE LOVED IT! WE OPENED THE DOOR TO THE BACK PATIO AND POGO'D AROUND LIKE FOOLS, ROCKIN' OUT AND CALLING ALL OUR FRIENDS.

Forming

✴ I was the first to get the short punk hair, first to lose the poodle do in What Is This? I saw a punk rock show at the Starwood, I was like, "This is where it's at!" I have always been late with everything. It was 1980 already! Me and Anthony would go there on a Tuesday night, hang out in the parking lot, go to the show. Try to hit on girls and never have any luck. Who cared? Just going out whenever I could to see bands — always exciting. **AT FIRST THE RAD HARDCORE THING REALLY FREAKED ME OUT — A SECTION OF BLACK FLAG'S AUDIENCE AT THE STARWOOD WAS SO VIOLENT, SO BRUTALLY VIOLENT, SO UGLY.**

Like if you see a guy with long hair there's ten chickenshit skinheads on his ass. Just like, stomping him upside the head with Doc Martens — and look, wow, some poor poophead getting carted off to an ambulance in bloody pulps! Musclehead brutes pounding on people because their hair isn't the right length? I remember thinking, "These assholes don't love punk rock music." Like it's an excuse for random beatdowns by dimwits who didn't make the football team or whatever.

✴ And sometimes by those that did. But whatever we thought about a small segment of Black Flag's audience was no reflection on how we felt about their sound and what they were doing as performers. The Black Flag guys were playing for keeps, committed to the end of earth, that's for sure. We loved that about them.

✴ Black Flag was like 150 percent committed to what they're doing. They were like a wonderful art band — they represented something so powerful, but it was like, damn — thugs and assholes keep following 'em around!! Worse, they're driving the girls away from punk, probably what these idiots wanted!

✴ We, on the other hand, were punk rockers who LIKED girls, worshipped their feminine presence. We wanted to see them at the gigs, we wanted to see them in the audience and up there playing in bands! Hello!!??

✴ **BACK AT THE CRIB I'D LISTEN TO THE GERMS' *GI* RECORD OVER AND OVER LYING ON THE FLOOR WITH HEADPHONES.** It was a spiritual awakening for me. Like one single chord with real passion and the right motivation is as valid as John Coltrane. I loved the vitality of punk rock, the attitude, the energy of the musicians, the explosiveness of it — the poetic side.

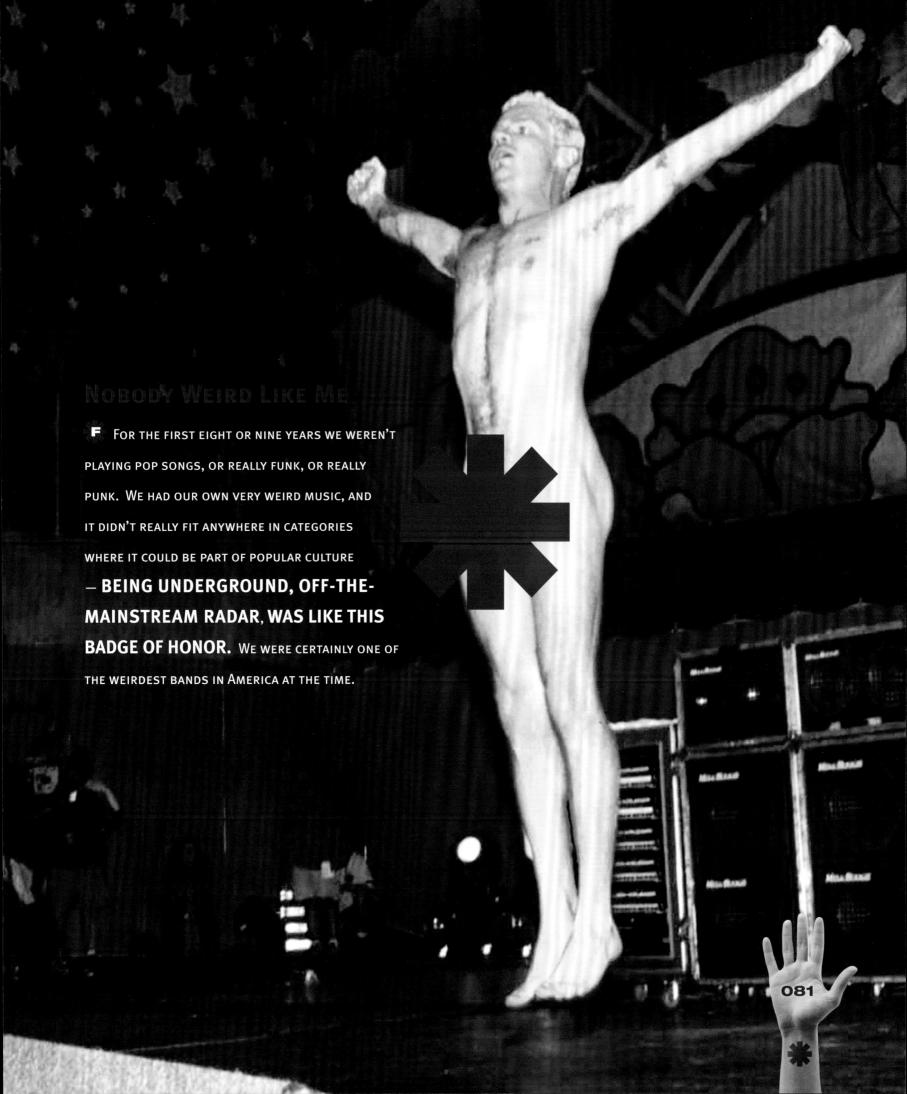

F FOR THE FIRST EIGHT OR NINE YEARS WE WEREN'T PLAYING POP SONGS, OR REALLY FUNK, OR REALLY PUNK. WE HAD OUR OWN VERY WEIRD MUSIC, AND IT DIDN'T REALLY FIT ANYWHERE IN CATEGORIES WHERE IT COULD BE PART OF POPULAR CULTURE **— BEING UNDERGROUND, OFF-THE-MAINSTREAM RADAR, WAS LIKE THIS BADGE OF HONOR.** WE WERE CERTAINLY ONE OF THE WEIRDEST BANDS IN AMERICA AT THE TIME.

Throw Away Your Television

F I discovered the C.A.S.H. space and moved in end of '81. Me, Anthony and JK had just been evicted from this house and were currently homeless. I'd become buds with this wonderful drummer, Joël Virgel, he and I were playing together there all the time. **JOËL AND MR. W THE SMACK DEALER WERE LIVING THERE, TOO. I WAS LIKE, "HEY, CAN I MOVE IN, TOO?"** I was dying to live at an after-hours illegal club space with these really arty dudes that I like who also love to shoot up. And I really wanted to play with Joël. Living there was wild — we were so into horrible drugs.

Janet Cunningham: I opened up C.A.S.H. [Contemporary Artist Space Hollywood] in April '81 because I wanted to get federal grant money for the arts. There was sly irony in the name, of course. I had already been involved with CETA programs in the '70s and watched the Contemporary Arts Space in New Orleans open up — I'd just moved here from New Orleans, where I was born and raised — so I thought I would do the same thing in Los Angeles. Get grant money, open up a performance space, put on shows, theater, live music, readings.

Laurence Fishburne (actor): During 1980 and '81 I would go to the Zero on Fridays and Saturdays, when John Pochna was running an illegal storefront club space for after-hours booze, like a modern-day speakeasy from the 1930s. A place to hang out and get a beer or two after 2:00 a.m. From there I stumbled onto C.A.S.H., which opened up next door about a year later, and Janet Cunningham introduced

herself. I met Joël Virgel, who was crashing there, always with his sticks and drum pads. He had two words of English then — "too much" — and it worked for everything, every question and every reply! He was a great musician, great percussionist. He eventually got into acting and I saw him in *10,000 B.C.* and lost my mind.

Janet: Laurence would come by, always kitted out in his Mr. Clean fatigues from *Apocalypse Now*. A wonderful, cool guy who volunteered to help out as an unpaid doorman when we had advertised shows.

Laurence: Janet fed us New Orleans style red beans and rice. She'd fix it up herself on Monday nights — $2.50, all you could eat with a piece of bread and a soda, too. I'd see Flea there all the time. I would fall by and act as an impromptu doorman if she had a special show going but I never lived there like some of the waifs she took in. This was fun times — I just wanted to give back a little to this crazy community. Flea — I knew him as Michael — was Joël's bud. They would clean up the next day in return for a place to sleep and a free practice space to try and get a band going. Who knew what was going on in Flea's mind at that time!

Joël Virgel (friend and musician): We were living in the C.A.S.H. space, practicing there all the time. We'd wake up and practice, then go steal some fruit from used-to-be Mayfair, come back, practice some more. All the time, eight hours straight, all night long, all the way through '82 into '83, playing, playing, playing. **FLEA WAS A SWEET, CARING KID WHO PLAYED BASS AND TRUMPET — WHO ONCE CRIED DURING *E.T.***

082

KEITH "TREE" BARRY (FRIEND AND MUSICIAN): WE FELL IN WITH
A FEW FRENCH FELLAS NAMED DAVID MAMOU AND THIERRY
FAUCHARD, WHO HAD A BAND CALLED NEIGHBORS' VOICES. JOËL
WAS THEIR REGULAR DRUMMER. MR. W WAS CLOSE FRIENDS
WITH THEM. GARY ALLEN — A PERFORMANCE ARTIST, SINGER AND
CLOTHING DESIGNER — WAS THEIR FRONTPERSON. THEY WERE
ALL PART OF THAT COMMUNITY WITH C.A.S.H.
AND THE LINGERIE AND THE PEOPLE THAT
WORKED THERE AND THE CATHAY.

LAURENCE: IT WAS A DIVERSE CROWD —
MUSICIANS MOSTLY, GRAPHICS PEOPLE, NOT
SO MANY ACTORS. I FELT LIKE I WAS ONE OF
THE FEW. **MOSTLY PERFORMANCE
ARTISTS AND MUSICIANS AT THE
BEGINNING OF THEIR CAREERS —
RUNAWAY STREET KIDS TRYING TO
FIGURE IT OUT. ALL OF THEM LOOKING FOR A PLACE
TO CONGREGATE, PARTY, EXPRESS THEMSELVES, AND
MAYBE NETWORK** — IF THAT IS THE PROPER PHRASE. DAVID LEE ROTH
FROM VAN HALEN ALSO HELD COURT THERE — REAL LOW-KEY FOR HIM, HAIR
HIDDEN, TIED BACK WITH A BASEBALL CAP SCRUNCHED DOWN OVER HIS FACE.
EL DUCE FROM THE MENTORS WAS ONE WAY-OUT-THERE MOTHERFUCKER, MAN!

JANET: C.A.S.H. WAS REAL TRANSIENT. I LIVED THERE LONGEST, FLEA SECOND
TO LONGEST. MICHAEL WAS PART OF A ROTATING CREW WHO WOULD MOP, CLEAN,
SWEEP UP CIGARETTE BUTTS AND BEER CANS, BOTTLES, BROKEN GLASS, ANY KIND
OF STUPID THING. EVERYBODY CLEANED UP. "YOU CAN LIVE HERE AS LONG AS
YOU CLEAN UP" — THAT WAS THE DEAL. WE WERE ALWAYS ALIVE, DAY AND NIGHT
— SOMETHING ALWAYS GOING ON. DIX DENNEY FROM THE WEIRDOS ALSO JAMMED THERE WITH TREE AND
MICHAEL. WHEN MICHAEL BECAME FLEA I THOUGHT IT WAS KIND OF DUMB. HE WAS MICHAEL WHEN I MET
HIM, AND HE WAS FLEA BY THE TIME HE MOVED OUT. I KNEW ANTHONY'S FATHER, BLACKIE DAMMETT, FROM
SOMEWHERE IN WEST HOLLYWOOD. HE WAS TRYING TO BE AN ACTOR. WHEN I DID MEET ANTHONY THROUGH
MICHAEL, SOMEONE TOLD ME HE WAS BLACKIE'S KID. NOBODY ELSE SEEMED TO HAVE ANY PARENTS.

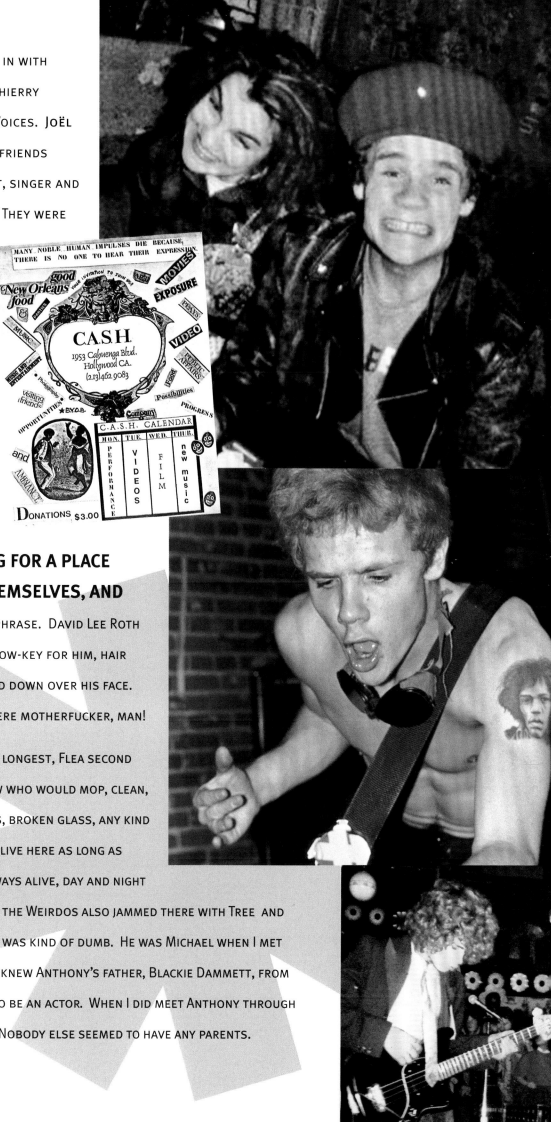

MANY NOBLE HUMAN IMPULSES DIE BECAUSE
THERE IS NO ONE TO HEAR THEIR EXPRESSION

good New Orleans food

ARTS MOVIES

EXPOSURE

PLAYS

VIDEO

PUBLIC AFFAIRS

MUSIC

C.A.S.H.
1953 Cahuenga Blvd.
Hollywood CA.
(213) 462 9083

MUSIC AND ENTERTAINMENT

Possibilities

Company

PROGRESS

visiting friends

B.Y.O.B.

OPPORTUNITIES

and AMBIANCE

C.A.S.H. CALENDAR
MON.	TUE.	WED.	THUR.
P E R F O R M A N C E	V I D E O S	F I L M	new music

DONATIONS $3.00

Fight Like a Brave

We met Bob and moved into his apartment right away. He was deejaying at the Cathay and playing a Defunkt song. I said for him to play the other side.

Bob Forrest (friend and musician): He bum-rushed my deejay booth and told me to flip the record — the hipper track was the other side of this 12-incher. Seemed like he was twelve years old. Such a child-like person, but I guess he must've been about twenty or twenty-one already, even if he didn't look it. You could see right away both Anthony and Flea were charismatic, powerful personalities. We started a friendship. We clicked real quick — we liked drugs, cocaine, we liked drinking, we loved girls. And then they were getting evicted from their apartment and I was getting a divorce. I said, "You can live at my house for $200 a month." Within a couple of weeks of knowing them they moved into my place on La Leyenda. I think they had a gig that first week.

All hell broke loose at this poor guy's apartment, we were just doing so many drugs like crazy. We were lowlife shitbags not paying rent.

Bob: I was this bookwormy nerdy kind of guy who likes a clean kitchen, clean everything. **I WAS LIKE, "OH MY GOD!" I DIDN'T REALLY WANT AMPS IN THE LIVING ROOM, SPRAY PAINT ON THE WALLS.** They were already into shooting coke a lot, and I got into it big-time with them. We shot coke all the time from the first few weeks on after they moved in. Flea had money for some reason. I think he got hurt on the set of *Suburbia* and got disability off it or something. I don't think we paid rent from March until we were evicted in November.

Finally in despair from getting no rent, the building manager took the door off its hinges to try and get us out.

WE SQUATTED THERE WITH NO FRONT DOOR TO THE APARTMENT — ANYONE COULD WALK IN AND TAKE OUR SHIT.

Then the manager shut off the water but that didn't matter. There was always some girl's shower and if you were extra lucky she had a laundry room in her apartment building and something to eat in her refrigerator.

We formed a one-off prank band with Bob and Anthony — the La Leyenda Tweakers. We played down at the studios where you could buy speed, and then we played a Blood on the Saddle show. They went off and we used their shit and Anthony went on right afterward for an encore. It must have been pretty bad.

We were horrible. Flea was the drummer, I was the bass and singing and Bob was the guitar player. We chased our tails practicing really bad music — then we decided to play in public the following day. We had been up way too long for our own good, and the only way we could get our amps to the Cathay was to push it a good two miles or so to the gig. We had that bad dirty speed energy — we just pushed these things down the boulevard until the wheels fell off.

Bob: They moved all their stuff by hand walking through Hollywood, rolling amps over the Walk of Fame star signs on Hollywood Boulevard with that really smooth surface. I'm like, "Dude, can't get a car — can't bum a ride off someone?" Three of us shunted Flea's gear up Hollywood Boulevard down to the Cathay de Grande, this huge bass amp and head. We're skatin' down Hollywood on the amp instead of a board. We were pushing it too fast. Anthony was squatting on top of it while Flea and I were pushing it and the fucking wheels melted under.

085

SPECIAL SECRET SONG INSIDE

BOB FORREST (FRIEND AND MUSICIAN): WE'RE UP ALL NIGHT SHOOTING DRUGS AND TALKING ABOUT FLEA AND I HAVING NEW HEROES EVERY DAY. GERMS, BLACK FLAG, THE CLASH, JOE STRUMMER — MOVING ON TO IAN MACKAYE AND THE STRAIGHT EDGE MOVEMENT IN D.C. WE ALSO HAD THESE SONGWRITER TYPE HEROES — I'VE GOT GRAM PARSONS, JOHN DOE, PAUL WESTERBERG, NEIL YOUNG, ELVIS COSTELLO, AND BOB DYLAN. ANTHONY USED TO SAY FLEA AND I WERE VERY HERO WORSHIPPY SO ONE TIME WE CORNERED HIM AND SAID, "DUDE! THERE'S NOBODY YOU LOOK UP TO? LIKE GRANDMASTER FLASH? IGGY POP? THERE'S NO ONE YOU IDOLIZE?" AND HE WAS LIKE, "NO." AND WE'RE LIKE, "COME ON, THAT'S RIDICULOUS. YOU HAVE HEROES, YOU JUST WON'T ADMIT IT." HE WAS LIKE, "NOPE, I ADMIRE PEOPLE'S WORK AND MUSIC, BUT I DON'T REVERE THEM THE WAY YOU GUYS DO." I WAS LIKE, **"THERE'S NOT ONE PERSON IN YOUR LIFE YOU LOOKED UP TO?" AND HE SAID, "WELL, MY DAD."**

I DO REMEMBER THAT CONVERSATION, AND I'M STICKING TO IT TWENTY-FIVE YEARS LATER. **WHEN YOU ARE LISTENING TO ARTISTS PLAY INSPIRED MUSIC OR YOU SEE A GREAT THEATRICAL PERFORMANCE, WHAT YOU ARE REALLY EXPERIENCING IS MAGIC — OR GOD — OR THE UNIVERSE — WHATEVER IT IS — WORKING THROUGH THESE PEOPLE.** YOU'RE TAPPING INTO SOMETHING THAT'S WAY BIGGER THAN A HUMAN. WHEN YOU MEET THAT PERSON YOU'VE ADMIRED FOR SO LONG, YOU'VE CONNECTED WITH THEIR MAGIC, YOU REALIZE, "OH SHIT, THAT'S JUST A DUDE!" THEY MIGHT BE SMART, THEY MIGHT BE PRODUCTIVE, BUT IT'S JUST A PERSON. I NEVER LOOKED AT THE ARTISTS THEMSELVES AS THE HERO — IT'S ALL ABOUT THE FORCES BEHIND THEM TO ME. I STILL LOVE AND ADMIRE CERTAIN ARTISTS, BUT THE WORSHIPPING PART HAS TO GO.

SUBWAY TO VENUS

A THE RED HOT CHILI PEPPERS TRANSITIONED BETWEEN PUNK ROCK AND THIS SORT OF ROCK-DISCO-GALLERY-FUNK NIGHTLIFE THING THAT SOMETIMES TOOK PLACE IN WEIRD BALLROOMS, WAREHOUSES, LOFTS AND GALLERIES IN DOWNTOWN L.A. IT WAS A VERY COOL, MULTIRACIAL MIXED CROWD — GAY, STRAIGHT, BI, TRANNIES, FASHION CASUALTIES, AND GENERAL MUSIC FANS SIDE BY SIDE.

F THIS SCENE WAS A REJECTION OF THE PAY-TO-PLAY GOINGS-ON AT THE TROUBADOUR AND THE SUNSET STRIP WITH THE POODLEHEAD METAL SCENE. PUNK ROCK HAD MOVED DOWN TO ORANGE COUNTY, MOSTLY FOR TEENS TOO YOUNG TO GET IN BARS AND REGULAR CLUBS, WHO COULD GET INTO THE OLYMPIC AUDITORIUM FOR MONTHLY EIGHT-BAND ALL-AGE SHOWS — THESE HARDCORE MARATHONS PROMOTED BY GARY TOVAR. GARY WAS LIKE THIS BIG-TIME POT DEALER SURFER DUDE, A REALLY NICE MAN FROM HUNTINGTON BEACH WHO STARTED UP GOLDENVOICE.

F WE WERE PLAYING WHAT WE THOUGHT WAS FUNK AND ANTHONY WAS RAPPING. HIP-HOP WAS STARTING TO INFILTRATE HIPSTER OUTLETS, AND THEY EMBRACED US. I REMEMBER GOING TO THE RADIO AND SEEING ICE-T, THE GLOVE . . .

A DOWNTOWN LOS ANGELES WAS A MUCH DIFFERENT ANIMAL THEN, THAN IT IS NOW. WHEN THE RADIO OPENED IT HAD A REAL ELEMENT OF DANGER WITH LURKING DRUG DEALERS AND OTHER CRIMS, RIGHT AROUND THE CORNER FROM MACARTHUR PARK, WHERE YOU MADE SURE YOU WATCHED YOUR BACK, ESPECIALLY AT NIGHT, GETTING TO AND FROM YOUR CAR. STROLLING UP TO THE WINDOW AND SEEING TRUDIE [ARGUELLES] AS THE TICKET SELLER FOR HIP-HOP WAS A GREAT JUXTAPOSITION. **THIS ULTRA-PALE BEAUTIFUL PUNK PRINCESS SELLING TICKETS FOR A HIP-HOP SHOW. I HAD GREAT TIMES THERE. ONE NIGHT I SHOWED UP IN A FULL-LENGTH BLACK DRESS AND COMBAT BOOTS AND A MOHICAN AND MANAGED TO FIND THE RIGHT MIXTURE OF DRUGS AND ALCOHOL — DANCING FROM 1:00 A.M. TO THE WEE HOURS.** ONCE I SAW BILLY IDOL VISITING, THAT WAS AN EXCITING BIG DEAL. HE HAD AN AURA AND CHARISMA ABOUT HIM. SAW EGYPTIAN LOVER PERFORM, WHICH WAS A VERY UNIQUE PERFORMANCE, SAW ICE-T HANGING OUT, AND THE GLOVE WAS JUST THE BEST DEEJAY EVER.

LYNN ROBB WAS PLAYING FUNK AT THE CONTINENTAL CLUB, ADJACENT TO THE OLD HOLLYWOOD BUS STATION. "THE FAKE CLUB," THEY CALLED IT ON FRIDAYS. WEIRD ENGLISH FUNK. NOT A CERTAIN RATIO, BUT MAYBE. THERE WAS ALSO A DEEJAY BOOTH IN THE BACK OF FLIP, THIS MASSIVE THRIFT SHOP SUPERSTORE ON MELROSE AVENUE NEAR OUR OLD SCHOOL. THIS SO-NOT-PUNK, NAMBY-PAMBY YET INTERESTING, SLINKY WEIRD POP FUNK STUFF WAS COMING OUT OF ENGLAND. POSEUR FUNK, IF YOU LIKE. MOST OF MY CREW CRIED CHEESEBALL, BUT I LIKED SOME OF IT ANYWAYS. PROBABLY "FASCIST GROOVE THANG" OR PIGBAG, OR SOMETHING. THERE WAS A BIZARRE, ODDBALL MIX OF CRAZY FUNK COMING OUT BACK THEN IN ENGLAND, IN NEW YORK AND ON THE WEST COAST, ALL AT THE SAME TIME — POST-PUNK SUBURBAN WHITE KIDS AND ART SCHOOLIES ITCHING TO START DANCEABLE FUNK BANDS.

F THEY CALLED SOME OF IT NO WAVE IN NEW YORK. I LOVED THE NO WAVE SCENE — THE CONTORTIONS WERE MY FAVORITE.

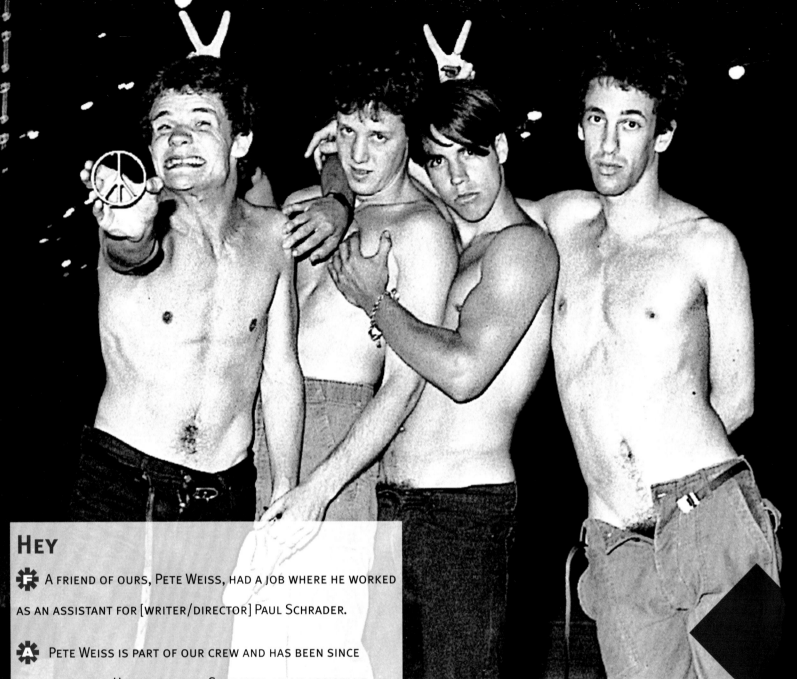

HEY

F A FRIEND OF OURS, PETE WEISS, HAD A JOB WHERE HE WORKED AS AN ASSISTANT FOR [WRITER/DIRECTOR] PAUL SCHRADER.

A PETE WEISS IS PART OF OUR CREW AND HAS BEEN SINCE THE BEGINNING. HE WORKED FOR SCHRADER AS AN ASSISTANT — WHICH MAY HAVE BEEN THE FIRST TIME I EVER HEARD OF SOMEBODY HAVING A PERSONAL ASSISTANT. HE SAID "I HAVE TO DRIVE ALL OF SCHRADER'S STUFF FROM A HOUSE IN WESTWOOD TO A HOUSE ON FIFTH AVENUE." THIS RYDER TRUCK HELD EVERY WORLDLY POSSESSION — FULL OF ART, TAPESTRIES AND RUGS, ANTIQUES AND DOODLES THAT RICH GUYS HAVE. SO HE SAID, "WOULD YOU COME WITH ME?" **FLEA AND I HAD NOTHING TO DO AND WE HAD A NEW DEMO TAPE, SO WE THOUGHT WE WOULD GO TO NYC** AND BOOK OURSELVES A TOUR BY GOING DOOR-TO-DOOR.

F WE GOT IN THE BACK — ME AND ANTHONY AND HILLEL. WE GOT THERE — WE HAD OUR FIRST DEMOS WE HAD MADE ON HOLLYWOOD AND WESTERN WITH SPIT STIX PRODUCING— AND WE WENT AROUND TO GET GIGS. WE WERE IN NYC TO GET GIGS OR RECORD DEALS OR WHATEVER WE COULD POSSIBLY GET.

A WE WEREN'T QUITE CLEAR ON THE WORKINGS OF THE MUSIC BUSINESS. WE JUST THOUGHT WE WOULD GO TO CLUBS.

F I REMEMBER JOE BOWIE [FROM DEFUNKT] WALKED IN AND WE WERE SO EXCITED. BUT WHEN WE WERE THERE WE WERE ALWAYS WALKING AROUND WITH A BOOM BOX, SO EVERY TIME WE SAW A LITTLE KID, THE PARENTS WOULD GRUMBLE AND THE KIDS WOULD GIGGLE AT US. WE DIDN'T END UP PLAYING ANYWHERE THOUGH.

A WE SMOKED A LOT OF WEED AND DROVE RECKLESSLY AND HAD A GREAT TIME.

091

THE BROTHERS CUP

✳ FLEA AND I GOT INTO A LITTLE BIT OF A FIGHT IN PARIS
— IT WAS OUR FIRST TRIP TO LONDON AND PARIS AND
AMSTERDAM — AND I DISAPPEARED FOR A FEW DAYS AND I
MET A DANISH GIRL. THIS IS '83 I'M GUESSING. I STILL LIVED
ON HOLLYWOOD WITH BOB FORREST. SO FLEA AND I WERE
IN A FIGHT AND HE WOULDN'T SPEAK TO ME, AND I SAW THIS
OLD FRENCH GEEZER SITTING ON THE STREET SELLING THESE
GORGEOUS OLD TIN CAMPING CUPS. AND I HAD A POCKET
FULL OF CHANGE AND BOUGHT THE CUPS, PUT THEM
ON FLEA'S JACKET — LIKE ON THE LAPELS — AND MINE,
AND HE LOOKED UP AT ME LIKE I WAS SO FREAKING
INSANE. HE WAS LIKE, "OKAY I CAN'T BE MAD AT
THIS GUY ANYMORE — HE'S PUTTING CUPS ➤

093

ON MY SHOULDERS." WE BECAME THE BROTHERS CUP, AND LATER WROTE A SONG ABOUT IT ON *FREAKY STYLEY*. WE WOULD LOOK AT EACH OTHER DEAD IN THE EYE AND SLAM OUR CUPS INTO ONE ANOTHER, AND IT MADE A GONGLIKE NOISE.

FLEA AND I WERE LIVING FROM STREET TO COUCH TO HOUSE — AND NOTHING WILL BOND YOU LIKE HAVING TO SLEEP ON A FLOOR NEXT TO SOMEBODY. WE WERE GETTING EVICTED FROM OUR HOUSE IN THE HOLLYWOOD GHETTO. **WE EACH HAD ABOUT $300 LEFT, AND WE COULD EITHER HUSTLE TO PAY THE RENT ONE MORE MONTH — OR BUY LEATHER JACKETS.** WE SAT DOWN AND HAD A LITTLE COUNCIL AS TO SHOULD WE PAY THE RENT OR GET LEATHER JACKETS? SCREW HAVING A PLACE TO LIVE, LET'S BUY LEATHER JACKETS AND WE'LL LIVE IN THOSE. WE WENT TO MELROSE TO BUY JACKETS FROM THIS ITALIAN AMERICAN GUY WITH THE BEST COAT SHOP, AND THEY WERE ALL $400. WE TOLD HIM WE ONLY HAD $300 AND HE WAS LIKE, "GET LOST — YOU AREN'T GETTING ONE OF MINE." SO WE HELD A PROTEST IN FRONT OF HIS STORE AND ACTUALLY GOT PICKETS. WE HAD THIS COMICAL PICKETING PROTEST AND AFTER A FEW DAYS HE GOT SICK OF SEEING US AND SOLD US THE COATS FOR $300, WHICH SEEMED A LOT TO US AT THE TIME.

095

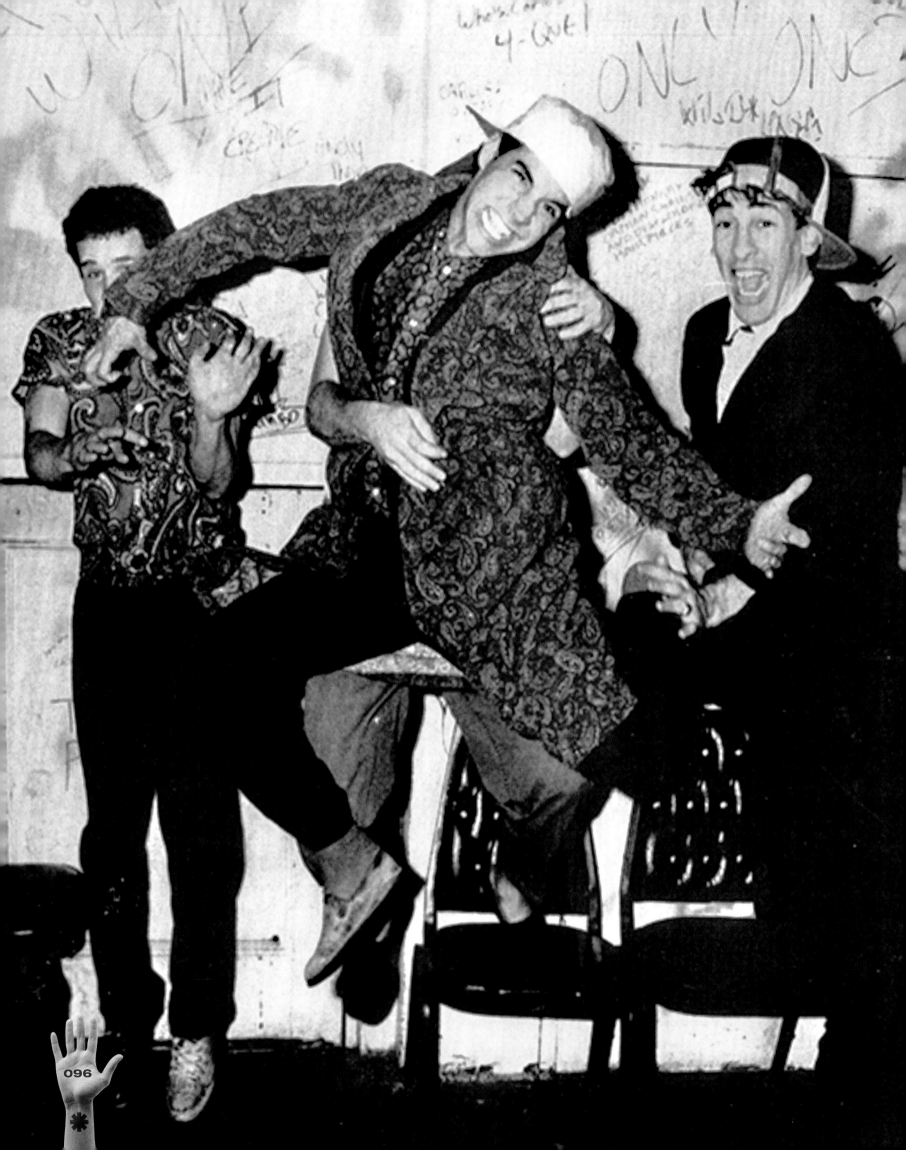

MAKE THE MUSIC GO BANG

BOB FORREST (FRIEND AND MUSICIAN): FLEA AND I WERE IN LOVE WITH EXENE [CERVENKA] — FUCKING OBSESSED WITH HER AND X. ONE NIGHT AFTER CLOSING TIME AT THE CATHAY WE INVITED HER AND JOHN DOE BACK TO OUR HOUSE, AND WHEN THEY ACTUALLY SHOWED UP WE WERE SHAKING, PETRIFIED! ME AND FLEA DASH INTO THE BEDROOM AND SHUT THE DOOR AND GO, "OMIGOD! THEY'RE IN OUR LIVING ROOM, OH MY GOD!"

WAYNE AND GARTH DOOF TIME. EVENTUALLY WE CALMED DOWN ENOUGH TO GO BACK OUTSIDE TRYING TO ACT ALL COOL AND COMPOSED.

BOB: I PUT ON SOME GEORGE JONES AND HANK WILLIAMS BECAUSE I KNEW THEY LIKED THEM AND MAYBE IT'D MAKE 'EM STAY A LITTLE LONGER. IT WORKED. JOHN WAS REAL RELAXED, SEEMED TO BE DIGGIN' THE MENTOR SPIEL. AN EDUCATION WAS PASSED FROM FIRST TO SECOND GENERATION BETWEEN JOHN AND ANTHONY THAT NIGHT.

IT JUST SEEMED LIKE ANOTHER NIGHT OF INTERESTING PEOPLE DROPPING IN. PETER HASKELL WAS WITH EXENE DURING THAT OCCASION. I WASN'T REALLY OF THE BRAIN-PICKING VARIETY AT THAT STAGE IN MY LIFE. I WASN'T THAT SCIENTIFIC ABOUT ANYTHING, JUST MORE SURVIVAL INSTINCT. MAYBE BOB WAS ANALYZING IT MORE, MAYBE I DIDN'T REALIZE IT WAS HAPPENING THAT WAY.

EVERYBODY WHO LOVED X THOUGHT THEY WERE GOING TO BE THE BIGGEST BAND IN THE WORLD.

IT'S LIKE 1983 — OUR YEAR — AND X WERE KINGS OF LOS ANGELES, BIG ENOUGH TO HEADLINE THE GREEK AMPHITHEATER THAT SUMMER WITHOUT A RADIO OR MTV HIT BEHIND THEM. THAT'S HOW WE SAW THE WAY FORWARD FOR US. **IT WAS POSSIBLE TO CIRCUMVENT THE DEADLOCK OF CONVENTIONAL FM RADIO OUTLETS AND NOW MTV IF YOU COULD JUST GET OUT THERE AND BUILD YOUR OWN FOLLOWING FROM SCRATCH.**

BLACKEYED BLONDE

✳ FORTUNATELY FOR ME **I DIDN'T KNOW VERY MUCH ABOUT ANDY WARHOL WHEN I MET HIM,** SO I WAS ABLE TO TREAT HIM LIKE ANY OTHER ARTIST. ALTHOUGH HE HAD A REPUTATION, TO ME IT WAS JUST LIKE MEETING SOMEONE AT THE C.A.S.H. CLUB — ANOTHER FUNKY STREET ARTIST TYPE. FLEA AND I WERE SUCH FANTASTIC HAMS AT THIS POINT IN OUR LIVES THAT IF SOMEONE HAD A CAMERA WE WERE MORE THAN WILLING TO OBLIGE!

099

HOLLYWOOD

✳ IT WAS VERY MUCH A MUSICAL COMMUNITY — A VERY DISTINCT, VERY L.A. MUSIC SCENE, AND IT WAS VERY QUIRKY AND ARTISTIC, BISEXUAL AND PUNK, AND AT THE SAME TIME, ANGRY, EFFEMINATE AND COOL. EVERYONE HUNG OUT TOGETHER — THERE WAS A LOT OF CAMARADERIE, A FAMILY-STYLE FEELING WITH ALL THE BANDS THAT WERE PLAYING AT THE CATHAY DE GRANDE, THE ANTI-CLUB, THE LINGERIE, THE MUSIC MACHINE, AND MANY OTHERS. ARTISTS LIVING IN LOFTS IN DOWNTOWN L.A. WENT OUT TO CLUBS AND BARS ALL THE TIME. CLUB PERFORMANCE ARTISTS LIKE JOHANNA WENT AND Z'EV WORKED THE BRAVE DOG, AL'S BAR. I LOVED ALL THOSE BANDS THAT USED TO PLAY DOWNTOWN — NEIGHBORS' VOICES, RED WEDDING, NERVOUS GENDER, ALL THESE WEIRD ART BANDS, BPEOPLE, MONITOR, HUMAN HANDS. I LOVED THEM. I USED TO SEE KOMMUNITY FK, CHRISTIAN DEATH. I THOUGHT 45 GRAVE WAS ONE OF THE BETTER DEATHROCK BANDS OFF OF THE *HELL COMES TO YOUR HOUSE* COMPILATION.

✳ *SCRATCH* WAS EVERY WEEK, THIS XEROX ZINE THAT CARRIED PICTURES AND DETAILS OF ALL THE COOL CLUB EVENTS FROM THAT WEEK.

✳ *SCRATCH* WROTE ABOUT US AND THE SCENE. ANYTIME THERE WAS AN OPPORTUNITY TO BE IN FRONT OF A CAMERA I WAS RIGHT THERE AND TURNING IT ON! ANTHONY, TOO. **WHATEVER IT TOOK TO GET NOTICED — WAVIN' OUR DICKS, MAKIN' DOPEY FACES, CRACKIN' JOKES WITH AN EIGHT-OUNCE TALL ONE.**

✳ WE WERE RELENTLESS, SO SHAMELESS ABOUT IT — MUGGING, GETTING IN PEOPLE'S FACES, DOING DAFT IMPROMPTU PUNCH AND JUDY SHOWS, GUERILLA STREET THEATER STYLE. WE WERE THE THREE STOOGES AND THE MARX BROTHERS COMBINED — ON THE STREET, IN THE CLUB, ON THE STAGE, THE PARKING LOT, AT THE PARTY . . .

✳ . . . IN THE ALLEY, UP ON THE ROOF, DOWN IN THE BASEMENT. WHEREVER, WHATEVER IT TOOK. WE WANTED TO ROCK IT ANYWHERE THEY'D LET US SET UP. I LOVED WHAT WE DID. I DIDN'T CARE ABOUT COMMERCIAL SUCCESS. WHEN WE GOT ACCEPTED INTO THE HOLLYWOOD SCENE I WAS SO PROUD AND EXCITED, CONVINCED WE WERE NOW REALLY AWESOME — EXCELLING IN THAT SCENE WAS THE GREATEST SUCCESS I COULD EVER HOPE FOR. WE WANTED TO BE A FORCE OF NATURE.

SCRATCH
MAGAZINE

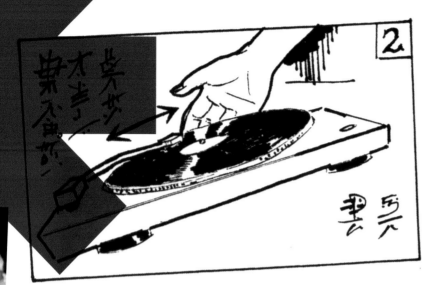

Vol. 10
Aug. 25, 1983.

PUTTING OUT THE FIRE

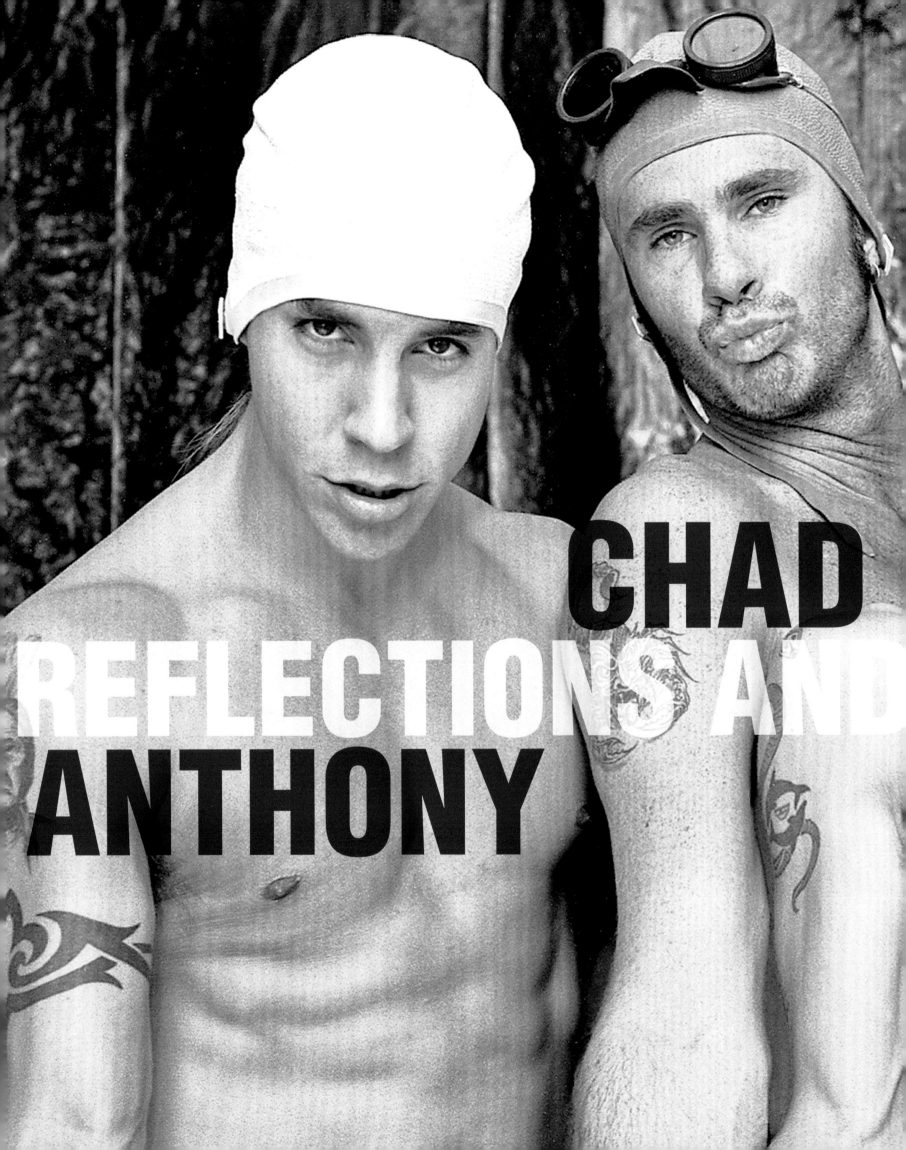

CHAD
REFLECTIONS AND
ANTHONY

RUMINATIONS
FLEA   JOHN

103

IF I LOOK AT US IN, SAY, 1988, I DON'T CONSIDER US TO BE ONE OF THE IMPORTANT BANDS TO COME OUT OF L.A. **I THINK THAT WE'RE PROBABLY ONE OF THE MOST INFLUENTIAL BANDS IN TERMS OF WHAT WE WERE DOING, WHAT WE SET UP IN TERMS OF FUNK AND ROCK BEING TOGETHER AND RAPPING AND ALL THAT SHIT,** AS OPPOSED TO THE SHITTY NU METAL BULLSHIT BANDS THAT HAPPENED. BUT AT THE TIME I DON'T THINK WE CAPTURED IT ON VINYL OR WERE VERY CONSISTENT WITH OUR SONGWRITING OR DEPTH THAT WOULD HAVE MADE US, TO ME, TO BE AS IMPORTANT AS, SAY, JANE'S ADDICTION OR THE DOORS IN THEIR HEYDAY. WE CERTAINLY DIDN'T CAPTURE IT ON VINYL — WE DIDN'T KNOW HOW.

IF

✳ I WAS ABOUT FOURTEEN OR FIFTEEN WHEN I GOT INTO ACTING. I WANTED TO BE AN ACTOR BECAUSE MY FATHER WAS DOING IT. I WAS MAYBE FOURTEEN WHEN THEY WERE DOING THE STORY OF ALAN FREED, THE ROCK AND ROLL RADIO DEEJAY. *AMERICAN HOT WAX* WAS A BIG-BUDGET FEATURE FOR PARAMOUNT. ONE OF THE STARRING ROLES WAS FOR A YOUNG MAN TO PLAY THE PRESIDENT OF THE BUDDY HOLLY FAN CLUB. I HAD ONLY EVER DONE SMALL ACTING JOBS BEFORE. I GOT AN AUDITION FOR THAT, AND MY FATHER HELPED ME THOROUGHLY PREP FOR IT. I WAS LISTENING TO BUDDY HOLLY, LEARNING HIS MUSIC AND LYRICS, DRESSING LIKE A GUY FROM THE 1950S. **I STARTED GOING ON THESE AUDITIONS, AND I KEPT ADVANCING TO THE NEXT ROUND** — PROBABLY STARTED OFF WITH A COUPLE HUNDRED KIDS. WITHIN A MONTH IT GOT NARROWED DOWN TO TWO OF US — MYSELF AND MOOSIE DRIER, A HUGE CHILD ACTOR AT THAT TIME. WE BOTH SCREEN TESTED, AND HE GOT THE PART. WHEN I ASKED WHY, THEY SAID, "WELL, HE'S GOT THE EXPERIENCE, AND EVEN THOUGH YOU'RE EQUALLY INTERESTING IN THE ROLE, IT'S A LOT OF WORK AND WE NEED SOMEONE WHO HAS DONE A MOVIE LIKE THIS BEFORE." THAT NIGHT I DROWNED MY SORROWS IN COCAINE AND ALCOHOL, TRYING TO MASK THE SENSATION OF REJECTION. **I'M MIGHTY GLAD I DIDN'T GET THE PART NOW.** WHAT IF I HAD BEEN A SUCCESSFUL CHILD ACTOR? SO SUCCESSFUL THAT I BECAME WRAPPED UP IN IT AND STARTED DOING TV OR SHOWS AND THEN MISSED MY TRUE CALLING — TO WRITE MUSIC WITH MY BEST FRIENDS.

YERTLE THE TURTLE

I first saw the Red Hot Chili Peppers on Alan Thicke's show [*Thicke of the Night*] and had this video of them. My friend Gerald made me a video mix tape with a lot of Residents, Sun Ra and other weird stuff. The first stuff I saw wasn't even with Hillel, but then Gerald made me a cassette mix tape of Captain Beefheart plus some other stuff I'd never heard like "Yertle the Turtle" from *Freaky Styley*. I really liked the guitar playing on that song.

First time I saw the Red Hot Chili Peppers live was at the Variety Arts Center, and that was really amazing. They had such a different sound — it was before *Uplift Mofo* came out. They were going for this real hard sound. They were really psychedelic in luminous body paint and everything. **HILLEL WAS DOING ALL THIS AWESOME FEEDBACK AND STUFF. IT WAS THE MOST MAGICAL EXPERIENCE I EVER HAD IN THE AUDIENCE OF A SHOW.** With the black light it felt like the band and the audience were one thing. After that I started seeing them as much as I could, every time they played L.A. or nearby. And I just always felt like I was a part of it. That same kind of thing when I heard Cat Stevens when I was four — the music was inside of me, and it wasn't that I felt particularly connected to the audience, but it just felt like everything there was one thing. It didn't feel like it was music being played to an audience — it was like anyone who was there was the music.

WHAT'S NEW WITH ALAN THICKE?
THE RED HOT CHILI PEPPERS THICKE OF THE NIGHT
Friday MARCH 16, 1984 11:30PM
KTTV 11
A Metromedia Station

109

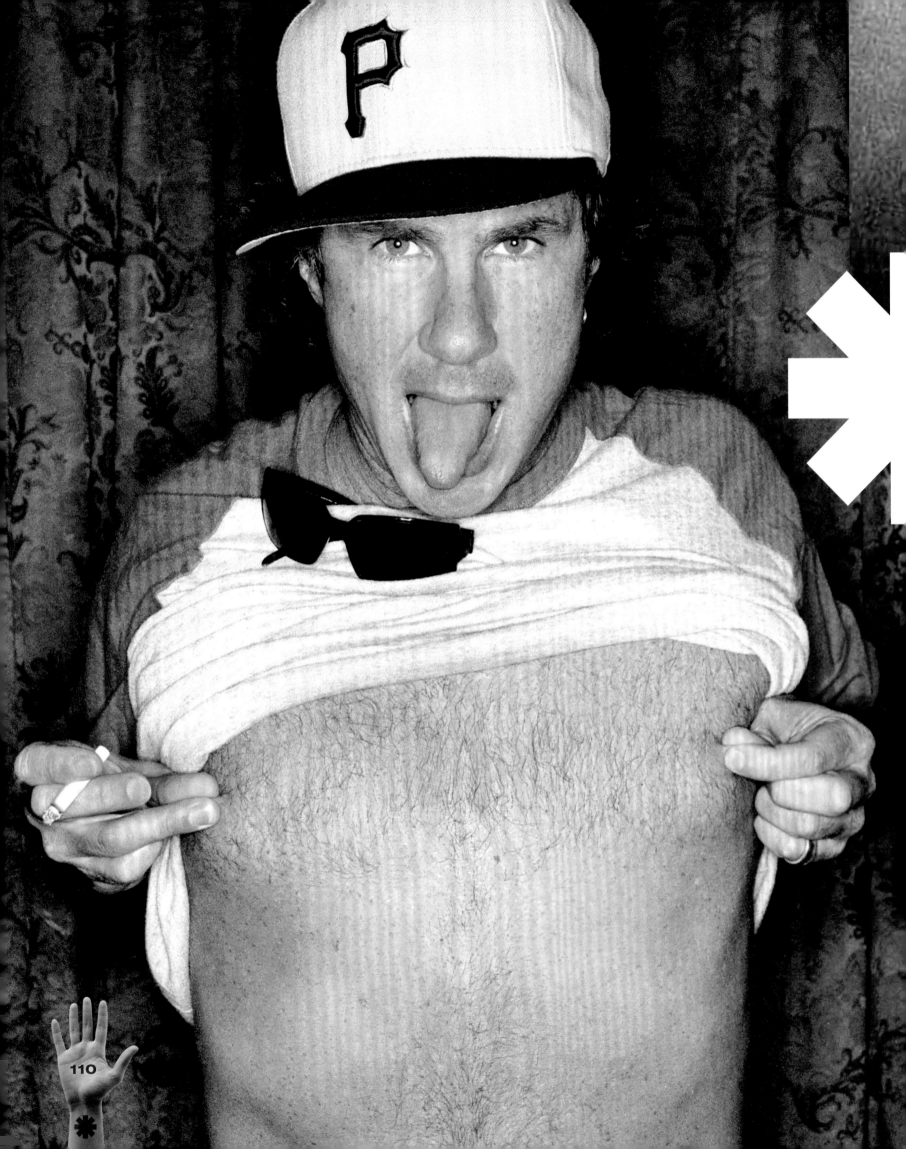

OPEN UP AND SAY . . . AHH!

I DIDN'T HAVE ANY MONEY. I TOLD MY PARENTS, "I WANT TO GO WEST," AND THEY SUPPORTED IT. THEY SAID, "MAKE SURE YOU BETTER YOURSELF AS A MUSICIAN, IF THAT'S WHAT YOU'RE GOING TO DO — WE THINK YOU SHOULD GO TO MUSIC SCHOOL." I WAS LIKE GREAT. I WASN'T ALL THAT KEEN, BUT IT WOULD BE A WAY FOR ME TO MEET PEOPLE, AND SO I SIGNED UP TO ATTEND MUSICIANS INSTITUTE, AT THE TIME $4,500 FOR A YEAR! THE SCHOOL PART, UNFORTUNATELY, NOT SO GOOD. I WAS LAZY, DIDN'T WANNA PUT IN THE WORK. I'D SHOW UP AND PUNCH IN BUT NEVER WENT TO THE CLASSES. I THOUGHT I COULD PLAY PRETTY GOOD, BUT THESE MI STUDENTS WERE A LOT OF COMPETITION. ALL THE GUITAR PLAYERS WANNA BE THE NEXT EDDIE VAN HALEN, THE NEXT STEVE VAI, THE NEXT SATRIANI CLONE. IT WAS VERY COMPETITIVE AND LAME. I WAS TWENTY-FIVE BY NOW, SEEING ALL THESE EDDIE-WANNABE KIDS POURING OUT OF EVERY HIGH SCHOOL. MI WAS VERY BRAINWASHY, LIKE A WEIRD CULT. I'M LIKE, "GET ME OUTTA HERE!" I'M ALL FOR LEARNING YOUR INSTRUMENT — NOT AGAINST THE CHOPS GUYS. I'M JUST NOT FEELIN' THIS PLACE, MAN. MANY OF THE PEOPLE THERE WERE SUCH DORKS. I WAS LIKE, "DAMN, THERE'S NO ONE HERE I'D WANNA BE IN A BAND WITH."

TO US, ALL THE HAIR BANDS WERE JUST RIDICULOUS. WE DIDN'T EVEN PAY ATTENTION. THE WHOLE METAL LITE THING JUST DIDN'T MAKE SENSE TO US.

WHEN I FIRST PULLED INTO TOWN, I WENT STRAIGHT TO THE CATHOUSE, LIKE '88 HAIR METAL HEAVEN — GAZZARRI'S ON SUNSET STRIP, POISON, MÖTLEY, GUNS AT THE TROUBADOUR — THAT'S WHAT I SAW. TUESDAY NIGHTS AT THE CATHOUSE, SLASH IS OVER HERE, THE GUY FROM THE CULT IS OVER THERE, MY MAN TOMMY LEE'S AT THE BAR. HOTTEST-LOOKING BABES I'VE EVER SEEN — A SEA OF 'EM! HOLY SHIT! ROCK 'N' ROLL HEAVEN! THE GENERICS, MY FRIEND GORDIE [GERMAINE]'S BAND, MADE NO MONEY. HE WAS SUPPORTING HIMSELF DESIGNING SETS FOR ROCK VIDEOS — HE BUILT THE FAKE MOUNTAINS IN THE BACKGROUND FOR KEITH RICHARDS. KEITH'S SITTING THERE DURING THE SHOOT, HUGE FUCKIN' BAG O' COKE AND LIKE THIS LONG-ASSED FUCKING ORNAMENTAL BLADE TO SNORT IT OFF OF, AND I'M LIKE, **"WHOA! FUCK!" KEITH RICHARDS PLAYING SLOPPY SLIDE GUITAR AND GETTING HIGH FROM A BEAUTIFUL GOLD DAGGER WITH A DIAMOND HANDLE** — AND I'M IN THE SAME ROOM!

Body and Soul

When my mom and dad split and he moved back to Australia, my mom started carrying on with this teacher at a music school she was going to. Walter Urban Jr. ended up becoming my stepdad. He was a jazz guy, and I became a musician primarily because of him. I lived for the jam sessions at the house in New York and later, in Los Angeles, when he'd come out. How fuckin' lucky was that? Every weekend there's a BBQ and all his jazz buds would come over to play standards and bebop and all this farther-out music, like they were really into 1940s and '50s bop. They played all these different tunes and it was so wild to me, so exciting, even as a child, to hear Charlie Parker songs, "Body and Soul," or whatever. They'd get together — sax players, other horn players, drummers, bass, piano, and start blowing some intense jazz. My first instinct was to roll around on the floor laughin' and laughin' — I was about eight or nine — just putting horns to their mouths and plucking on strings and making **THIS MUSIC WAS PURE, UNBELIEVABLE, SHOCKING MAGIC TO ME. THE GREATEST THING I COULD EVER IMAGINE SEEING.** Walter was definitely a questionable character, a real difficult Jekyll/Hyde guy. I don't want to rake him over the coals because in a lot of ways he was a kind, nice man — he just had this addiction problem. At this point in my life I forgive him for all of his problems, and want to affirm he was the one who lit me up with the gift of music — and for that I'll always be grateful.

I will rock your motherfuckins world

Break on Through

❋ I discovered punk when I was about nine. I liked Devo, the Ramones, B-52's, and then I got the Germs' album in '79 when it came out. From that I gradually focused more on radical punk, early West Coast skatecore stuff. Up to then Devo was my favorite band, but that switched to the Germs, X, Black Flag, Circle Jerks, Wasted Youth, Adolescents and so on and on. I listened to Rodney [Bingenheimer]'s radio show every Saturday and Sunday on KROQ-FM — I would record it and sit on my bed relistening to everything hours after the show was over. Sometimes Rodney even played cassette demos! It was inspiring more kids to think they could do it, too. **WEST COAST HARDCORE WAS TEENAGE MUSIC BY AND FOR OTHER TEENS — THAT WAS THE POINT OF IT.**

Before we moved to Mar Vista, we lived in Santa Monica and I was going to the Marina skate park every weekend. I had short hair and would spike it up. I would overhear the older people talking in lines about this band or that band. From nine till eleven, I was into skateboarding. That's how I heard about new music. If I would have had my way, I woulda been there all day, every day, straight after school, but my mom wouldn't allow it. I'd walk to Mrs. Gooch's in Mar Vista because I had older friends who worked there, twenty-three

years old or whatever. I met my first punk friend there. When I started liking punk, a couple of friends didn't want to be friends with me anymore. I definitely had kids turn on me a lot. I wasn't able to go to shows when I was into punk — my mom wouldn't let me go. Jumping around in the slam pit and losing your mind and dancing — seemed a very beautiful thing to me, but not her. This guy Craig who worked at Gooch's and his best friend had a little brother, my age, also into punk. Our first conversation was, "So, dude, I hear you like the Flag?" and I said, "Fully."

I filled up a jar of pennies so I could buy vinyl records — back then you could get them for $3.99. I was at this record store in Santa Monica getting a Ramones record when I met this girl, probably eighteen years old, and she told me she knew Darby Crash and that she liked the Doors — and that Darby and Jim Morrison were these great poets. She was telling me I should buy a Doors album, so next chance I bought this really good compilation, some greatest hits album, I think it was. **PUNK NOW SEEMED LIKE DARBY AND JIM MORRISON WITH IGGY AND BOWIE IN BETWEEN.** I also had books around the house. My dad was really into philosophy, a subject was always being discussed in the house so, luckily, I had him or a couple of friends I could talk about it with. My new discoveries — Eno, Byrne had an intellectual slant to everything they did and so studying the nature of the mind gradually became more and more important.

Fly Like an Eagle

My first vivid memories of music are after moving back to Michigan when I was five or six. I heard "Heart of Gold" for some reason, by Neil Young, and it moved me so much I insisted my mother buy me the 45. I remember playing that on my little white plastic turntable. At the same time I heard "Brand New Key." I got into that song, and got the 45. **AND THEN I JUST BECAME A COMPLETE LOVER OF AM RADIO. I REMEMBER DRIVING AROUND WITH MY MOTHER JUST ADORING THESE SONGS — PRETTY GOOD POP RADIO AT THE TIME.** I remember buying some hits-compilation album with The Hollies' "Long Cool Woman in a Black Dress" on it — something about that groove played over and over. Only

These psychedelic care packages with beads and T-shirts, records, magazines, notes about his trips — all this cool, exciting stuff. Dad started sending me weird records from Hollywood he wanted me to hear. One of them was an early Steve Miller Band record. These were down-and-dirty records. Not that I didn't like the hits — his hits got me later, in high school. Like a lot of other kids at the time, I took LSD and tripped out to "Time keeps on . . . slippin' slippin' slippin . . . haha . . . " I was ten when I saw Bowie in 1972 during one of my visits to dad. That had such a profound effect on me because it was such a great combination of artistic theatrics, as opposed to theatrics for the sake of, "Oh, we gotta do something." It was a real artist's presentation. Dad also took me

later on I understood it's like a Creedence-Clearwater-goes-T-Rex groove. I remember waking up late one night in my bed, turning on the radio, and "Frankenstein" by Edgar Winter Group was playing. I went into a trance, like I've never heard anything like this — what is this music? My father was in California and we'd go visit each other for extended periods. In between he'd send me

to an Iggy Pop show at the Whisky — another great experience. I remember Iggy's leopard print pants and he's bare-chested onstage. At the time, I never thought to myself, "Oh, I could do that" or "I wanna be that." It just got filed away. There are no rules to what it is to be a performer or musician.

ZOOT ALLURES

✳ MUSIC ALWAYS MEANT MORE TO ME THAN IT MEANT TO OTHER PEOPLE. FOR OTHER PEOPLE IT WAS SOMETHING TO WEAR ON THEIR ARM, BUT IT FULFILLED ME IN A WAY THAT REALLY CAN'T BE EXPLAINED. **I WOULD HEAR MUSIC IN MY HEAD EVEN THOUGH I DIDN'T KNOW HOW TO PLAY AN INSTRUMENT YET.** I'D HEAR SONGS I NEVER HEARD BEFORE AND IT WOULD SOUND REALLY GOOD, AND I'M LIKE EIGHT YEARS OLD WALKING DOWN THE STREET HEARING THIS BEAUTIFUL MUSIC IN MY HEAD. I'D THINK, "WOW, IF I KNEW HOW TO SING WHAT I HEAR IN MY HEAD OR HOW TO PLAY AN INSTRUMENT, I COULD MAKE THESE SOUNDS. I COULD MAKE REALLY GOOD MUSIC!" I GOT INTO SKATEBOARDING AND THOUGHT I WOULD BE A SKATEBOARDER. I REMEMBER BEING IN SCHOOL WRITING THAT I WANTED TO BE AN ACTOR. BUT ANYTIME I WOULD DO THESE THINGS, THE VOICE WOULD COME IN MY HEAD LIKE, "WELL, YOU'D LIKE TO DO THOSE THINGS, BUT YOU AREN'T GOING TO — YOU'RE GOING TO BE A ROCK STAR."

MY FIRST MEMORY OF HEARING MUSIC AND ACTUALLY FEELING IT WITH MY OWN FEELING AND NOT MY MOM'S OR DAD'S FEELINGS WAS AT A NEIGHBOR'S HOUSE — THE LIGHTS WERE DIM IN HIS LIVING ROOM AND IT WAS A CAT STEVENS RECORD PLAYING, I WAS ONLY FOUR YEARS OLD, BUT I COULD FEEL THAT THIS MUSIC RELATED TO ME AND MY SOUL AND MY LIFE IN A REALLY DIRECT, PROFOUND WAY. I'D ALWAYS HEARD IT IN A WAY WHERE IT SOUNDED OUTSIDE OF ME — THIS TIME IT WAS AS IF THE MUSIC WAS PLAYING IN MY HEAD, INSIDE OF ME.

THE DAY I STARTED PLAYING GUITAR I WROTE THIRTY PUNK SONGS IN A ROW — THE MUSIC WAS ALREADY THERE INSIDE. IT JUST TOOK LEARNING AN INSTRUMENT. PUNK WAS NOT INTIMIDATING IN A WAY THAT JIMMY PAGE OR SOMEBODY WOULD BE. ANYONE COULD DO IT. AS SOON AS I REALLY TOOK IN THAT KIND OF MUSIC, I JUST PULLED OUT AN ACOUSTIC — I DIDN'T EVEN CARE IT WASN'T ELECTRIC. INITIALLY I WANTED TO PLAY ELECTRIC — BUT MY PARENTS WOULDN'T GET ME ONE. THEY DIDN'T THINK I'D STICK WITH IT. **I NEEDED TO DO IT SO BADLY I DIDN'T CARE IF I WAS FORCED TO PLAY PUNK ROCK ON AN ACOUSTIC.**

MY TASTES RAN TO ARTY THINGS — ENO, DAVID BYRNE, TALKING HEADS, LAURIE ANDERSON. AND KING CRIMSON. PROGRESSIVE ROCK AND ARTY ROCK. I LIKED BOWIE AND YES, I REALLY GOT INTO FRANK ZAPPA, ALL DAY, EVERY DAY, STUDYING HIS MUSIC AND PLAYING ALONG WITH HIS RECORDS. WHEN I WAS FIFTEEN OR SIXTEEN I HAD A GOOD NINETY-MINUTE REPERTOIRE OF REALLY COMPLICATED ZAPPA STUFF. MOSTLY HIS SOLO STUFF FROM THE '70S. SOMEETHING LIKE "THE BLACK PAGE." I KNEW HIS MUSIC REALLY WELL ON GUITAR. IT WAS A WAY FOR ME TO GAIN SOME CONFIDENCE, BECAUSE I FELT LIKE IF I COULD PLAY THIS, I COULD DO WHATEVER I WANTED.

118

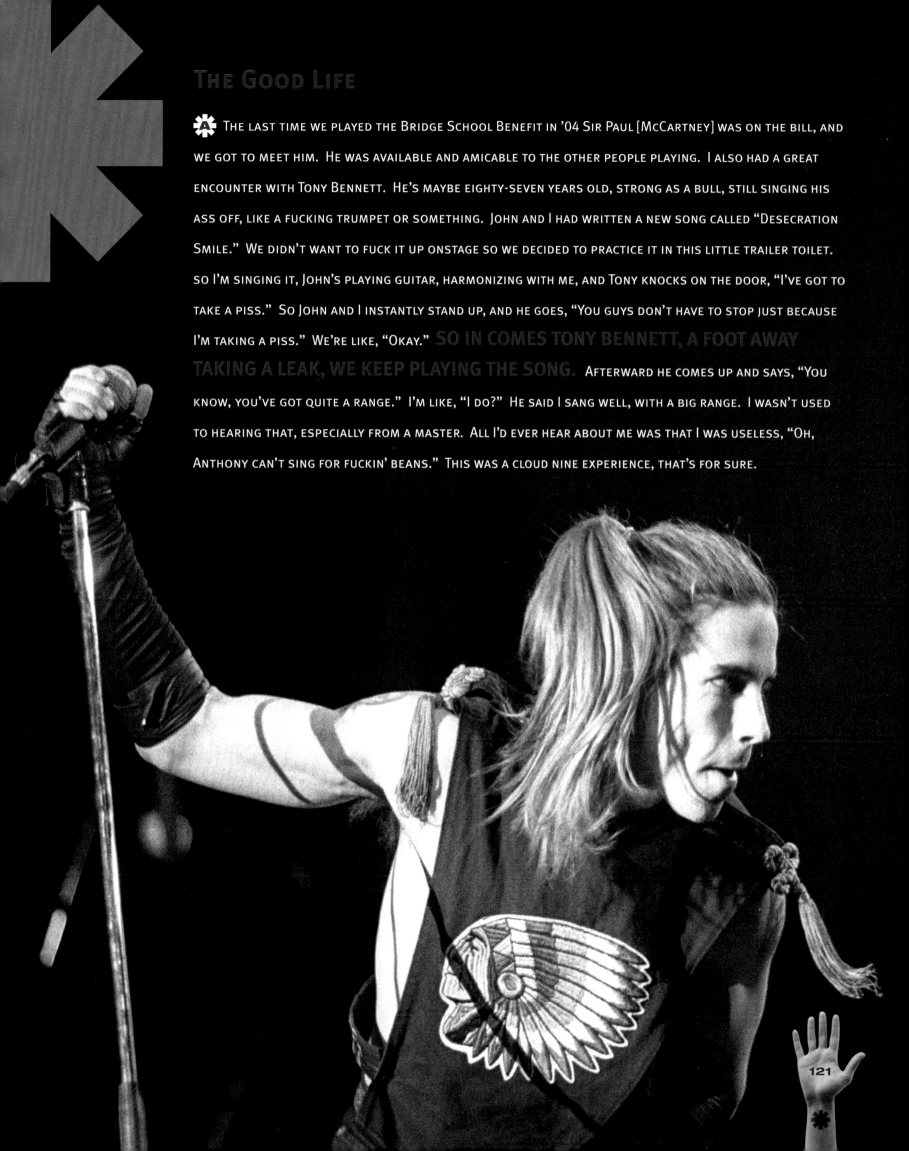

THE GOOD LIFE

A THE LAST TIME WE PLAYED THE BRIDGE SCHOOL BENEFIT IN '04 SIR PAUL [MCCARTNEY] WAS ON THE BILL, AND WE GOT TO MEET HIM. HE WAS AVAILABLE AND AMICABLE TO THE OTHER PEOPLE PLAYING. I ALSO HAD A GREAT ENCOUNTER WITH TONY BENNETT. HE'S MAYBE EIGHTY-SEVEN YEARS OLD, STRONG AS A BULL, STILL SINGING HIS ASS OFF, LIKE A FUCKING TRUMPET OR SOMETHING. JOHN AND I HAD WRITTEN A NEW SONG CALLED "DESECRATION SMILE." WE DIDN'T WANT TO FUCK IT UP ONSTAGE SO WE DECIDED TO PRACTICE IT IN THIS LITTLE TRAILER TOILET. SO I'M SINGING IT, JOHN'S PLAYING GUITAR, HARMONIZING WITH ME, AND TONY KNOCKS ON THE DOOR, "I'VE GOT TO TAKE A PISS." SO JOHN AND I INSTANTLY STAND UP, AND HE GOES, "YOU GUYS DON'T HAVE TO STOP JUST BECAUSE I'M TAKING A PISS." WE'RE LIKE, "OKAY." SO IN COMES TONY BENNETT, A FOOT AWAY TAKING A LEAK, WE KEEP PLAYING THE SONG. AFTERWARD HE COMES UP AND SAYS, "YOU KNOW, YOU'VE GOT QUITE A RANGE." I'M LIKE, "I DO?" HE SAID I SANG WELL, WITH A BIG RANGE. I WASN'T USED TO HEARING THAT, ESPECIALLY FROM A MASTER. ALL I'D EVER HEAR ABOUT ME WAS THAT I WAS USELESS, "OH, ANTHONY CAN'T SING FOR FUCKIN' BEANS." THIS WAS A CLOUD NINE EXPERIENCE, THAT'S FOR SURE.

121

In the Light

✺ I GET IN THIS BAND AROUND '84–'85 CALLED TOBY REDD. GOT A RECORD DEAL — IT TOOK A LONG TIME, PLAYING IN CLUBS FOREVER. IT WAS SO EXCITING FOR A DETROIT BAND PLAYING ORIGINAL MUSIC. **NO ONE COMES TO DETROIT TO SIGN BANDS. IT WAS LIKE, "WE'RE SO**

FUCKIN' LUCKY, A MAJOR LABEL, WOO-HOO!" RCA, YOU KNOW, THE ROMANTICS. SAME LABEL. WE'RE ALL THINKING, "BIG TIME, WEEE!" SIX MONTHS LATER WE'RE BACK PLAYING CLUBS AGAIN DOING IGGY AND CLASH COVERS. I'M LIKE, "I GOTTA GET OUTTA HERE NOW!" I'M TWENTY-THREE OR TWENTY-FOUR, PLAYING WITH OLDER GUYS, SQUEAKING BY ON $180 A WEEK, PLAYING COVER SONGS EVERY NIGHT. ALSO GOT INTO A FEW SCRAPES — A FEW DUIs AND A LITTLE TROUBLE WITH THE LAW. I NEEDED CHANGE. I DESPERATELY NEEDED SOMETHING NEW.

123

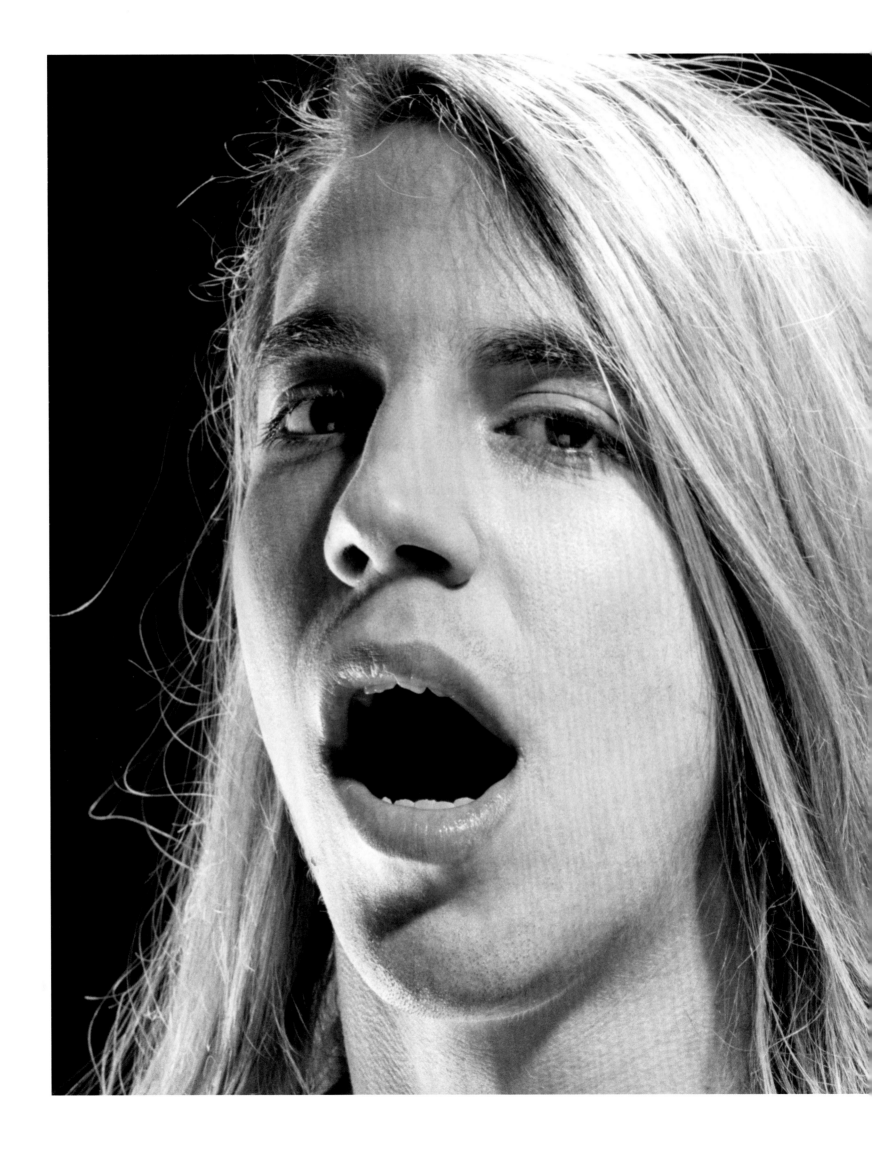

SNOW (HEY OH)

✳ I CAN TELL YOUNGSTERS WHAT HAPPENED TO ME, LIKE, "OH, WHEN I WAS TWELVE I SMOKED TOO MUCH POT AND IT MESSED ME UP! LIKE I COULDN'T THINK STRAIGHT OR DEVELOP RIGHT OR HAVE A CLEAR PICTURE OF EVERYTHING I NEEDED TO BE AWARE OF." SO, YOU KNOW, OF COURSE YOU CAN IF YOU WANT TO BUT THERE IS A CONSEQUENCE. IT'S PRETTY FUCKING FUN AT THE BEGINNING, BUT YOU'LL ALSO WRECK YOUR MIND A LITTLE BIT — YOU MAKE THE CHOICE. IF IT IS SOMEONE YOU HAVE AN INTIMATE RELATIONSHIP WITH THAT YOU ARE MEANT TO COUNSEL, **THE BEST YOU CAN DO IS TELL THEM OF THE CONSEQUENCES FROM YOUR EXPERIENCES. HELP THEM KNOW — YOU CAN DO THAT, THIS IS WHAT WILL HAPPEN.** FOR ME THE CONSEQUENCES WERE IT MADE ME WANT TO TAKE OTHER DRUGS. IT MADE ME TREAT PEOPLE HORRIBLY AND MADE ME FORGET ABOUT THINGS AND MADE ME A SELFISH, FUCKED-UP PERSON. BUT PEOPLE HAVE TO DO IT THEMSELVES TO KNOW WHAT IT IS. SO ROLE MODEL, NO. I LOVE KIDS AND FEEL VERY CONNECTED TO THEM, AND I FEEL THAT I'M PACKING A LOT OF LOVE INTO THE STREAM OF LIFE AND PEOPLE CONNECT WITH THAT, SO WHEN I SEE KIDS I DON'T HAVE TO TELL THEM ANYTHING.

125

J BY THE TIME I WAS FIFTEEN OR SIXTEEN I KNEW THE MUSIC I WAS WRITING WAS GOOD. I JUST KNEW I WAS GOING TO DO IT FOR A LIVING. EVEN THOUGH MY DAD DIDN'T BELIEVE IN ME AS MUCH AS I DID, HE SAW THAT I BELIEVED IN MYSELF WHEN I TOLD HIM I WAS CERTAIN I WAS GOING TO BE A MUSICIAN. I ASKED TO TAKE THE PROFICIENCY TEST SO I WOULD NOT HAVE TO GO TO HIGH SCHOOL. HE AGREED, AND WHEN I PASSED IT I WANTED TO MOVE AWAY. MY FATHER AGREED TO PAY MY RENT AND GIVE ME FOOD MONEY EVERY MONTH BUT ONLY IF I TOOK SOME MUSIC CLASSES AT UCLA OR SMC OR VALLEY COLLEGE OR WHATEVER. I WENT TO EACH ONE OF THOSE FOR A FEW DAYS, BUT WASN'T INTERESTED IN HOW THEY WERE TRYING TO BEND MY BRAIN. MY FRIEND WAS ENROLLED AT MUSICIANS INSTITUTE AND I SAW YOU COULD JUST PUNCH IN THERE AND THEY DIDN'T TAKE ROLL IN THE MORNING CLASSES. AS LONG AS YOU PUNCHED IN, YOU WERE CREDITED AS BEING THERE. I FIGURED I ALREADY KNEW A LOT OF THE STUFF AND THAT I COULD GET AWAY WITH JUST GOING TO CLASSES ONCE IN A WHILE AND TAKING THE QUARTERLY TEST. I DID PASS THE FIRST TEST THAT WAY. I MIGHT HAVE PASSED THE SECOND — BY THEN IT WAS FINALLY STARTING TO GO BEYOND ME. I WENT THERE AT THE HIGHEST LEVEL YOU COULD, PROBABLY WOULD HAVE BEEN EASIER IF I HAD PRETENDED LIKE I SUCKED WHEN I DID THE AUDITION. THEN I WOULD HAVE BEEN IN EASIER CLASSES WITH EASIER TESTS. AS IT WAS, I REALLY SHOWED OFF. BY THE SECOND OR THIRD TEST I COULDN'T PASS. I WAS GOING A LITTLE BIT TO CLASSES JUST TO SEE WHAT THEY WERE DOING, BUT AFTER A FEW MONTHS I WASN'T GOING AT ALL. THIS SCHOOL WAS HELPING

MY MUSIC GET OUT INTO THE WORLD A LITTLE MORE AND TO BE AROUND PEOPLE. THE MAIN THING I USED THAT SCHOOL FOR WAS TO JAM. FREE REHEARSAL ROOMS, DRUMS WERE ALREADY THERE, AND YOU'D WORK ON A SONG, BUT THEY ALSO HAD A PERFORMANCE CLASS WHERE YOU PLAY FOR THE STUDENTS.

ROBERT HAYES WAS THE FIRST MUSICIAN I EVER REALLY CONNECTED WITH, THE FIRST WHO WAS ON THE SAME LEVEL AS ME AT MY AGE. WE USED TO PLAY HENDRIX SONGS, CHILI PEPPERS AND FISHBONE. ROBERT AND I JAMMED A LOT, WE WERE BOTH INTO JAZZ, ANYTHING WITH GOOD MUSICIANSHIP, BUT WE ALSO LIKED

SOME RAWER HARDCORE. WE WERE PERCEIVED AS WEIRDOS AT MI, NOT ONLY FOR LIKING PUNK — THERE WAS NOBODY ELSE WHO EVEN LIKED JIMI HENDRIX THERE. KIDS THERE THOUGHT HENDRIX WAS SIMPLE — THAT WAS OLD SHIT. ROBERT AND I WERE THE ONLY STUDENTS WHO THOUGHT THE WAY WE THOUGHT. I ADMIT WE LIKED HEARING SOMEBODY PLAY FAST, BUT NOT AT THE EXPENSE OF THE SOUL, THE EMOTIONAL SPIRIT OF IT — THE ENTIRE POINT

OF OUR FELLOW STUDENTS. KIDS WERE TRAINED LIKE MINDLESS, ROBOTIC DRONES TO JUDGE MUSIC ON HOW FAST SOMEBODY PLAYED, HOW MANY TECHNIQUES THEY WERE DOING AT ONCE.

WHEN I HEAR FAST GUITAR PLAYERS, WHAT THEY ARE DOING RHYTHMICALLY AND ACCENT-WISE ISN'T VERY COMPLEX IN TERMS OF THE STRUCTURE NATURE OFFERS. THE POTENTIAL PLACES NOTES CAN GO. AND WHEN THEY PLAY FAST THEY USUALLY PLAY NOTES CLOSE TOGETHER. YOU HEAR MOST FAST PLAYERS FROM THE '80S, THE NOTES ARE CLOSE AND THERE'S NOT A LOT OF THOUGHT GIVEN TO PLACEMENT — JUST SQUEEZE IN AS MANY AS POSSIBLE IN THE SHORTEST SPACE POSSIBLE BY MOSTLY RUNNING THROUGH SCALES AND VARIOUS EXERCISES. WHAT THEY DO HAS NO MUSICAL VALUE IN TERMS OF HOW IT RELATES TO THE TONAL AND RHYTHMIC

OPTIONS AVAILABLE. LEARNING THEORY AND READING MUSIC WELL ARE BIG THINGS AT MI. THEY HAVE CLASSES SPECIFICALLY FOR PLAYING FAST, BUT THEY ALSO HAVE CLASSES FOR HARMONY, IF YOU DIDN'T MIND LEARNING AND MAKING MUSICAL SYMBOLS AND THEORETICAL TERMS. IF YOU WANTED TO MAKE THAT YOUR FOCUS — THEN IT WAS A REAL FINE PLACE TO BE. I HAD SPENT SO MUCH TIME PRACTICING IN MY BEDROOM, I WAS MORE INTERESTED IN WALKING AROUND HOLLYWOOD BOULEVARD DOING COKE, HANGING WITH PEOPLE.

HEY, I WAS ONE OF THOSE HOLLYWOOD BOULEVARD KIDS CHECKING MYSELF OUT IN THE WINDOW, HAULING THE GUITAR AROUND OUT OF THE CASE. THAT WAS ME! I WALKED DOWN THE STREET PRACTICING MY GUITAR ALL THE TIME. I'D SPENT SO LITTLE TIME AROUND PEOPLE. I ONLY HAD A FEW FRIENDS I ENJOYED WHO DIDN'T SEEM JEALOUS OF ME THE WAY KIDS DID WHEN I WAS YOUNG. I DIDN'T CARE IF I WAS GOING TO BE A RICH AND FAMOUS ROCK STAR, OR IF I WAS GOING TO BE AN ANONYMOUS SESSION MUSICIAN. ALL I KNEW WAS THAT I WAS GOOD AT PLAYING GUITAR. I WASN'T GOING TO GET A NORMAL JOB, I WASN'T GOING TO APPLY FOR ANYTHING. I FELT CONFIDENT I WAS GOING TO DO WELL MAKING MUSIC.

Venice Queen

During the late '80s I went to see this woman speak about sobriety — an elderly lady who wore all black, had silver hair. A real pistol. Most people that talk about that kind of thing are a little goody-two-shoes, but she was anything but that — foul-mouthed, smart and brutally to the point, but funny, above all. She'd been living in a bungalow cottage in Venice since the '60s. She told me, "The only things I have up at my house are a poster of Neil Young and a poster of the Red Hot Chili Peppers wearing socks on their dicks!" I'm like, "Wow, we're on the wall with a heavyweight like Neil Young." I became friends and really looked up to her as the years went by. During the difficult times when I went back to using, no one could get up to my locked house, but Gloria would send me these postcards. I was up there just passed out, dying, smack- and crack-headed. I hadn't answered my phone in months, and so she'd send me cards with pictures of Native warriors. She'd write, **"ANTHONY, I KNOW YOU AREN'T GOING TO DIE OVER THIS. YOU ARE A WARRIOR. I KNOW WHO YOU ARE AND I WON'T GIVE UP ON YOU."** She truly inspired me to get sober again. But then she ended up getting cancer and was pronounced terminally ill. She had no money — she wasn't able to take care of herself and the basic needs. We did a benefit at the Hollywood Palladium to get her medicine and food, to get her in a nice apartment where she could see the ocean during her final days. I very randomly — just for the heck of it — decided to call Neil Young to ask him to play this benefit for a dying woman who considered him her number one artist. Gloria Scott. I thought he'd just say "no," or "Thanks for asking, but I've got another gig." I went into shocked delight when he said, like, "Sure, just tell me where to be, and I'll be there." I nearly dropped dead!

I got the thrill of telling Gloria, "Oh, by the way, Neil Young is playing your benefit show — and he's bringing Crazy Horse with him!" We were both ecstatic about it. It was near the end — she was in a wheelchair by now — but she got to meet Neil and see him perform on her behalf. It was very powerful, really emotional.

128

HOUSES OF THE HOLY

F DUDE, I NEVER STOPPED LIKING LED ZEP. I WAS
NEVER COOL ENOUGH, NOR PUNK ENOUGH TO NOT.
WHEN I WAS IN FEAR, YOU WEREN'T SUPPOSED TO
LIKE 'EM AT ALL, AND I'M ALL, "I LIKE LED ZEPPELIN."
I LOVED THEM SO MUCH, AND I LOVED PUNK ROCK
SO MUCH, TOO, BUT THEN **PUNK ROCKERS
WERE ALL TRYING TO MAKE ME NOT
DIG ZEPPELIN . . . ARRR!**

The Great Divide

I ONCE MET WILLIE NELSON IN NEW YORK DURING A PHOTO SHOOT WITH ANNIE LIEBOVITZ AND A BUNCH OF OTHER PEOPLE FOR *VANITY FAIR* — ONE OF THESE MUSICIAN SPECIAL THINGS — AND WILLIE IS THERE DOING THIS, TOO, BUT HE'S NOT SHARING A DRESSING ROOM WITH ANYONE. HE'S STAYING IN HIS BUS ON THE STREET. I'M LIKE THIS IS MY ONLY CHANCE. I'M GONNA GO KNOCK ON THAT DOOR, AND WHEN I DO HE'S LIKE, "YEAH?" AND I'M LIKE, "HI, MY NAME IS ANTHONY. I'M TAKING A PICTURE WITH YOU TODAY AND JUST WANTED TO SAY HI." HE'S LIKE, "OH, OKAY." MY FOOT IN THE DOOR OF WILLIE'S BUS, TELLING HIM I KNOW WOODY HARRELSON, KNOWING FULL WELL HE AND WOODY ARE GOOD BUDS. HE GOES, "OH, YOU'RE FRIENDS WITH WOODY! WELL, COME ON IN," **AND SUDDENLY I'M INSIDE WILLIE'S TOUR BUS — A MASTERPIECE OF '70s WORKMANSHIP — FACE-TO-GRIZZLED-FACE WITH WILLIE, HAIR SET IN INDIAN PIGTAILS, MARCHING TOWARD THE WEED BOX GOING, "FRIEND OF WOODY, WELL, LET'S FIRE UP!"** AND HE STARTS ROLLING THIS MONSTER RASTA-SIZED FATTY, AND HERE AM I, THIS WEIRD SOBER GUY, AND I LOOK AT HIM LIKE, "BUT I DON'T SMOKE" AND HE WENT, "OH WELL, SEE YOU INSIDE!" DISAPPOINTINGLY FOR ME, THAT BOND COULD NOT TAKE PLACE, SOMETHING AS A SOBER GUY I HAVE TO DEAL WITH ON A REGULAR BASIS. PEOPLE THAT DON'T HAVE MUCH IN COMMON, THE MINUTE THEY SMOKE WEED TOGETHER, THEY GOT A LOT. WHICH IS A BEAUTIFUL THING — A GREAT BONDING MECHANISM. SUDDENLY YOU GOT A NEW FRIEND, AND WITHOUT THAT IT IS HARDER TO MAKE THEM. SAME WITH ALCOHOL, ANY SUBSTANCE. "HEY, BUDDY, WANNA GO GET DRUNK?" "LET'S FUCKIN' DO IT!"

YOU'RE FRIENDS. ONE GUY SAYS HE DOESN'T DRINK — YOU AREN'T FRIENDS. SUDDENLY YOU DON'T HAVE THAT THING THAT MAGICALLY MAKES YOU ACCEPT EACH OTHER. I RUN INTO THAT ALL THE TIME — PEOPLE I WANT TO HAVE THE OPPORTUNITY TO HANG OUT WITH, BUT ENERGETICALLY IT'S JUST NOT MEANT TO BE.

READYMADE

✱ There's always these dynamics in a band situation — this power struggle, you know. I wasn't more friends with one or another. I always kept more to myself. I was never really into those dynamics — the band and my personal life were separate, whereas I think with the other guys it was intertwined more. They hung out socially more. I mean I did, but not as much. It was the way it was. I never felt it was weird, though. I came in and did my thing I loved. And my role, maybe still to this day, is someone you can depend on, who is solid. Maybe it is my upbringing, but it is what I do. **I'M THE DRUMMER.**

Behind the Sun

JOHN FRUSCIANTE AND I WERE SPENDING ALL KINDS OF TIME TOGETHER, JUST BEING BAND MEMBERS IN A BAND. HE HAD JUST JOINED THE BAND BUT I DON'T THINK WE HAD RECORDED ANY MUSIC TOGETHER. WE GOT THESE TATTOOS — I DESIGNED THE SYMBOL. **OUR MANAGER TOLD US WE NEEDED A LOGO FOR A T-SHIRT AND I LITERALLY PICKED UP A SCRAP OF PAPER AND DREW THAT.** WE WERE ALL DRAWING A LOT AT THAT POINT — HILLEL AND FLEA AND I, AS PART OF OUR EXPRESSION. I DON'T KNOW WHY, BUT IT CAME OUT OF THE PEN AND I HANDED IT TO OUR MANAGER. BOB ROBERTS GAVE ME MY TATTOO, AND THE GIRL WORKING FOR HIM GAVE JOHN HIS. THEY WERE IDENTICAL ALTHOUGH MINE WAS HEAVY — IT IS DARKER TODAY THAN JOHN'S. INK SEEMS PAINFULLY COMMON THESE DAYS, BUT IN THE LATE '80S IT WAS UNCOMMON AND I HAD NEVER SEEN A BACK TATTOO BEFORE IN MY LIFE. I GOT ONE WHILE IN AMSTERDAM BASED ON DIFFERENT IMAGES FROM THE LIBRARY. GOT EVERYTHING INTO THIS TOTEM POLE — ONE SITTING OF FIVE-AND-A-HALF HOURS, WHICH WAS VERY PAINFUL. I DIDN'T TELL MY GIRLFRIEND, IONE [SKYE], ABOUT IT. I CAME BACK FROM TOUR, AND SHE FOUND IT DURING A LOVEMAKING SESSION. SHE ALMOST CRIED BECAUSE IT SEEMED A BIT MUCH TO HER AT THE TIME.

136

THE CREATIVE IN THE STUDIO

138

PROCESS

ON THE ROAD

ROCK WITH YOUR ✳ OUT

CLIFF MARTINEZ (RHCP DRUMMER 1983–86): ROID ROGERS AND THE WHIRLING BUTT CHERRIES WAS THE PRODUCT OF TOO MUCH COFFEE AND A GAGGLE OF NONMUSICIAN FRIENDS — ALL THESE GREAT ARTISTS AND PEOPLE LIVING IN THE SAME HOUSE ON HILLHURST WHERE I USED TO HANG OUT WITH MY GIRLFRIEND. IT MUST HAVE BEEN SPYDER MITTLEMAN WHO MADE UP SUCH A SICK NAME. SPYDER MITTLEMAN WAS WELL-KNOWN AND LOVED FOR BEING OUTRAGEOUS AND FLAMBOYANT ONSTAGE AND OFF. MAY HE REST IN PEACE. MYSELF, SPYDER AND OUR FRIEND BOB MANN WERE BORED MUSICIANS DEFINITELY UP FOR A BIT OF OUTRAGEOUS, ANYTHING TO GRAB ATTENTION — NEVER MIND HOW CHEAP OR LOWLIFE — WAS THE MAIN PLOT.

BOB MANN (MUSICIAN AND COMPOSER): THE LOCAL CLUB CIRCUIT AND THE BANDS THAT PLAYED IT NOWADAYS SEEMED HUMDRUM. THE CHILI PEPPERS GOT BOOKED INTO THE KIT KAT AND SOMEHOW WE WERE ON THE BILL. WE CAME OUT BUTT-NAKED BUT FOR LEATHER CHAPS AND JOCK STRAPS, WHICH MAY HAVE INSPIRED THEM TO GO ONE BETTER WITH THE SOCKS LATER THAT NIGHT.

✳ WE USED TO DO IT AT HOME AS A JOKE, LIKE SOCK PUPPETS. IT WAS SPUR OF THE MOMENT.

WE WERE ALWAYS TRYING TO UPSTAGE EVERYBODY. WE WERE ALWAYS GOING TO MAKE A STATEMENT TO THE POINT OF BEING OBNOXIOUS.

CLIFF: I DON'T KNOW IF WE INSPIRED THEM, OR IF IT WAS THE ENVIRONMENT OF THE KIT KAT WITH THE TOPLESS DANCERS — BOTH, PROBABLY.

LINDY GOETZ (MANAGER): A FRIEND CALLED AND ASKED IF I WANTED TO GO SEE THIS BAND AT THE KIT KAT, THIS STRIP JOINT ON SANTA MONICA BOULEVARD NEAR WEST HOLLYWOOD. I'D ACTUALLY NEVER BEEN TO THE KIT KAT BEFORE THAT NIGHT. THE AUDIENCE WAS A CROSS SECTION OF THE TRENDY CROWD, THE ROCKABILLIES AND THE METAL CROWD. I DIDN'T THINK THE CHILI PEPPERS SOUNDED LIKE HENDRIX. THEY WERE JUST WHAT THEY WERE — NASTY, SHARP RHYTHM SECTION WITH THIS CRAZY, EXHIBITIONISTIC RAPPER AND ACROBAT FOR A FRONT GUY, SHIRT OFF LIKE IGGY, HAIR NOT LONG ENOUGH YET TO DO HIS TRADEMARK HAIR FLAILING. THEY ONLY HAD FOUR OR FIVE SONGS. A SHORT SET WAS PART OF THE CHARM — NO TIME FOR BOREDOM. ANTHONY WAS RAPPING OVER AN INCREDIBLE HYPERANIMATED RHYTHM SECTION. THEN THEY WENT OFF AND SOME OF THE STRIPPERS CAME OUT AND THEN THEY CAME BACK OUT AND DID THE SOCKS. THAT WAS IT. CROWD WENT WILD.

JUNGLE MAN

✳ WE WERE SOUND-CHECKING AND THAT CHRIS CAMPBELL GUY WHO DID THE JAMES BROWN TRIBUTE ACT LATER THAT NIGHT WAS SAYING TO ANTHONY, "HEY, IF YOU WANT TO BE TRULY FUNKY, YOU GUYS GOTSTA SLOW IT DOWN A LITTLE." WE WERE ALL BAM BAM BAM! FAST AND HARD.

✳ I REMEMBER THINKING HE MIGHT HAVE A POINT, BUT WE DIDN'T CARE, WE DIDN'T WANT TO SOUND LIKE ANYONE ELSE, WE JUST WANTED TO SOUND LIKE US.

PETE WEISS (FRIEND AND MUSICIAN): I WALKED INTO THE CATHAY AND THEY WERE ALREADY ONSTAGE. THE LAST TIME I'D SEEN THAT BOUNDLESS ENERGY ONSTAGE WAS THE WEIRDOS — BUT THESE GUYS WERE SOMETHING ELSE. **IMAGINE TAKING A MEXICAN JUMPING BEAN AND SHOOTING IT FULL OF METH. THEY WERE JUST FLAILING AND BOUNCING OFF THE FUCKING WALLS.** IT WAS A PINBALL GAME. AND THEN ANTHONY IS HANGING OUT WITH NINA HAGEN ACTING ALL BIG-TIME AND SHIT.

✳ THE CATHAY WAS A REALLY GOOD SHOW, ONE OF THE GREAT MOMENTS OF THE CHILI PEPPERS. WE HAD ENOUGH SONGS, FIVE BY THEN, AND AT THAT POINT WE JUST EXPLODED. HOLLYWOOD SCENESTERS ARE THERE — JUST THESE PEOPLE WHO HUNG AROUND.

✳ WHOEVER IT WAS, IT JUST FREAKING EXPLODED, THIS NATURAL FORCE OF ENERGY TOOK OFF.

✳ ANTHONY WAS SPINNING AROUND AND WAVING BEER IN THE AIR, SPIRAL FOAM SPLATTERING EVERYWHERE. SO FUN, NO THOUGHT INVOLVED. WILD EXPRESSION ONLY.

✳ WAYZATA [DE CAMERONE, WHOSE BAND PLAYED THE SAME BILL] ATTEMPTED TO RENEGE ON A $40.00 GUARANTEE. I PUSHED HIM INTO A URINAL UNTIL HE COUGHED UP.

✳ WENT HOME WITH $10.

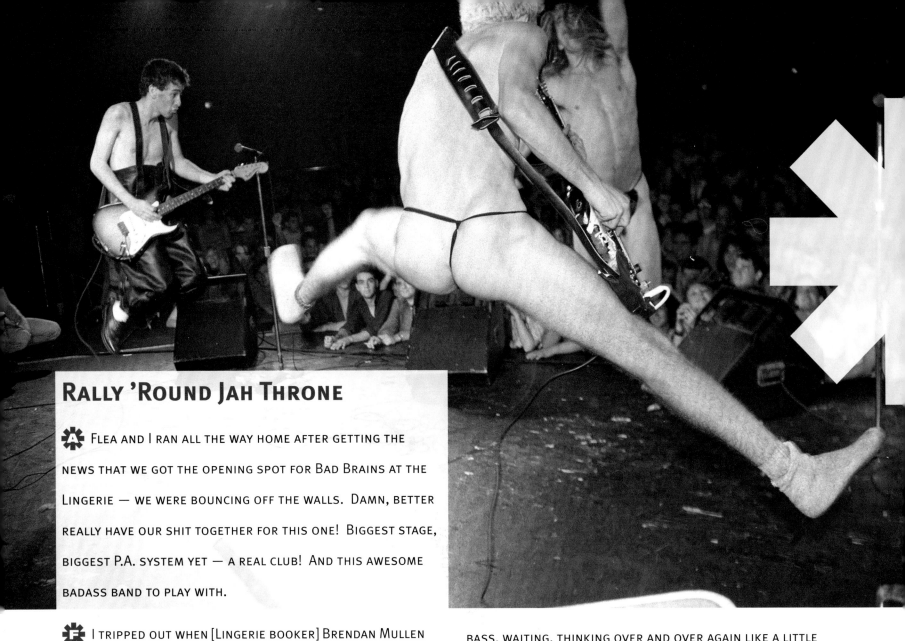

RALLY 'ROUND JAH THRONE

✳ FLEA AND I RAN ALL THE WAY HOME AFTER GETTING THE NEWS THAT WE GOT THE OPENING SPOT FOR BAD BRAINS AT THE LINGERIE — WE WERE BOUNCING OFF THE WALLS. DAMN, BETTER REALLY HAVE OUR SHIT TOGETHER FOR THIS ONE! BIGGEST STAGE, BIGGEST P.A. SYSTEM YET — A REAL CLUB! AND THIS AWESOME BADASS BAND TO PLAY WITH.

✳ I TRIPPED OUT WHEN [LINGERIE BOOKER] BRENDAN MULLEN OFFERED US THE SHOW. **HELL, YEAH. I LOVED BAD BRAINS. *ROCK FOR LIGHT* HAD JUST CAME OUT, AND I WAS JUST SO EXCITED — THOUGHT THEY WERE TOTALLY THE FOREFRONT OF ROCK MUSIC AT THE TIME.** I LIVED OVER IN THIS PLACE NEAR THE LINGERIE OFF OF MCCADDEN ON LELAND WAY, JUST BELOW SUNSET, AND IT WAS CALLED POT ALLEY BECAUSE THEY SOLD A LOT OF DRUGS OUT OF THERE. ONE BIG APARTMENT BUILDING WAS A CRACK HOUSE, AND THIS OTHER BUILDING, THEY JUST SOLD WEED OUT OF, AND THERE WERE ALL THESE GUYS IN THE STREET HUSTLING DRUGS. I WAS PSYCHED SITTING THERE IN MY CRIB PRACTICING BASS, WAITING, THINKING OVER AND OVER AGAIN LIKE A LITTLE KID, OMIGOD, WE'RE PLAYING WITH BAD BRAINS TONIGHT, CAN'T FUCKING BELIEVE IT, CAN'T FUCKING BELIEVE IT. WE'RE PLAYING WITH BAD BRAINS TONIGHT, AND THEN LOOKING OUT MY WINDOW AND SEEING [BAD BRAINS' LEAD SINGER] H.R. COME ROLLIN' DOWN THE STREET LOOKING TO BUY HERB. HOW THE FUCK DID HE DIVINE SO FAST WHERE THE ACTION WAS? I WAS HAPPY AS HELL TO SEE HIM. I WENT OUTSIDE AND HOOKED HIM UP — WE GOT STONED OUT AND THEN PLAYED THAT NIGHT, AND IT WAS A BLAST.

✳ WE WENT ON FIRST AND THEY INVITED US SPONTANEOUSLY TO PLAY WITH THEM AT THE END OF THEIR SET. THEY WERE SO RELAXED ABOUT IT, SUPERCOOL GUYS, LIKE IT'S JUST A SHOW, LET'S JUST PLAY. I LOVED HOW DOWN-TO-EARTH THEY WERE FOR ALL THEIR MIGHT AS MUSICIANS AND THE GREAT ARTISTS THEY ARE.

144

MONDAY, JULY 18

Four black guys, dreadlocks flying, playing white-heat punk rock? Yes, it's **Bad Brains**, from Washington D.C., who can skid from blistering sonic convulsions into smooth skankin' roots/dub reggae without missing a beat. The Rastafarian thrash outfit is joined by L.A.'s answer to the punk-funk question: **The Red Hot Chili Peppers**, four white boys that sound like Captain Beefheart playing James Brown. All this hyper-activity can be found at Club Lingerie, 8507 Sunset (at Wilcox). Call 466-8557 and prepare for some musical disruption.

MONDAY **(JULY 18)**
ONLY L.A. APPEARANCE
BAD BRAINS
PLUS SPECIAL GUESTS
RED HOT CHILI PEPPERS

MIDNIGHT

WE GOT A SLOT OPENING FOR SUICIDAL TENDENCIES HIGH OFF THEIR MTV HIT "INSTITUTIONALIZED" AT THE OLYMPIC AUDITORIUM, AN OLD BOXING AND WRESTLING ARENA IN DOWNTOWN L.A. BUT ANTHONY IN ALL HIS JUNKIE SPLENDOR DID NOT SHOW UP. KEITH MORRIS FROM THE CIRCLE JERKS SAID, "I'LL SING" AND SO WE WENT OUT WITH HIM. KEITH'S YELLING OUT, "PUT YOUR LEFT HAND IN THE AIR, PUT YOUR RIGHT HAND IN YOUR UNDERWEAR . . . AND SCREAM!!!" WE WERE JUST PLAYING THE SONGS AND HE WOULD YELL OUT STUFF LIKE THAT — WHATEVER HE COULD. HE DID ALL THE WAVE YOUR HANDS SIDE TO SIDE AND SHIT AND HE WAS GREAT. CLEARLY NOT AS GOOD AS ANTHONY. **I WAS MUCH MORE HAPPY-GO-LUCKY ABOUT IT. I WAS SO ANTI "BEING PROFESSIONAL" IN ANY WAY. THE SPIRIT OF PUNK ROCK LIVES NO MATTER WHAT.** HONESTLY DID NOT GIVE A FUCK! I THOUGHT HE SHOULD HAVE SHOWED UP, BUT WE GOT PAID. ANOTHER TIME ANTHONY DIDN'T SHOW UP — NORTHRIDGE — SO PEOPLE FROM THE AUDIENCE GOT UP AND SANG, INCLUDING [MANAGER] LINDY [GOETZ]'S BROTHER, STUART. IT WAS RIDICULOUS — IT WAS FUNNY AND PATHETIC AT THE SAME TIME. I WAS LIKE FUCK IT, THIS GIG WAS PAYING $2,000! ANTHONY WAS BEING SUCH A PATHETIC JUNKIE, I WAS GOING TO GO BACK TO WHAT IS THIS? I WAS LIKE, "FUCK THIS!" BUT WHEN HE SAID HE WAS GONNA BE THE JAMES BROWN OF THE '80S, THAT WAS SO FUNNY, I COULDN'T HELP LAUGHING.

FLEA CHASTISED ME WITH A GOOD DRESSING-DOWN, "DUDE, THEN QUIT BEING THE FUCKING SLY STONE OF THE '80S — SHOWING UP LATE AT GIGS, IF AT ALL, IS SO FUCKIN' LAME!"

POLICE HELICOPTER

✳ IT'S EASY TO SAY WOULDA, SHOULDA, COULDA . . . FOR OUR FIRST RECORD, *THE RED HOT CHILI PEPPERS*, I THINK WE HAD THE SONGS, THE ENERGY, AND THE ORIGINALITY TO MAKE A RECORD THAT WOULD HAVE MADE US ONE OF THE MOST IMPORTANT BANDS AT THAT TIME, AS IMPORTANT AS JANE'S ADDICTION OR THE DOORS. I REALLY THINK WE COULD HAVE, AND THAT MIGHT BE A POMPOUS THING TO SAY, BUT WE REALLY BLEW IT WITH THE FIRST ALBUM. JACK AND HILLEL BOTH LEFT AND THEN IT BECAME IMPOSSIBLE — NOTHING AGAINST THE OTHER GUYS WE GOT, BUT THOSE WERE THE GUYS THAT MADE IT HAPPEN. WE ALSO HAD NO IDEA WHAT WE WERE DOING IN THE STUDIO, AND WE GOT THE WRONG PRODUCER.

CLIFF MARTINEZ (RHCP DRUMMER 1983–86): THEY WANTED A PRODUCER WHO'D MADE A RECORD THEY REALLY LIKED. ANDY GILL, JIMMY PAGE CAME UP, GANG OF FOUR ESPECIALLY — IT WAS MORE REALISTIC THAN GETTING PAGE, WAY OVER OUR HEADS. MORE PRAGMATICALLY, EVERYONE LOVED *ENTERTAINMENT!* AND WE ALL THOUGHT ANDY GILL WAS A REALLY COOL IDEA, BUT WE DIDN'T KNOW MUCH ELSE ABOUT HIS TRACK RECORD.

✳ WE GOT ANDY GILL BECAUSE WE LOVED GANG OF FOUR, BUT THEN HE WAS DISSING THE FIRST GANG OF FOUR RECORDS — NOW HE'S SAYING, "OH, I DIDN'T KNOW WHAT I WAS DOING."

✳ WE THOUGHT THESE WERE GREAT RECORDS, ESPECIALLY HILLEL. ALARM BELLS WENT OFF WHEN ANDY TRIED TO DISTANCE HIMSELF FROM THE EARLY GO4 RECORDINGS. IF THAT'S WHAT HE DID WHEN HE DIDN'T KNOW WHAT HE WAS DOING, NOW THAT HE THOUGHT HE DID, WHAT WAS HE GOING TO DO WITH US? FLEA GOT PRETTY WIGGY ABOUT IT.

CLIFF: THE FATE OF THESE SESSIONS WAS DOOMED AFTER ANDY DISMISSED THE *ENTERTAINMENT!* RECORD. HE'S LIKE, "I DON'T LIKE THAT RECORD, THAT'S NOT WHERE I'M AT ANYMORE." HE'S HOLDING UP HIS FOURTH ALBUM, BUT WE THOUGHT THEY'D DONE AN ABOUT-FACE WITH THIS POLISHED TEMPO THING. WE WERE LIKE, "WE HATE THAT!" ANDY WANTED IT MORE SLEEK, MORE COMMERCIAL. HE JUST COULDN'T RELATE TO THE RAW POWER ROCK ENERGY OF WHAT WE DID LIVE. NONE OF US HAD MUCH STUDIO EXPERIENCE. WE WERE SO INTIMIDATED BY THE CLICK TRACK THAT ANDY INSISTED ON — A LOT OF IT COMES OFF STIFF AND SERIOUS, MECHANICAL, DUMB-SOUNDING LIKE THAT!

✳ THIS DEMO WE DID IN THREE HOURS ONE DAY WITH SPIT STIX WAS SO MUCH BETTER THAN THE RECORD WE MADE WITH ANDY. IF WE HAD ONLY JUST GONE INTO A REALLY GOOD STUDIO AND TAKEN OUR TIME AND MADE A GOOD RECORD — PLAYING LIVE, GETTING THAT LIVE-IN-THE-ROOM FEELING. IT COULD HAVE BEEN A REALLY, REALLY IMPORTANT RECORD, BUT WE JUST DIDN'T.

CLIFF: ANDY HAD A NOTEBOOK WHERE HE HAD THE TITLE AND NOTES ON EVERYTHING. AS SOON AS HE'D LEAVE THE ROOM WE'D JUMP ON IT AND SCAN THROUGH IT. LENGTHY NOTES ABOUT CHANGES, FLIPPING THROUGH WE'D SEE, "POLICE HELICOPTER. SHIT!" WE NEVER QUITE TRUSTED ANDY AFTER THAT. WE LIKED THAT SONG! ANDY SAW THE LACK OF SONGS AS THE CORE PROBLEM. HE'D SAY, "YOU GUYS NEED SONGS, NOT JUST GROOVES. YOU CAN'T GO ON JUST DOING BASS GROOVES WITH WEIRD WHITE-BOY RAPS." NOT VERY MARKETABLE, HE DIDN'T THINK — WE NEEDED AT LEAST ONE SONG FOR RADIO.

✳ WE JUST BLEW IT WITH THAT FIRST RECORD. I'VE ALWAYS WANTED TO RE-RECORD IT WITH JOHN AND EVERYONE.

CLIFF: WE WORKED ON THIS ONE SONG FOR A LONG TIME CALLED "HUMAN SATELLITE" AND HE SPENT A LOT OF TIME ON THAT, ANDY'S CREATION. FROM HINDSIGHT IT WOULD HAVE BEEN NICE TO HAVE A HIT SONG, BUT IT HAD NO CONNECTION TO WHAT WE WERE DOING. ANDY WAS PISSED BECAUSE WE WERE LIKE, "NO WAY IS THAT GOING ON THE RECORD!" BUT ANDY DID MAKE BIG CONTRIBUTIONS — SOME GANG OF FOUR INFLUENCES IN THE INSTRUMENTAL THINGS. THE HORNS AND PERCUSSION OVERDUBS AND SOME POLISH. IT WASN'T A REAL HAPPY MARRIAGE THOUGH.

✳ BOB FORREST TURNED US ON TO HANK WILLIAMS WITHOUT A DOUBT. WHEN WE WERE PREPARING TO RECORD OUR FIRST RECORD, HE MORE OR LESS INSISTED WE COVER ONE OF HIS SONGS, AND SO WE DID "WHY DON'T YOU LOVE ME." THAT WAS PURE BOB AND HIS DIRECTION. UP TO THAT POINT I HADN'T EVEN CONSIDERED LISTENING TO OLD COUNTRY MUSIC. NOW WE WERE HOOKED ON HANK.

✳ ANTHONY SAID MANY YEARS LATER, **"IF THAT RECORD WOULD HAVE BEEN GREAT WE WOULD NEVER BE TOGETHER TODAY."** HE'S DEAD RIGHT. WE NEVER WOULD HAVE SURVIVED THIS LONG, AND BECAUSE OF IT WE'VE GROWN OVER TIME.

✳ NOT HAVING A WHOLE LOT OF SUCCESS TOO SOON WAS THE BIGGEST BLESSING IN DISGUISE OVER THE LONG HAUL.

149

TRUE MEN DON'T KILL COYOTES

 SOON AFTER RELEASE OF THE FIRST ALBUM, *THE RED HOT CHILI PEPPERS,* JOHN LYDON OFFERED FLEA A JOB IN PIL. FLEA HAD BEEN JAMMING WITH LYDON & CO., AND LATER PLAYED TAPES FOR HILLEL AND ASKED FOR PERSPECTIVE. HILLEL, STILL A FULL-TIME MEMBER OF WHAT IS THIS?, LISTENED TO THE PIL JAM TAPES AND TO WHAT THE CHILI PEPPERS WERE DOING AND TOLD FLEA TO STAY RIGHT WHERE HE WAS.

LINDY GOETZ (MANAGER): WE'D COME UP WITH A FINISHED ALBUM [THE LABEL] WEREN'T SURE WHERE TO GO WITH. IT WAS A NO-BRAINER AT THE TIME — COLLEGE RADIO. PLUS, WE WERE ALWAYS SOLID ON TOURING, I KNEW WE COULD CAPITALIZE ON THOSE TWO THINGS. WE BUILT IT THE RIGHT WAY, LIKE A LADDER, ONE STEP AT A TIME AND IT GOT BIGGER. IT WAS EASY TO SEE THAT IF THEY COULD

BUILD A FOLLOWING, RADIO WOULD COME, BUT YOU HAVE TO BET THE FOLLOWING WILL STAY WITH YOU AFTER YOU HIT RADIO. WE WANTED TO PLAY FOR KEEPS.

CLIFF MARTINEZ (RHCP DRUMMER 1983–86): **EMI JUST KNEW THERE WAS A GROUNDSWELL OF INTEREST IN US AND THEY DIDN'T KNOW WHAT TO DO WITH IT.** JAMIE COHEN WAS OUR GUY, HE WAS A CHAMPION, HE MAY HAVE BEEN THE ONLY ONE. THE SOLE SUPPORTER, AND ONCE HE LEFT . . .

 THE RECORD MAY HAVE TANKED FAST, BUT NOT BEFORE LEAVING A SLIGHT SMUDGE ON COLLEGE RADIO WITH "TRUE MEN DON'T KILL COYOTES." X WAS LOOSELY THE LYRICAL INSPIRATION FOR THIS SONG.

LINDY: THERE WERE SOME ALTERNATIVE STATIONS BUT THEY WERE FEW AND FAR BETWEEN. WE WEREN'T GETTING KROQ PLAY, BUT AGAIN, WE WERE GETTING TONS OF PRESS. NO MTV, BUT WE'RE

150

GETTING ALL THE LOCAL MEDIA MTV VERSIONS. I STAYED ON THE ROAD WITH THEM FOR THE FIRST EIGHT YEARS. I DON'T THINK I EVER MISSED ANY SHOW. IN THE EARLY DAYS, WE WORKED HARDER THAN ANYBODY, THAT'S FOR SURE — SIX DAYS A WEEK NONSTOP FOR AS LONG AS POSSIBLE. WE BUSTED OUR ASSES TO PROMOTE OURSELVES AND THE RECORD. WE DID EVERYTHING WE COULD WHILE WE WERE OUT THERE — PRESS, PRESS, PRESS. NO INTERNET YET, BUT EVERY CITY HAD AN INDEPENDENT TV STATION.

✱ WE DIDN'T GET ON MTV — OUR CHEAPO VID CLIPS WERE A LITTLE TOO LOW-BUDGET FOR THEM — BUT WE GOT ON ALL THESE SMALL LOCAL STATIONS, ANYWHERE LINDY COULD TALK THEM INTO HAVING AN IN-PERSON. FLEA AND I WOULD SHOW UP AT RADIO STATIONS AND PULL THE RAMBUNCTIOUS MARX BROTHERS SHTICK ON THE STAFF.

✱ WE'D DO THESE CRAZY ROUTINES OVER THE AIR.

LINDY: I INSISTED ON IT. ADVANCING THE TOUR, DOING IT RIGHT. WE DIDN'T JUST GLIDE INTO A CITY AND CHECK INTO THE NEAREST SKEEZE BAG MOTEL 6. WE'D HEAD STRAIGHT TO THE LOCAL TV STATION, STOP AT THE CAMPUS RADIO STATION, DO ANYTHING TO GET

SEEN TO HELP BUMP TICKET SALES FOR THE GIGS THAT NIGHT. **THE GUYS SURE HATED ME! DRAGGING THEIR BUTTS OUT OF BED BEFORE NOON THE DAY AFTER A GIG WHEN THEY'D BEEN UP ALL NIGHT. I RODE THEM LIKE DOGS,** BUT I WAS DOING THE SAME THING. IN THE EARLY DAYS I WAS DRIVER, THE MANAGER — I WAS DOING THE LIGHTS AND THE SOUND IN HALF THE PLACES. IT WAS JUST US — FOUR GUYS AND ME, UNTIL EVENTUALLY BEN MARCH BECAME OUR FIRST TOUR MANAGER AND BOB FORREST WAS A ROADIE.

CLIFF: THE FIRST TOUR WAS WHISKY A GO GO–SIZED ROOMS AROUND THE COUNTRY. ALWAYS HEADLINING, ALTHOUGH WE HAD A COUPLE DISASTROUS OPENER GIGS LIKE SPARKS AT THE GREEK. MOSTLY HEADLINING GIGS AND COLLEGE RADIO TOWNS, 500-SEATERS OR LESS. WE TOURED IN A VAN. WE HAD A PAIR, ONE FOR EQUIPMENT, ONE FOR US. THAT'S TOUGH.

Why Don't You Love Me

The Chili Peppers will treasure Bob Forrest forever — most ridiculous roadie of ALL TIME. His legacy is forever sealed for showing up all drunk and pissed off because we now had a pro tour manager! He's like, "I thought I was gonna be tour manager!" But every night when it was time to go to work, Bob would hand over his $20.00 per diem to some other guy and then go get wasted while the other kid did all the work. "Dude, why the fuck would we hire you to be our tour manager?" We're like in NYC and The Replacements are there, and Bob is just sucking up to them real bad. Suddenly we're not cool any more, like embarrassing cousins you don't wanna be seen or associated with.

Just what we needed in the middle of our first tour — a drunk punk rock roadie, one of our best friends, to boot, telling us how much we suck, now announcing, "I don't do amps. I don't do van windows."

"YOU GUYS ARE A BUNCH OF CORPORATE SELLOUTS! ROCK STAR WANNABES!" BOB'S HOLLERIN' INSANE SHIT AT US, LIKE DROOLIN' EVERYWHERE, DRUNK AS A SKUNK. Next day I see him sliding into the hotel behind [Replacements' singer/guitarist Paul] Westerberg, carrying his guitar for him. Dude, I just flipped, cracked up laughin' — it was just so funny to see him like that.

LINDY GOETZ (manager): We're getting ready for a long drive down to New Orleans and Bob's going off on another of his crazy fucked-up rants, "You guys suck, I don't even wanna work for fuckin' sellouts already!"

I'm like, "Bob, how the fuck are we corporate sellouts, when the evil corporation in question wants precious little to do with us? We're building this shit up brick by brick, pretty much by ourselves from scratch, dude! We're gonna get our own following, our own culture of fans despite them, not because of them. We're gonna beat them, why are we so derided and punished for that?"

Finally even Lindy couldn't take it anymore and he pulls over and says, "Bob, get the fuck out, get out of the van!" Lindy took Bob's suitcase and threw it out onto the sidewalk! So Bob gets out, and we drove away, and he was just standing there. He ended up sleeping at Grand Central Station — made it home a month later.

LINDY: We gave him money to get home. We dumped him in front of some hotel in midtown Manhattan. When we got back I went on to manage Bob in Thelonious Monster — he's a great, loveable guy. You just can't stay mad at him for long.

FUNK TO DEATH

DON'T BE   SILLY
THEREDHOTCHILLIPEPPERS
E A
[WAYZATA BAND]

RESTLESS NATIVES

153

FIRE

✱ I BEFRIENDED PERRY FARRELL RIGHT BEFORE JANE'S ADDICTION SIGNED WITH WARNER BROTHERS. I KNEW ABOUT IGGY BUT NOT A LOT, AND HE REALLY GOT ME INTO IGGY AND A BUNCH OF DUB STUFF. HE USED TO PLAY ME THESE ADRIAN SHERWOOD ON-U-SOUND THINGS. I FIRST HEARD ABOUT PERRY WHEN WE PLAYED A JIMI HENDRIX TRIBUTE AT THE ROXY. HILLEL AND I GOT THIS HENDRIX BAND TOGETHER WITH A BUNCH OF DIFFERENT PEOPLE. I CAN'T REMEMBER WHO PLAYED DRUMS, PROBABLY JACK.

JACK IRONS (ORIGINAL RHCP DRUMMER): YEAH, THAT WAS ME, BUT I THINK FISH [NORWOOD FISHER] MIGHT ALSO HAVE PLAYED SOME OF IT.

✱ AND THEN THE FISHBONE GUYS WERE IN ON IT. WE ORGANIZED THIS WHOLE HENDRIX THING, AND I WORKED SO HARD ON IT. I TOOK ACID, AND THOUGHT I PLAYED THE GREATEST SHOW OF MY LIFE, AND THEN THE NEXT DAY IN THE NEWSPAPER THERE'S A BIG PICTURE OF PERRY FARRELL. "PERRY FARRELL SINGS AT HENDRIX TRIBUTE!" I DIDN'T EVEN SEE HIM PLAY, AND I WAS LIKE "WHO THE FUCK IS PERRY FARRELL?" I REMEMBER CALLING UP THE NEWSPAPER REALLY PISSED

OFF. I'M LIKE "I WORKED SO HARD ON THIS HENDRIX THING. I HAD THE BEST SHOW OF MY LIFE AND THERE'S A PICTURE OF SOME GUY WHO SHOWS UP WITH A FUCKING HARMONICA." WOW. PERRY ALREADY HAD THAT MAGNETISM, THE ONE THAT GOT ALL THE ATTENTION.

NORWOOD FISHER (FISHBONE BASSIST): THE NIGHT ENDED WITH A TOPLESS GIRL GETTING ONSTAGE. WE'RE FINISHING UP WITH "FIRE" — EVERYONE WAS UP JAMMING TOGETHER ALL AT ONCE AND THE GIRL LOOKED LIKE SHE WAS SUPPOSED TO GET UP, LIKE IT WAS PLANNED. AND WHICH MOFO WOULD PLAN SUCH A THING? ONLY ONE, IN ANTHONY'S GIRLFRIEND'S MIND! **JENNIFER BRUCE GOES NUTS, SNAPS, COMPLETELY LOSES HER SHIT, MAN, WHEN THE TOPLESS GAL STARTED SHAKING HER ATTRIBUTES AT HIM.** JENNIFER RUNS ONSTAGE AND STARTS WHALIN' ON HIM, BEATIN' THE SHIT OUT OF POOR ANTHONY IN FRONT OF THE AUDIENCE!

✱ HOW FUCKING WEIRD WAS THAT?

BOB FORREST (FRIEND AND MUSICIAN): HOW MANY MAJOR ROCK 'N' ROLL GUYS HAVE GOTTEN THRASHED ONSTAGE BY THEIR GIRLFRIENDS AND LIVED ON TO HAVE A CAREER AFTERWARDS? NOW THAT'S PUNK ROCK!!

NORWOOD: GOTTA LOVE THIS ANTHONY GUY — BOUNCES BACK EVERY TIME.

155

One Nation Under a Groove

GEORGE CLINTON (MUSICIAN AND PRODUCER): I WAS ON THE NEW MUSIC SEMINAR IN NEW YORK WITH TOM SILVERMAN FROM TOMMY BOY RECORDS AND HAD MADE A STATEMENT THAT FUNK WAS GOING TO COME BACK FIFTEEN TO TWENTY YEARS AFTER THE MOTHERSHIP AND IT WAS GONNA BE LIKE ENGLAND AND THE FIRST ROCK INVASION. FLEA AND ANTHONY CAME UP TO THE PLATFORM AND THEY GO, "WHY DOES IT HAVE TO COME FROM ENGLAND? IF YOU PRODUCE OUR RECORD, WE'LL DO IT FROM HERE! WE'LL INVADE THEM WITH IT FROM THE U.S.!" I LIKED THIS, LOVED THIS ATTITUDE ALREADY. AND THEY MADE MENTIONS OF JAMES BROWN AND SLY STONE AND EVERYTHING. I SAID COME OUT TO MY FARM IN MICHIGAN AND WE'LL WORK IT OUT AND SO A FEW MONTHS LATER THEY SHOW UP THERE! THEY ENDED UP STAYING TWO OR THREE WEEKS — WE RODE SNOWMOBILES AND STUFF, THEN THEY WENT HOME AND SAID THEY WERE GONNA COME BACK AND WORK IT OUT.

✳ LINDY AND I FLEW TO MICHIGAN TO MEET WITH GEORGE CLINTON. HE WAS SO EASY-GOING, COOL AND FRIENDLY. EVERYONE WAS BLACK AND DRESSED TO THE NINES. WINTER. EVERYONE HAD BEAUTIFUL FUR COATS AND LOOKED NICE. I'M THIS PUNK, AND LINDY'S WEARING LINDY CLOTHES, A COUPLA WHITE NERDS.

GEORGE: WE WORKED OUT A DEAL WITH THE RECORD COMPANY, AND THEY INDEED DID COME BACK, AND THIS TIME WE DID THE PRE-PRODUCTION OF THE ALBUM AT ONE STUDIO AND THEN WENT TO UNITED SOUND AND DID THE FOR-REAL ALBUM, *FREAKY STYLEY*.

✳ THE MAKING OF THE ALBUM WAS A GREAT EXPERIENCE. I JUST WANTED TO PLAY GROOVES AS WELL AS I COULD. I **LOVED HANGING OUT WITH THE P-FUNK GUYS AND FEELING LIKE A PART OF THAT SCENE — IT WAS SUCH A COOL THING,** A POWERFUL SUPERCREATIVE MUSIC SCENE SO DIFFERENT THAN THE CULTURE WE WERE FROM. BLACK INNER-CITY DETROIT. DIFFERENT WORLD FROM WHITE PUNK ROCK HOLLYWOOD. WHAT A FUCKING HONOR TO HANG WITH THESE FELLAS.

✳ GEORGE WAS A COMPASSIONATE GENIUS WHO APPEARED AMUSED AND DELIGHTED BY THE CHILI PEPPERS, ESPECIALLY HE WAS A FAN OF HILLEL'S PLAYING.

GEORGE: BASICALLY THEY CAME IN AND PLAYED ALL THE STUFF AND CALLED THE SHOTS. I DIDN'T TRY TO CHANGE THEM, I JUST SORT OF IMPLEMENTED WHAT THEY WANTED TO DO.

✳ WE WERE DOING A LOT OF COKE, FREEBASING, WHATEVER GOD-AWFUL DRUGS WE COULD THE WHOLE FUCKING TIME — AND THAT WAS ANOTHER DISASTER. BUT I THOUGHT WE STILL MANAGED TO PLAY REALLY WELL. WE'D REHEARSED REALLY HARD, HAD A BUNCH OF GOOD SHIT. ORIGINALLY "BLACKEYED BLONDE" WAS WRITTEN BY HILLEL AND I WITH JOHN MURRAY FOR HIS PROJECT.

CLIFF MARTINEZ (RHCP DRUMMER 1983–86): GEORGE WAS WORKING WITH ANTHONY A LOT. WE DID THE BASICS AND HILLEL DID GUITAR WORK. BUT THE VOCALS WERE VERY INCOMPLETE, LYRICS WERE ADDED LATER AROUND THE TRACK, WHICH IS STRANGE. GEORGE HAD A LOT TO DO WITH CRAFTING THE VOCALS SINCE A BIG PART OF HIS MELODIC SOUND IN P-FUNK IS VOCAL HARMONIES.

GEORGE: WE PARTIED AND PARTIED. THEY WERE LIKE THE FUNKADELIC GUYS WHEN THEY WERE REAL YOUNG. BUT AT THE SAME TIME WE MADE SURE THEY WORKED HARD ALL WEEK BEFORE THEY COULD GO OFF TO HAVE THEIR FUN. THEY'D BE GOING DOWN INTO THE 'HOOD AND SOME OF MY FRIENDS THAT USUALLY WOULD ROB YOU WOULD BRING THEM BACK AND SAY, "NEXT TIME THEY COME DOWN TO THE HOOD LOOKING FOR A PARTY, I'M GONNA ROB 'EM MYSELF!" THIS NAVARRO DUDE — JUST THE ONE NAME — QUITE A BIG GANGSTER WITH A WHITE ROLLS-ROYCE, HAD A LITTLE

STUDIO WHERE WE DID PREPRODUCTION. HE LIKED THEM SO MUCH — HE THOUGHT THEY WERE GONNA BE THE NEXT ROCK 'N' ROLL SUPERSTARS. AND HE WAS RIGHT.

CLIFF: DETROIT WAS KIND OF A CULTURAL FUN ZONE, TOO. FIRST THING I SAW WAS A COP IN BROAD DAYLIGHT CHASING A BLACK MAN DOWN AN ALLEY WITH HIS GUN DRAWN. FIRST GAS STATION WE GO TO THEY'RE SELLING FREEBASING SUPPLIES! BEAKERS AND Q-TIPS. A CAR FULL OF BROTHERS PULLS UP TO US, AND THEY ROLL DOWN THE WINDOW AND GO, "YOU GUYS ARE WHITE!" DETROIT WAS A WORLD UNTO ITSELF. GUESS WE STOOD OUT. ARETHA FRANKLIN WAS WORKING DOWN THE HALL, WE WERE PROUD TO BE THERE. IT WASN'T A SUCCESSFUL ALBUM, BUT STILL . . .

GEORGE: NAVARRO TOOK 'EM TO SEE ARETHA FRANKLIN. WE ALL WENT. HE SAID, "YOUR LITTLE WHITE BOYS FROM L.A. ARE GONNA GET IN TROUBLE COMING DOWN TO THE HOOD," BUT EVERYONE WAS WATCHING OUT FOR THEM FOR ME. THEY DIDN'T EVEN KNOW I HAD PEOPLE LOOKING OUT FOR THEM EVERYWHERE! LOUIE WAS THE LOCAL WEED DUDE, HE WAS WITH US FOR YEARS DOING RAPPING, AND HE WAS LIKE A LITTLE BABY WHO DIDN'T KNOW NOTHING ABOUT NOTHING. I DON'T KNOW WHERE HE GOT THE NERVE, BUT HE WANTED TO BE A RAPPER SO BAD, AND THEY LET HIM BE ON "YERTLE THE TURTLE."

CLIFF: FRED WESLEY CAME IN ONE WEEKEND AND WROTE HORN ARRANGEMENTS AND PLAYED THEM — WE THOUGHT THE HORNS WERE SUCH A COOL ADDITION TO THESE SIMPLE SONGS. NO OTHER PRODUCER COULD HAVE PULLED IT OFF. GEORGE HAD A PARTY ATMOSPHERE IN THE STUDIO ALL THE TIME, BUT A PRODUCTIVE PARTY ATMOSPHERE. YOU TOOK CARE OF BUSINESS, BUT HE MADE SURE YOU HAD A LOT OF FUN DOING IT. **I THINK THE FUN WAS CAPTURED IN THE GROOVES. IT WAS A GREAT EXPERIENCE. WE SMOKED A TON OF POT — DRUGS WERE ALL OVER THE PLACE — TO CREATE A SPIRIT OF JOY AND FUN.** GEORGE WAS INSPIRING WITH HIS STORIES AND IDEAS.

GEORGE: FUNK WAS GETTING POP, AND ROCK WAS CHANGING. HIP-HOP WAS COMING ON STRONG WITH WHITE FOLKS AS WELL AS BLACK PEOPLE AND HIP-HOP IS A PART OF FUNK. THE ATTITUDE OF ROCK WAS IN HIP-HOP, THAT'S WHERE IT WAS NATURALLY HEADED, THAT ATTITUDE THE RED HOT CHILI PEPPERS WERE REPRESENTING. THEN YOU HAD FEAR AND THE PUNK ROCKERS, THOSE DUDES WERE ROCKING AND FUNKY. IT WASN'T METAL, IT WASN'T ALTERNATIVE, IT WAS SERIOUS BANGIN' SHIT. "KNUCKLEHEAD MUSIC," I CALL IT.

157

RED HOT CHILI PEPPERS

DICKIES

WITH

GUNS N' ROSES

AND

THELONIOUS MONSTER

8:00PM OCTOBER 31st HALLOWEEN NIGHT

BLACK MAGIC

 JAMES WHITE WAS REALLY FUN — I LOVED PLAYING WITH HIM. WE WERE GETTING READY FOR A GIG AND THE FIBONACCIS' DRUMMER JOE [BERARDI] AND HILLEL AND I ARE LIKE, "JAMES, WE'RE GOING TO GO DOWN TO THE SHOW," AND WE GO AND HANG OUT, DRINK BEERS. IT IS TIME TO PLAY, AND JAMES ISN'T THERE. THE STAGE MANAGER WAS LIKE, "GET ON." SO JOE CALLS HIM. "HEY JOE, GOD THAT WAS A GREAT SHOW TONIGHT — SOOO GOOD." JAMES HAD PASSED OUT — HAD A DREAM HE DID THE SHOW AND THOUGHT HE WAS BACK AT THE HOTEL. HE THOUGHT HE WAS DONE. **DREAMT HE HAD DONE THIS AWESOME SHOW. WHICH TO ME, FUCK, THAT IS AS GOOD AS DOING THE SHOW!** WHAT'S BETTER — A DREAM SHOW OR A REAL ONE? SO HE GOT DOWN THERE RIGHT AWAY, ROCKED HIS FUCKING ASS OFF, AND DID AN ENCORE TEN-MINUTE-LONG CASIO SOLO. GREAT ENTERTAINER. IF HE WANTED TO PLAY STRAIGHT HE COULD BE JACKIE WILSON.

159

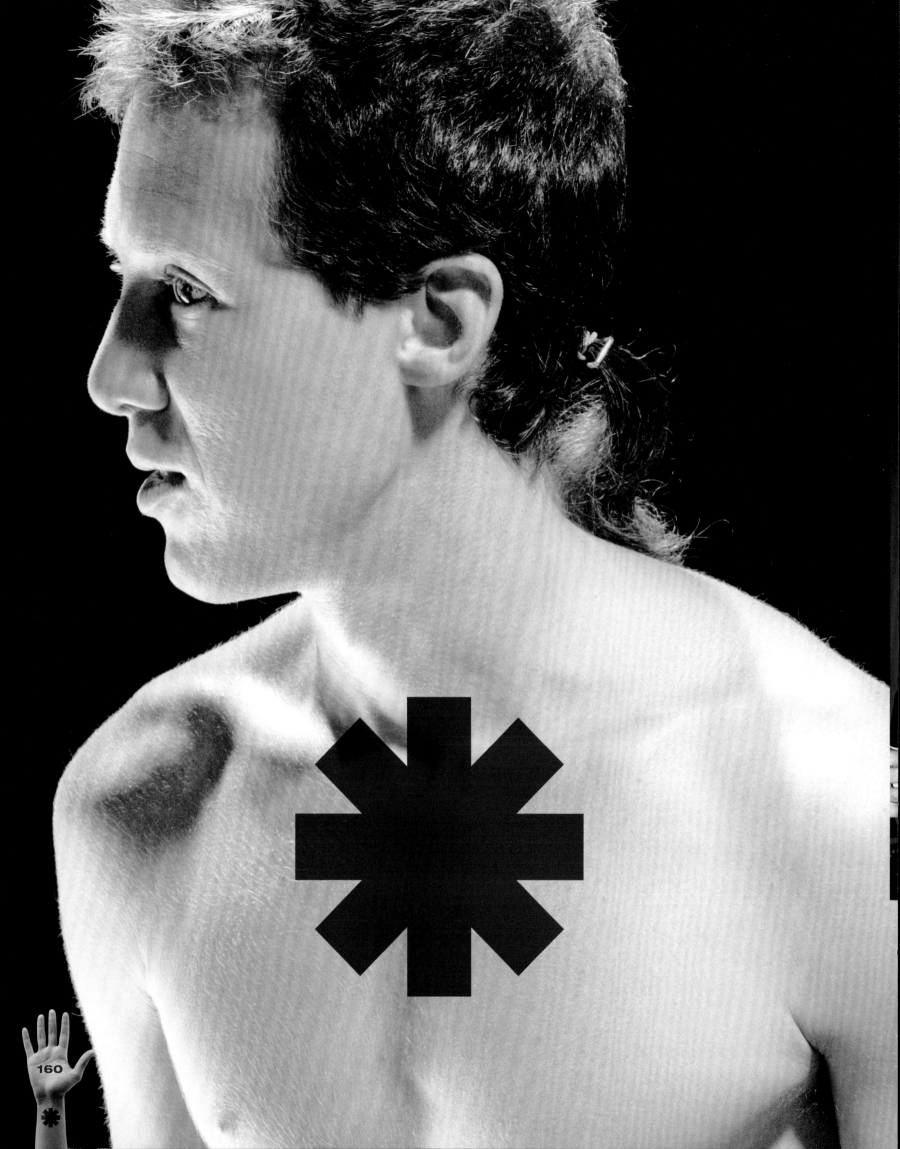

Funky Crime

✱ IT WAS A FANTASTIC FEELING TO HAVE JACK [IRONS] BACK. IT LED TO A LOT OF THE INSPIRATION FOR *UPLIFT MOFO* — A LOT OF THE JUBILATION IN THE LYRICS OF THAT RECORD ARE ABOUT BEING REUNITED.

JACK IRONS (ORIGINAL RHCP DRUMMER): WE GOT MICHAEL BEINHORN FROM NEW YORK TO PRODUCE. AND SO MICHAEL COMES TO TOWN AND HE'S A TYPICAL MANHATTANITE WHO CAN'T DRIVE EVEN A BASIC AUTOMOBILE. AND THE POOR GUY HAD NO IDEA WHAT HE WAS GETTING IN FOR — ANYBODY THAT WAS GOING TO PRODUCE OUR BAND WAS GOING TO HAVE TO SAVE US AS WELL.

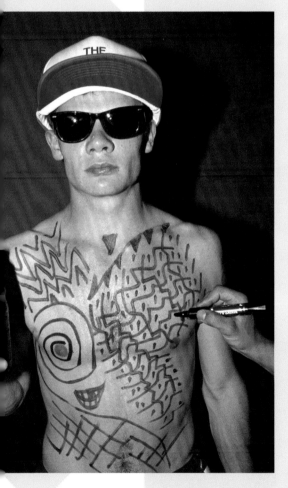

LINDY GOETZ (MANAGER): WE MET WITH MICHAEL AND I THOUGHT HE WAS A COOL GUY, SEEMED TO HAVE A GOOD FEEL FOR IT. THIS WASN'T THE KIND OF BAND SOMEONE LIKE MUTT LANGE WOULD BE ABLE TO TAKE ON.

MICHAEL BEINHORN (PRODUCER): BY 1983 I'D HAD NO REAL COMMERCIAL SUCCESS WITH ANYTHING I'D DONE SO FAR. I WAS DOWN ON MY LUCK, OUT OF A GIG, BEATING DOWN DOORS AT RECORD COMPANIES TRYING TO GET PRODUCTION WORK, BUT I'D NEVER HEAR BACK FROM ANYONE. ONE DAY I WENT OVER TO EMI AND SOME GUY THERE SAID, "WE GOT THIS BAND NO ONE KNOWS WHAT TO DO WITH THEM — THE RED HOT CHILI PEPPERS."

THOUGH THEIR MUSIC ALL SEEMED KIND OF ABSTRACT, THERE WAS DEFINITELY AN EXCITEMENT TO IT. I THOUGHT THEY NEEDED A LOT OF ARRANGEMENT HELP. I WROTE DOWN SOME IDEAS AND ASKED TO MEET UP WITH THE GUYS, BUT RATHER THAN A FORMAL MEETING — WHICH I'M SURE WOULD HAVE GONE RIDICULOUSLY — WE MET UP AT TIPITINA'S, IN NEW ORLEANS, THIS AMAZING CLUB IN HONOR OF PROFESSOR LONGHAIR, WHERE DR. JOHN, THE NEVILLE BROTHERS, THE METERS STILL JAMMED REGULARLY. I HAD NEVER SEEN ANYTHING LIKE THE RED HOT CHILI PEPPERS, THAT'S FOR DAMN SURE. IT WAS HYSTERICAL, EXPLOSIVE — EVERYONE IN THE PLACE WAS GOING APE SHIT HAVING FUN, GIRLS AND GUYS ALIKE. IT WAS EXCITING TO SEE SUCH RAW, UNTAPPED POTENTIAL. THEY CHANGED THE LYRICS TO "AFRICA" BY THE METERS TO "HOLLYWOOD," AND THE LOCALS LOVED IT. **I ALSO QUICKLY LEARNED THAT EXECS AT THE RECORD LABEL ACTUALLY HATED THE CHILI PEPPERS, LIKE OPENLY REVILED THEM SO BAD THEY DIDN'T EVEN WANT THEM TO SUCCEED. IT WAS THE WEIRDEST THING.**

✱ IF THEY DIDN'T LIKE US, I DIDN'T CARE. I JUST THOUGHT WE WERE GREAT, AND THAT'S ALL THAT COUNTED.

✱ WE RAN IN NAKED TO A HIGH-LEVEL MEETING OF EMI SUITS.

✱ ME AND ANTHONY GALLOPED UP TO THEIR RECEPTIONIST, COCKSURE DROOGIES, LIKE, "WE WANNA MEET THE PRESIDENT — WE WANNA MEET THE TOP BIG SHOTS." SHE GOES, "OH, THE PRESIDENT IS HAVING A MEETING WITH THE INTERNATIONAL HEADS OF BLAH BLAH AND HE'S BUSY IN THE BOARDROOM. MAYBE ONE DAY NEXT MONTH YOU CAN MEET WITH THE JUNIOR GUY IN THE MAILROOM." SO WE'RE SLIDIN' OUT, LOSER CHUMPS, ➤

➤ TAIL BETWEEN THE LEGS, AND ANTHONY'S LIKE, "NOT SO FAST! DUDE, WE GET OFF ALL OUR CLOTHES AND DANCE ON THE TABLE NAKED AND RUN OUT!" I SAID, "GREAT IDEA!"

✳ WE ALREADY HAD A REP AS COMPULSIVE STREAKERS, EXHIBITIONISTS, SHAMELESS LIMELIGHT HOGS. IT REALLY WASN'T ANYTHING NEW FOR US. **LOVE US OR HATE US, YOU AIN'T GONNA IGNORE US.**

✳ WE STRIPPED DOWN, GOT BUTT-NAKED AND BURST IN THE DOOR. ALL THESE SUITS ARE SITTING AROUND THIS LONG-ASSED BOARDROOM TABLE — BIG-TIME CORPORATE SHIT. SO WE JUMP UP ON THE TABLE MAKING STUPID FACES, WAVING OUR COCKS AROUND. JUMPED OFF THE TABLE, RAN OUT, GRABBED OUR CLOTHES, BOOKED OUT, AND HEADED TO THE PARK TO SMOKE A JOINT.

MICHAEL: THEY WERE EXTREMELY OUTRÉ WITH THEIR PERSONALITIES, AND THE EMI GUYS JUST DIDN'T DIG THEIR SHIT AT ALL. WORSE, THEY DIDN'T RESEMBLE ANYTHING OR ANYONE ELSE OUT THERE. THEY WEREN'T TRYING TO BE A HAIR BAND OR SOME LAME POSER POP GROUP. THERE WAS NO RELATIVITY BETWEEN THEM AND ANY OTHER ARTIST ON EMI'S ROSTER — ROXETTE, RICHARD MARX, TINA

TURNER. THEY'D HAD A BIG HIT WITH BOWIE'S "LET'S DANCE" SINGLE BUT THAT WAS LIKE A SLEEK CHIC GROOVE. THE CHILI PEPPERS WERE MORE RAW, AGGRESSIVE, WITH A HARD ROCK FEEL.

✳ EMI WAS NOT TAKING US SERIOUSLY LIKE THEY TOOK RICHARD MARX AND KAJAGOOGOO. THEY WERE PUTTING ALL THEIR CASH INTO BILLBOARDS AND POSTERS FOR THEM. **FOR SURE WE WERE THE UGLY STEPCHILDREN.**

LINDY: EMI HAD ACTS THAT WERE SELLING WELL BUT PLAYING VENUES HALF THE SIZE OF WHAT THE PEPPERS WERE USED TO. WE DIDN'T HAVE SUCCESS WITH RECORD SALES — WE WERE ONLY SELLING ALBUMS IN THE 30,000 RANGE, BUT WE WERE PLAYING THE SAME VENUES AS GROUPS WITH 400,000 IN SALES. AT LEAST WE HAD THAT GOING. WE TOURED AND WE TOURED TO DEATH. DOING INCREDIBLE AMOUNTS OF PRESS, SO IN THE END THEY HAD TO GIVE US WHAT WE WANTED — WASN'T LIKE THE GROUP WAS A TOTAL FAILURE EVEN IF IT WAS SOMETHING THEY WEREN'T USED TO WORKING WITH.

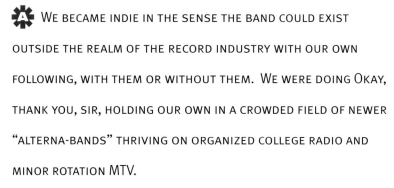

✳ WE BECAME INDIE IN THE SENSE THE BAND COULD EXIST OUTSIDE THE REALM OF THE RECORD INDUSTRY WITH OUR OWN FOLLOWING, WITH THEM OR WITHOUT THEM. WE WERE DOING OKAY, THANK YOU, SIR, HOLDING OUR OWN IN A CROWDED FIELD OF NEWER "ALTERNA-BANDS" THRIVING ON ORGANIZED COLLEGE RADIO AND MINOR ROTATION MTV.

The Mofo Uplift Party Plan

Michael Beinhorn (producer): There were points in pre-production [of *The Mofo Uplift Party Plan*] . . . where I really thought the record wasn't gonna get made. I remember sitting in [manager] Lindy [Goetz]'s car at some intersection, his hands are off the steering wheel, and he looks off into space going, "I don't know what to do! I just don't know what the fuck to do!"

For *Uplift* I would go sober for fifty days and congratulate myself by calling the dope dealer. At the same time I realized we were writing really cool songs, songs I believed in and showed our true nature and it was revealing itself, our chemistry that got us started in the very beginning. The energy, the love and joy was coming through.

Jack Irons (original RHCP drummer): **PEOPLE WOULD GET STRAIGHT FOR A WEEK OR TWO. THEY'RE ALL, "FUCK THAT, YOU'RE RIGHT, IT'LL BE GOOD" AND THEN YOU KNOW, STRAIGHT AWAY, RIGHT BACK. WE JUST COULDN'T FINISH THE RECORD, WE DIDN'T KNOW WHAT TO DO FOR MONTHS ON END.** When Anthony doesn't show up to rehearsals we got to find him, dig him up, call his girlfriend. We could get Hillel down there more often. Dramas — at least three or four months at a time. We were rehearsing in the backroom at EMI Studios. Flea and I did a lot of preproduction, just the two of us with Michael. Eventually we didn't know what to do. We were like, "Okay, we're spending all this time," so we made a decision to fire Anthony and get another singer — which is really funny looking back.

I would disappear for a week and go, "Man, I can't fucking do this." For the first time I was getting loaded knowing that there was, in fact, a solution to that dilemma and I was ignoring it. I was loaded and I didn't have to be. Before I was loaded and lost and confused, really didn't know what was wrong — why am I insane on a staircase downtown hallucinating? During *Uplift* things started to come into focus.

JACK: When we were tracking "Fight Like a Brave" —we played that song so many times — but Michael kept saying "You're off. No, man, you're off." If it wasn't me, it was Hillel. If it wasn't Hillel, it was Flea — like, someone's always off. I remember getting really irritated. Michael is very particular — he wants what he wants. If he doesn't think it is good enough it's not gonna fly. No fooling around, he wants to make the best record he can make. I like that he pushes like that.

✱ Michael was trying to open us up to another level of songwriting. We were obstinate, self-important and not really so open-minded. It is really awkward when you are used to going with your intuition and flow when writing lyrics and making music — even if it is unorthodox — but it feels natural to you. When a producer starts suggesting you do it another way, it is a little awkward, like that doesn't feel like me. I had a conversation with Michael about a song called "Behind the Sun" and I remember him suggesting, "Why don't you sing some melody here, instead of just rapping all the time?" and me going, "Melody-schmelody, why would I do that?" But, in the end there's a sappy melody in that song, but at least it was trying something new.

MICHAEL: It wound up turning into, like, a seven- or eight-month ordeal of uncertainty and frustration. We got spread thin very, very fast on the money the record label allocated us. There were many twists and turns where it almost didn't get made. This was a crazy, crazy record. That it even came out at all is a miracle considering the diverse personalities.

JACK: We were definitely overworked, and considering everyone's drug issues, I started to become unglued too, just from exhaustion and my own mental health issues. The touring just drove it to the ground. Drama would be every day, one day would be slightly better than the other, but it would never really straighten out. It didn't straighten out for a long time. I don't remember how we got through that next year and a half. We were on autopilot or something. I was.

MICHAEL: Everything is meant to go the way it is meant to go. That's the way it went, so that's how it was meant to go. In the end, we made a fantastic record. For me, there's never been a sense of, "Aw, shit, it should have been like this, should have been like that." It's a great record. No matter what happened with Anthony or Hillel, when push came to shove they both took care of their shit.

✱ **DURING THE *UPLIFT* TOUR I REMEMBER ACTUALLY FEELING A CHANGE TAKING PLACE NOT JUST IN THE AMOUNT OF PEOPLE SHOWING UP AT THE GIGS BUT THE INTENSITY OF THE FAN BASE,** the number of people who cared and knew our songs and vibe. We were a popular club band, but every dive was the same size, same amount of people, which was cool, but now the momentum was changing. Started getting a little bit bigger — by the end of the tour we played a theater in Denver, probably a 1,000-seater, a huge diff from 100. I remember one ecstatic moment with Hillel, "We sold this place out! Like, What's goin' on? I'm liking this a lot!"

✱ We were in love with those songs and how much fun we were having playing them.

165

Abbey Road

I APOLOGIZED TO AN OLD LADY ON THE CORNER FOR FLAUNTING MY GENITALS AND SHE RETORTED, **"YOU THINK I'VE NEVER SEEN A WILLY AT MY AGE, LUV?"**

JACK IRONS (ORIGINAL RHCP DRUMMER): IT WAS FUN, WE WERE HIDING OUT IN OUR TRENCH COATS, IN THE BUSHES WAITING FOR THE RIGHT MOMENT TO JUMP OUT THERE WITHOUT GETTING CAUGHT FOR INDECENT EXPOSURE OR WHATEVER.

Summertime Rolls

J We played a show with Jane's Addiction at the Palace, a legal fund benefit for [Fishbone bassist] Norwood Fisher. Up till that point their music hadn't hit me.

F The first time I saw Jane's Addiction play electric was at the Father's Rights Benefit for Norwood Fisher at the Palace.

C We'd heard so much about Jane's. Our records were coming out at the same time. Fishbone played, we did, then Jane's. I was like, "Wow — powerful and big! Awesome!" Right up my fuckin' alley. **PERRY [FARRELL] AND THOSE GUYS WERE DANGEROUS-LOOKING. HEAVY, YEAH, OUT THERE! ZEPPELIN IN A WAY — WHAT A GREAT SHOW.** Perry glided by me at the side of the stage with his pink George Clinton dreads, a perfumed freak in these silver gloves up to the elbows, looking like a fucking alien from Jupiter. As soon as they go into "Mountain Song," people go berserk.

J That night was one of the most magical rock shows I've ever seen — a life-changer. The air was so thick you could cut it with a knife — this darkness and this magical glow that was beyond the music. This other energy beyond human beings onstage playing music. I can only imagine that would be the same kind of energy that was around Jesus Christ or Lucifer. Perry was gazing into the audience like there were lights shooting out of his eyes.

F As soon as they started playing, the crowd was hypnotized. A lot of the songs start with just the bass. As soon as Eric [Avery] would play two notes of the bass line the crowd would just go nuts. That was when I really realized the power of them as a live band.

J Perry looked to the side of the stage where I was standing and stared at me with this really scary look and then he looks out at the audience and this light comes from his eyes. Wherever he looks there's this huge burst of energy. Up to this point rock music for me was something that was fun. The Chili Peppers was about being crazy, jumping around. But Jane's was at this whole other level. I

168

REALIZED WE WEREN'T SHIT. IT JUST SEEMED LIKE THEY WERE A BUNCH OF MURDERERS ONSTAGE. IT WAS SO BEYOND ANYTHING I THOUGHT A BAND COULD BE. I WAS SO FREAKED OUT. I WENT HOME IN A DAZE, LIKE SOMEBODY HAD OPENED UP THE DOOR TO THIS WORLD OF DARKNESS AND MADNESS I DIDN'T KNOW EXISTED. IT TOOK SOME DOING FOR ME TO CHANGE ENOUGH TO BE ABLE TO FEEL LIKE I COULD BE A PART OF THE ENERGY OF SOMETHING LIKE THAT. SOON THEY BECAME MY FAVORITE BAND AND I'D GO SEE THEM EVERY CHANCE I GOT. I'M LIKE, "THIS IS THE BEST BAND IN THE WORLD! THE MOST POWERFUL A BAND CAN BE ONSTAGE." JANE'S ADDICTION GUIDED ME IN WAYS THAT WOULD BE KIND OF EMBARRASSING TO EXPLAIN IN DETAIL BUT THEIR MUSIC WAS IMPORTANT TO ME FOR THAT WHOLE PERIOD.

✱ AFTER THAT NIGHT, IT WAS LIKE FISHBONE, CHILI PEPPERS, JANE'S ADDICTION, THELONIOUS MONSTER — FOUR L.A. BANDS DOING DIFFERENT MUSIC BUT OF THE SAME FAMILY. IT WAS NEVER A COMPETITION THING, MORE LIKE, "OH, WHAT'S JANE'S DOING, WHAT'S ANGELO [MOORE OF FISHBONE] DOING?"

✱ **IT WAS THROUGH ERIC AND PERRY THAT I STARTED LISTENING TO JOY DIVISION AND BAUHAUS, SAME THING ECHO AND THE BUNNYMEN.** I REMEMBER DRIVING WITH THEM IN THEIR VAN FROM THE LAST CALIFORNIA SHOW, THE SAN FRANCISCO LOLLAPALOOZA. WE DROVE BACK TO THE HOTEL AND WE WERE LISTENING TO THE CROCODILES ALBUM. EVERY TIME I HEAR THAT ALBUM IT BRINGS ME BACK TO THAT VAN.

Knock Me Down

A The seeds of the "Get More Melodic Plan" that were planted during *Uplift* continued on with *Mother's Milk*.

J *Mother's Milk*, the first album we did together was me going, "Okay, what does this band's audience need from me?" The most important element of it — your own individual soul — ends up immobilized with that type of thinking. You've got to just follow your heart and follow your interests. You can't be thinking in terms of what the band members want from you or their fans, but I did anyway.

C John had never been in a studio before or knew what anyone wanted. He loved Hendrix and Hillel. They battled in the studio over string tones. Michael Beinhorn, the producer, wanted a lot of Les Paul–sounding, "chugging metal," if you will. We got labeled as funk-metal and all that bullshit. I think Michael pushed John to go that way. He had an idea what the sound should be and since John didn't know how to be in the studio someone had to take charge.

J Flea wrote more of the music than me. I probably wrote 30 percent of it. Everything back in those days we put together as a band, and with the help of whoever was producing us in terms of arranging. We would do it all together, but the initial ideas were always Flea or I. But I just felt cut off from myself — I was so scared to do something that would not be acceptable to them.

F Michael Beinhorn did some good things, but he tried to make us fit into something that would be successful. Trigger drum sounds and all this other jive stuff to try and make us sound like a big-budget pro studio band.

C Michael was very supportive of me from the beginning. I'm forever grateful, but in the studio he had his own ideas. I put my trust in him — he was like a member of the band doing his thing. I liked him. He is a cool guy. When we were cutting the basics it was pretty good — it was after that that it started to get kind of funny. Though he did have some great ideas, some of his mixes were just too bombastic and he lost focus. He triggered drums and talked about Led Zeppelin, but it lost the dynamic in the execution. When triggered drums are the loudest thing in that type of metal mix it just sounds dumb and mechanical. Personally, I was like, Whatever. Me and John were the new guys, and so I just kept my mouth shut and played my drum parts.

F **I WAS VERY EXCITED ABOUT THE RED HOT CHILI PEPPERS ALL OVER AGAIN. JOHN BROUGHT THIS REAL MELODIC SENSE WITH CHORDS AND MELODIES, SORT OF A NEW THING FOR US, A WHOLE NEW ELEMENT.** Anthony had his lyrics and John had chord structures and ideas, and they sat down together and worked out "Knock Me Down."

C "Knock Me Down" was the first single, the first video off the *Mother's Milk* album. It was more of a real song structure. If you listen closely, John and Anthony sing. I don't know who came up with the melody, maybe John. That song turned a whole new melodic corner for the Chili Peppers compared to just a bass groove with raps over the top.

F John and Anthony definitely evolved into a wonderful creative relationship.

170

MOTHER'S MILK

LINDY GOETZ (MANAGER): WHEN *MOTHER'S MILK* CAME OUT EMI GOT DIFFERENT PEOPLE WORKING ON IT. THEY HIRED KIM WHITE TO HANDLE IT. COLLEGE RADIO WAS NOW GETTING CALLED ALTERNATIVE MORE AND MORE.

KIM WHITE, THE COLLEGE RADIO PERSON THEY FINALLY GOT THERE IN TIME TO PROMOTE *MOTHER'S MILK*, WAS REALLY NICE AND SWEET AND SEEMED TO CARE ABOUT US.

KIM WHITE (EMI PROMOTION): I HAD A BACKGROUND IN COLLEGE RADIO PROMOTION WHEN I WAS HIRED ON AT EMI AT THE TIME OF THE *MOTHER'S MILK* RECORD. THEY'RE LIKE, "WE DON'T REALLY HAVE A BIG ALTERNATIVE ROSTER. **WE HAVE THIS ONE ALTERNATIVE BAND BUT THEY'RE DISGUSTING. THE RED HOT CHILI PEPPERS, AND IF THEY COME TO THE OFFICE DON'T LET THEM SIT ON ANY OF THE COUCHES."** THEY GO, "IF YOU SHAKE HANDS WITH THEM, WASH YOUR HANDS." NO ONE CARED ABOUT THE BAND'S FEELINGS — THEY WANTED NOTHING TO DO WITH THEM. RHCP WERE STRICTLY COLLEGE RADIO PRE–*MOTHER'S MILK*. WE HAD A SUMMIT ABOUT CONTEMPORARY RADIO PROMOTION IN A HOTEL CONFERENCE ROOM IN NEW YORK. IS IT GOING TO BE ALTERNATIVE, NEW MUSIC, COLLEGE RADIO? EVERYBODY VOTED ON ALTERNATIVE — SERIOUSLY, IT WAS THIRTY PEOPLE SITTING IN A CONFERENCE ROOM VOTING. ALTERNATIVE WAS ALL ABOUT UNITING, CONSOLIDATING WHAT HAD PREVIOUSLY BEEN COLLEGE RADIO AND THEN MODERN ROCK OR NEW MUSIC. AS SOON AS A LOT OF COMMERCIAL STATIONS STARTED CONVERTING TO ALTERNATIVE, OR WHATEVER, THEY WERE LIKE, WE NEED TO BE IN ONE TENT, UNDER ONE NAME.

LINDY: ALL OF WHICH HELPED PUT RHCP IN PRECISELY THE RIGHT PLACE AT THE RIGHT TIME.

OUR BAND HAD NOWHERE ELSE TO GO. CYNICS WERE SAYING, "WHO WANTS TO BE DUMPED IN A LOW-WATT CMJ GRAVEYARD FOR JUNK THAT CAN'T GET PLAYED ELSEWHERE, MUCH OF IT FOR GOOD REASON?" TO OTHERS, LIKE US AND OUR FRIENDS, ORGANIZED COLLEGE RADIO WAS A REAL MOVEMENT FOR SOCIAL EVOLUTION — COLLEGE RADIO EXPOSURE HELPED US THROUGH THE MANY LEAN YEARS.

OUR BAND IS ETERNALLY GRATEFUL FOR THAT SUPPORT.

LINDY: EMI WAS SUCH A STRUGGLE. THEY WERE A VERY POP LABEL AND WE WERE STILL SO FAR OFF TO THE LEFT. THEY WEREN'T GEARED UP TO WORK THIS KIND OF ACT BECAUSE THEY DIDN'T HAVE A STRONG ALTERNATIVE DEPARTMENT. NO COLLEGE DEPARTMENT AT FIRST, NOTHING TILL KIM WHITE CAME ON BOARD. ALL THE SUDDEN EVERYTHING STARTED COMING OUR WAY. WE'RE GETTING RADIO AND

TV ADS LIKE CRAZY AND WE'RE ON THE COVER OF *ROLLING STONE*, *SPIN*. I WENT AND HAD A GOLD ALBUM MADE WITH A QUARTER OF IT CUT OUT — LIKE A PIE SLICE — AND MAILED IT TO THE PRESIDENT OF EMI. INSTEAD OF "CONGRATS ON THE SALE OF ONE MILLION" IT WAS JUST A GOLD RECORD WITH A CHUNK CUT OUT, AND THE ENGRAVING SAID, "WHAT'S MISSING HERE?" IT EMBARRASSED THE SHIT OUT OF EVERYBODY, BUT IT WORKED. WHATEVER THAT MAGIC BUTTON THEY TALK ABOUT RECORD COMPANIES PUSHING — HE PUSHED IT. "HIGHER GROUND" BECAME A HUGE RADIO HIT. THE MESSAGE OF STRIVING AGAINST ALL ODDS WAS UNIVERSAL.

✳ "KNOCK ME DOWN" FIRST CRACKED THE DOOR TO "COMMERCIAL ALTERNATIVE" RADIO — AND THEN "HIGHER GROUND" KICKED IT WIDE OPEN FOR US.

✳ KIM WHITE WAS SINGLE-HANDEDLY RESPONSIBLE FOR THE SUCCESS OF *MOTHER'S MILK* BY SHOVING IT DOWN THE THROATS OF COLLEGE RADIO. HER LIFE BECAME SITTING IN THAT OFFICE MAKING THOSE CALLS. THERE WAS A SQUIRRELLY A&R GUY IN NEW YORK WHO WAS OBSESSED WITH DOING EDITS OF OUR SONGS TO MAKE THEM MORE RADIO FRIENDLY. I JUST REMEMBER GETTING SUCH A DISGUSTING FEELING, LIKE **WHO IS THIS GUY THAT LIVES IN HIS MOTHER'S SPARE ROOM THAT THINKS HE CAN DECIDE WHAT TO EDIT OF OUR SONGS? WE WROTE IT — IF IT IS TOO LONG, THEN FUCK IT. THAT'S THE SONG.** THAT'S WHERE MY HEAD WAS AT THAT POINT IN TIME.

KIM: A FEW ASSHOLE RADIO GUYS SAID, "I WILL NEVER PLAY THIS SONG OR THIS BAND — STOP CALLING ME." THEY ENDED UP ADDING IT THOUGH, BECAUSE IT WAS THE BIGGEST RECORD IN THE COUNTRY. WE'RE LIKE, "DUDE, SONG IS NUMBER ONE, NOW WHAT'S YOUR PROBLEM?" THERE'S A LOT OF PUMPED-UP ASSHOLES IN RADIO. THAT'S WHY THEY'RE IN RADIO, LET'S FACE IT. "THEY HAVE A FACE ONLY RADIO COULD LOVE," IS WHAT I ALWAYS SAY.

Storm in a Teacup

✱ *MOTHER'S MILK* WENT GOLD — NOW WE WERE FINALLY A REAL, FUNCTIONING BAND WRITING SONGS, RECORDING AND TOURING. WE WERE COMING INTO A NEW CHAPTER. ANTHONY AND LINDY WERE FIRM THEY DIDN'T WANT TO GIVE EMI THE NEW THING.

✱ WE SHOPPED AROUND TO ALL THE LABELS, WE WERE COMING OFF A GOLD ALBUM AND KIND OF HOT — SEVEN YEARS LATER, WE ARE FINALLY THIS HOT NEW OVERNIGHT SENSATION THING.

✱ ANTHONY IS OH SO AMBITIOUS, WHICH FLEA AND I ARE NOT. ANTHONY WAS ALWAYS HEADING THE IDEA OF GETTING US OFF EMI. FLEA AND I WOULD HAVE DONE WHATEVER, WHEREAS ANTHONY WAS VERY SPECIFIC, EXTREMELY FOCUSED, "I AM NOT GOING TO GIVE THIS RECORD TO EMI." WE WERE UNANIMOUS WITH HIM ON THAT ONE. WE ALL THOUGHT THE MUSIC WAS TOO GOOD — WE COULDN'T PUT IT IN THEIR HANDS.

✱ EMI HAD BEEN SO BAD FOR US FOR SO LONG, THAT WHEN THEY FINALLY BROKE OUR RECORD AND WE GOT A LITTLE TASTE OF POWER, WE WERE LIKE, "OKAY NOW — SCREW YOU GUYS! YOU REALLY TREATED US LIKE UGLY STEPCHILDREN FOREVER AND NOW THEY ARE LISTENING TO US, AND THEY WANT US — WE'RE GONNA BAIL ON YOU."

✱ WE WANTED OUT, WE WERE ON TO SOMETHING NEW AND WE KNEW IT. NEW BAND, NEW SONGS — WE JUST KNEW WE'RE COMING ON, EXCITED ABOUT WHAT WAS HAPPENING. WE JUST HAD TO TRY SOMEWHERE ELSE, SOMEWHERE FRESH.

✱ IT WAS SUCH A BATTLE ROYALE, I THINK WE ONLY HAD ONE ALBUM LEFT WITH EMI AND FOR THE FIRST TIME EVER IN OUR SIX-YEAR HISTORY, WE HAD RECORD COMPANIES THAT WANTED US — AFTER *MOTHER'S MILK* AND THE SUCCESS OF "KNOCK ME DOWN"

AND "HIGHER GROUND." IT WAS A BIT OF A FEEDING FRENZY, HENCE OUR DETERMINATION TO GET RID OF THAT COMPANY THAT HADN'T WANTED US FOR SO LONG BECAME VERY STRONG. I WAS SUMMONED BY JOE SMITH WHO RAN CAPITOL WHICH WAS PART OF EMI. HE'D HEARD I WAS FIGHTING TOOTH AND NAIL TO GET OFF EMI AND HE'D MADE UP HIS MIND HE WASN'T LETTING US GO. IT WASN'T A QUESTION IF WE WERE GOING OR NOT, IT WAS JUST A MATTER OF TIME AND FIGURING IT OUT. HE SAT ME DOWN AT HIS BIG OFFICE AT

CAPITOL AND SAYS, "YOU'RE NOT GOING ANYWHERE" AND I LOOKED AT HIM AND SAID, "WELL, WE ARE, THERE'S NOTHING YOU CAN DO," AND HE SAID, "WELL YOU CAN'T, I'M NOT LETTING YOU." I SAID, "CONSIDER IT DONE, WE ARE LEAVING." WE HAD THIS AWFULLY TEDIOUS BACK AND FORTH THING — A VERY CONFRONTATIONAL DISCUSSION. THERE WAS JUST NO WAY THEY WERE GOING TO MAKE US STAY. WHOEVER WAS GOING TO BE OUR NEW COMPANY WOULD HAVE TO SOMEHOW MAKE A DEAL WITH EMI TO GET US OFF AND OUT OF THAT FINAL RECORD. THAT'S HOW ADAMANT WE WERE. THE WHOLE BAND UNANIMOUSLY BACKED ME UP IN MY STAND.

✱ WE WERE COURTED BY ALL THE MAJOR LABELS, WE MET WITH DAVID GEFFEN AND MO OSTIN, VIRGIN RECORDS, NOW THEY ALL

WANTED US. ERIC [GREENSPAN, RHCP'S ATTORNEY] GOES, "WELL, YOU GUYS GOT AN OFFER FROM EPIC, AND IT'S A MILLION DOLLARS MORE THAN EVERYONE ELSE," AND WE JUMPED UP "ALL RIGHT! EPIC! THAT'S OUR LABEL!" WE MET WITH TOMMY MOTTOLA, WHO GAVE US A SIGNED GUITAR BY THE ROLLING STONES. SO WE SAID EPIC, BUT WE OWED EMI ONE MORE RECORD AND WE HAD TO GET OFF EMI TO CLOSE THE DEAL, BUT THEN NEGOTIATIONS BETWEEN EMI AND EPIC STALLED. ONCE WE EVEN CAME OUT TO TAKE PICTURES FOR TRADE MAGAZINES LIKE, "RED HOT CHILI PEPPERS SIGN WITH EPIC." WE'RE LIKE, "MAN, THIS FUCKING EPIC DEAL IS DRAGGING." MORE AND MORE EPIC JUST DIDN'T FEEL RIGHT. OUR MANAGER'S LIKE, "WOULDN'T THAT BE THE COOLEST IF I COULD JUST DRIVE DOWN TO BURBANK AND DEAL WITH THEM AT WB?"

LINDY GOETZ (MANAGER): WHAT HAPPENED WITH TOMMY'S DEAL WAS THAT WHEN THE EPIC CONTRACT FINALLY ARRIVED IT WASN'T WHAT THEY WERE PROMISED DURING NEGOTIATION. A BAIT-AND-SWITCH JOB. THEN VIRGIN RECORDS SUDDENLY CALLS. [RICHARD] BRANSON HIMSELF WANTING TO FLY ME TO THE BAHAMAS OR WHEREVER IT WAS, TO COME HANG OUT, BUT VIRGIN WASN'T A LABEL I THOUGHT WAS RIGHT OR INTERESTING AT THE TIME. IT WAS DOWN TO SONY/EPIC OR WB, AND WB JUST FELT SO RIGHT, BUT THE SONY ADVANCE WAS SO MUCH BIGGER.

THEN MO CALLS EVERYONE AT HOME, "I HEARD YOU'RE GOING WITH EPIC, AND I WANTED TO SAY GOOD LUCK AND HOPE EVERYTHING WORKS OUT GREAT — IT WAS A PLEASURE MEETING YOU GUYS." WE'RE ALL BLOWN OUT, SUCH A REAL CLASSY MOVE, JUST TO CALL, TO SAY GOOD LUCK — TO EACH OF US. WE STARTED LOVIN' THE IDEA MORE AND MORE OF WB. IT WAS L.A.-BASED AND ITS REP WAS HIGH FOR BEING ARTIST-ORIENTED.

LINDY: THEY HAD PRINCE, THEY HAD TALKING HEADS, DEVO, THE RAMONES, SEX PISTOLS, JANE'S ADDICTION, THE BLASTERS, AND MANY OTHER GREATS — THE GUYS WERE VERY EXCITED ABOUT BEING ASSOCIATED WITH THOSE ARTISTS.

WE WERE BEING COURTED BY GEFFEN, EPIC, WB, AND MAYBE SONY. WE GOT TO HANG OUT WITH THE BIGWIGS. WE REALLY HADN'T PAID TOO MUCH ATTENTION TO THE BUSINESS SIDE UP TO THAT POINT. IT WASN'T PART OF WHAT WE DID, BUT IN THE PROCESS OF INVESTIGATING WHO EXACTLY WE WERE GOING TO END UP IN BED WITH, WE MET SOME VERY INTERESTING PEOPLE — MAINLY MO OSTIN — BUT ALSO TOMMY MOTTOLA, AND ALL THESE OTHER PEOPLE. BUT THE GUY WHO WAS A WARM, MUSIC-LOVING LIKEABLE GUY WAS MO OSTIN. WE CERTAINLY MILKED IT FOR A LOT OF GOOD MEALS. WE TOLD MO IF HE COULD GET US OFF EMI, WE'D GO WITH HIS COMPANY. IT TOOK HIM LESS THAN A MONTH TO MAKE A DEAL WITH THE EMI GUY — MO SURE GOT US OFF THE LABEL FAST. WE SIGNED WITH WARNERS FOR LESS MONEY, AND THE EPIC PEOPLE WERE PISSED!

175

UNDER THE BRIDGE

✲ WHEN ANTHONY FIRST CAME UP WITH THE IDEA FOR "UNDER THE BRIDGE," HE SAID HE HAD WRITTEN SOMETHING BUT IT WASN'T SOMETHING THAT WOULD BE FOR THE CHILI PEPPERS. WE STILL HAD THIS FIXED IDEA OF WHAT A CHILI PEPPERS SONG COULD AND COULDN'T BE.

✲ "UNDER THE BRIDGE" SOUNDED LIKE US PLAYING IN A ROOM. [PRODUCER] RICK [RUBIN] HELPED US REINFORCE THE STRENGTHS OF US PLAYING TOGETHER. **RICK'S CONCEPTS FOR MAKING SONGS ARE ALWAYS GOOD.** MAKE EVERY SONG AS GOOD AS IT CAN BE. RICK IS GREAT, VERY CLEARHEADED, EXTREMELY RELAXED — A PERFECT COUNTERPOINT TO OUR CHAOS.

✲ IT WAS CERTAINLY A HIGHLIGHT OF OUR CAREER WHEN MO OSTIN, BIG CHIEF OF WARNER BROS RECORDS, WHO HAD BEEN AROUND THE INDUSTRY SINCE THE 1950S, ASKED, "WHAT ARE YOU GUYS WRITING ABOUT ON THE RECORD?" THAT'S THE FIRST TIME ANYONE FROM ANY RECORD COMPANY HAD EVER ASKED A QUESTION LIKE THAT. I WOULD TELL HIM, AND THEN LATER HE WOULD COME TO THE STUDIO TO VISIT AND SAY, "YOU KNOW

RICK RUBIN (PRODUCER): "UNDER THE BRIDGE" WAS A REVELATION. UP TILL THEN THEY ALL HAD A VISION OF WHAT THE CHILI PEPPERS WERE SUPPOSED TO BE, WHICH I THOUGHT WAS LIMITING THEM FROM BEING WHAT THEY COULD BE. THAT SONG TORE DOWN THE WALLS OF CLOSED FORMATS.

YOU WERE TELLING ME ABOUT THIS SONG AND THE LYRICS WENT LIKE THIS . . ." AND WE ENDED UP RECORDING "UNDER THE BRIDGE." HE WAS LIKE, "I WANNA HEAR THAT SONG — SOUNDED INTERESTING TO ME." I WAS LIKE, **"OH, RICK, CAN WE PLAY IT FOR MO?" IT WAS JUST SO GREAT TO BE WORKING WITH SOMEONE WHO WAS SENSITIVE AND REAL.**

Blood Sugar Sex Magik

✳ *Blood Sugar* was John's second record with us — where everything just came together. It was the first time we recorded with the same lineup two records in a row. **THE JAMMING, THE WRITING, THE PLANNING, THE MAKING OF *BLOOD SUGAR* WAS ONE OF THE PUREST, FUNNEST, CREATIVE TIMES IN THE ENTIRE HISTORY OF THE BAND.** That feeling of all for one.

✳ By *Blood Sugar* about half the things were brought in by me and half by Flea. A good amount just came from us jamming with Chad and Anthony.

✳ I knew we were going to make a good record. When we made *Blood Sugar*, I wanted to be as big as Led Zep. I wanted to have a profound effect on culture like them.

✳ We began rehearsing and working with [producer] Rick Rubin at Alley Studios in North Hollywood. We got the stuff written and arranged there.

✳ Rick realized we were a jamming band, a rock band, and he worked on the song structures as good as he could, then he wanted to record it and make it sound like us. That was the first time anyone said that to us.

✳ Rick told us, **"YOU GUYS SHOULD JUST DO WHATEVER YOU DO, THAT SHOULD BE THE BAND."** He didn't have a fixed idea of what the band's sound should be — he wasn't interested in super-imposing any producer's magic stamp.

✳ Thankfully, Rick had no legendary producer's signature sound in mind for us.

✳ We all heaved a huge sigh of relief.

➤ ✺ WE WERE ALREADY EXPANDING OUR CONCEPT AND SOUND, AND RICK WAS THERE TO HELP US DO THAT FURTHER. IT WAS THE HEALTHIEST THING A PRODUCER COULD DO — GIVING YOU LICENSE TO BE YOURSELF.

✺ RICK ISN'T A MUSICIAN, HE JUST HAS A REALLY KEEN SENSE OF ARRANGEMENT. HE DOES WHAT FEELS GOOD — THINGS LIKE, TRY MAKING THE CHORUS LESS THIS, CUT OUT THE BRIDGE HERE, YOU DON'T NEED IT. TRY THIS INSTRUMENTATION THERE.

RICK RUBIN (PRODUCER): I NEVER THOUGHT THE RECORDS WERE GREAT, BUT LIVE I THOUGHT THEY WERE INCREDIBLE. ACROSS THE BOARD — MUSICIANSHIP, ENERGY, SENSE OF COMMUNITY. **EVEN THOUGH I HAD BEEN COMING TO L.A. BEFORE I BEGAN WORKING WITH THEM, I FELT LIKE BEING AROUND THEM WAS MY REAL INTRO TO THE L.A. MUSIC SCENE.** I ALWAYS FELT LIKE AN OUTSIDER BEFORE WORKING WITH THEM AND BEING THEIR FRIEND AND SEEING THEIR WORLD.

✺ WE HAD A LOT OF MUSIC FOR *BLOOD SUGAR*. AND SO THEN IT WAS LIKE, "WHERE ARE WE GOING TO RECORD?" STUDIOS WITH DENTIST-OFFICE LIGHTS CAN BE STERILE. RICK SAID, "LET'S GO SOMEWHERE WHERE WE'RE NOT DISTRACTED AND THERE'S NO OTHER BANDS OR PEOPLE AROUND. LET'S GO TO A HOUSE AND LIVE THERE AND MOVE EQUIPMENT IN, LIKE SUMMER CAMP." SO WE MOVED EVERYTHING INTO A MANSION IN LAUREL CANYON FOR THE OFFICIAL RECORDING. [ENGINEER] BRENDAN O'BRIEN AND RICK SET UP ALL THE RECORDING GEAR THERE.

RICK: I FOUND THE HOUSE. WE WERE UP THERE MAYBE SIX WEEKS. IT SHOULDN'T EVEN HAVE BEEN THAT LONG— WE WERE REALLY WELL PREPARED.

✺ A LOT OF HISTORY IN THAT PLACE WITH THE BEATLES AND HENDRIX HANGING OUT THERE. THEY DIDN'T RECORD THERE.

HOUDINI'S MANSION WAS ACROSS THE STREET. WE SAW A LITTLE OF THE HAUNTED STUFF. I HAD JUST MET MY FIRST WIFE — WE WERE HANGING OUT A LOT. I DIDN'T REALLY WANT TO STAY AT THE HOUSE. I WANTED TO BE WITH HER. SO THE OTHER GUYS ARE GIVING ME A HARD TIME, CALLING ME CHICKEN, SCARED OF GHOSTS. BUT IT WAS MAINLY BECAUSE I LIVED CLOSE AND COULD RIDE MY MOTORCYCLE TO MY HOUSE TO BE WITH MY LOVELY WIFE. BUT, IN THE SPIRIT OF THE BAND I PICKED A ROOM, THOUGH I WASN'T IN THERE MUCH. THE OTHER GUYS HAD POSTERS ON THE WALL AND STEREOS, FUTONS, BEDS. ONE DAY, FOR ENTERTAINMENT VALUE, WE GOT THESE TWO KOOKY GHOST PEOPLE TO CHECK OUT THE PLACE FOR SPIRITS, AND THEIR DIVINING WATER ROD WAS A FUCKING COAT HANGER! FLEA'S BROTHER-IN-LAW IS FILMING IT. ALL OUR EQUIPMENT IS SET UP IN THE BALLROOM READY TO PLAY AND ONE OF THEM'S ALL, "OH, MY, I FEEL THERE'S BEEN A LOT OF MUSIC IN HERE" AND WE'RE ROLLING OUR EYES LIKE, "WHAT A GENIUS." THE OTHER ONE'S PEERING AT CATERING IN THE KITCHEN GOING, "OOH, I SEE FOOD AND PARTIES AND DRINKING" AND HE GOES UPSTAIRS AND INTO MY ROOM. I HAD NOTICED THE BATHROOM WAS REALLY ICE COLD AND SO I ASK THEM TO CHECK IT OUT, "OOOOH SOMETHING TERRIBLE HAS HAPPENED IN HERE, LIKE SOMEBODY KILLED THEMSELVES OR SOMETHING!" THEY WERE LIKE THE SISKEL AND EBERT OF THE GHOSTBUSTIN' WORLD.

RICK: DURING *BLOOD SUGAR* ANTHONY WAS AT THE TOP OF HIS GAME LYRICALLY AND MUSICALLY.

✺ MUSICALLY AND CREATIVELY, THE *BLOOD SUGAR* SESSIONS FLOWED GREAT! ME AND JOHN REALLY CONNECTED. HE WAS COMING INTO HIS OWN. ON *MOTHER'S MILK* HE WAS MORE WANTING TO FIT IN TO THE RIGHT THING FOR THE CHILI PEPPERS.

✺ WE COULD JUST RECORD WHATEVER WE WANTED — USE DIFFERENT ROOMS, ONE KIT HERE AND ONE THERE. A LOT OF

TILE FLOORS AND WINDOWS. "FOUR MICROPHONES IS ALL YOU NEED," SAYS BRENDAN O'BRIEN. JOHN WOULD DO ACOUSTIC STUFF IN HIS ROOM, AND WE'D RECORD IN THE FOYER. STUFF YOU COULDN'T DO IN A REGULAR STUDIO. WE HAD THIS EX–PLAYBOY BUNNY, OUT OF HER MIND, COOK — ALL OUR FRIENDS WOULD HAVE DINNER AT NIGHT.

A JOHN WAS FINDING HIS OWN VOICE. WHAT HE'D STARTED WITH *MOTHER'S MILK* NOW BEGAN TO BLOOM IN THE SUN.

RICK: JOHN FOUND HIS VOICE, THAT'S FOR SURE. BUT GUITAR-WISE *BLOOD SUGAR* I STILL THINK IS HILLEL-ESQUE. IT WAS A SELF-IMPOSED THOUGHT BY JOHN, BECAUSE I DON'T THINK ANYONE ELSE REALLY WANTED TO PUSH HIM INTO THAT WAY OF PLAYING.

J RICK MAINLY WORKED WITH VOCALS AND DRUMS. LIKE, HE DIDN'T REALLY EVER SUGGEST ANYTHING TO ME ON GUITAR, OR CHANGE ANYTHING. WHEN I RECORDED MY GUITAR PARTS, HE WASN'T THERE. IT WAS JUST ME AND BRENDAN O'BRIEN ENGINEERING. I WAS GRADUALLY LEARNING ON THE JOB HOW TO PRODUCE MYSELF.

C BRENDAN O'BRIEN IS A WORLD-CLASS ENGINEER — RICK'S MAIN GUY — A DREAM COME TRUE FOR ANY MUSICIAN. HE GOT GREAT SOUNDS AND TONES, BRILLIANT MIC SELECTION AND PLACEMENT, MIXING, EDITING, EVERYTHING. THE MAN.

J BRENDAN UNDERSTOOD THE VALUE OF MISTAKES, AND IMPERFECTIONS — DIDN'T TRY TO FIX OR PUT A LOT OF COMPRESSION ON THINGS. HE WAS JUST RECORDING THINGS THAT WERE ALREADY IN THE AIR. ME NOT KNOWING ANYTHING ABOUT RECORDING TECHNIQUES OR ENGINEERING BACK THEN, I WAS REALLY HAPPY TO BE IN SOMEONE'S HANDS WHO WASN'T TRYING TO CHANGE IT, BUT WHO KNEW HOW TO FIT THINGS TOGETHER BY JUST RECORDING THEM WELL.

WHAT CAME OUT OF THE SPEAKERS WAS EXACTLY WHAT WE WANTED TO HEAR — US PLAYING LIVE MUSIC TOGETHER ON REAL INSTRUMENTS IN A ROOM WITH A FEW WELL-PLACED MICS.

F WE KNEW IT WAS GOOD. WE KNEW RIGHT AWAY THE NEW SHIT WAS GOOD.

C JOHN WAS STARTING TO BECOME HIS OWN PERSON, MORE CONFIDENT AS A MEMBER OF THE BAND AND A SONGWRITER, AS A GUITAR PLAYER.

J WITH "I COULD HAVE LIED" THE INTENTION WAS TO WRITE A GUITAR PART WITH THE SAME VIBE AS THE BASS LINE ON JANE'S ADDICTION'S "THREE DAYS." THEY START WITH THE SAME TWO NOTES AND THEN THEY GO IN DIFFERENT DIRECTIONS. I WAS FIGURING OUT WHAT KIND OF FEELINGS I WANTED MY MUSIC TO REPRESENT. THERE WAS SOMETHING VERY SENSUAL ABOUT THAT BASS LINE.

C WE RECORDED A ROBERT JOHNSON COVER OUTSIDE ON TOP OF THE HILL — ON THE RECORD YOU CAN HEAR THE CARS IN LAUREL CANYON GOING BY. RICK SAID, "LET'S TAKE EVERYTHING OUTSIDE." WE JUST WANTED TO TRY DIFFERENT THINGS. BRENDAN WAS SO GOOD AND FAST — IT WASN'T LIKE IT TOOK ALL THIS TIME TO SET UP. HE'D JUST THROW UP A MIC, AND WE'RE GOOD TO GO. IT FELT LIKE EVERYBODY WAS IN SYNC AND THE SOUND WAS REALLY GOOD. I THINK IT WAS THE FIRST TIME THE SOUND OF THE BAND HAD BEEN CAPTURED PROPERLY — POWERFUL BUT ORGANIC AND NATURAL. LIKE YOU ARE STANDING IN THE ROOM WITH THE GUYS PLAYING.

181

Smells Like Teen Spirit

✳ Until that whole breakthrough with *Blood Sugar* we stayed at the same level for a long time, from *Freaky Styley* onwards. For years and years we were doing okay playing 2,000-seat theaters. Suddenly all these amazing bands opening up for us were becoming huge — like Nirvana, Pearl Jam, Alice in Chains, Soundgarden, Smashing Pumpkins, GN'R.

✳ The Pumpkins I really liked. Me and Jimmy [Chamberlin] really hit it off. He is an amazing drummer to watch, definitely one of my favorites, and we'd go out all the time. He had this alter ego, Brutal Jim. He'd stand by with a bottle of vodka, all, "Chad, my good man — where we going out tonight?" And Jimmy can get pretty, you know, rowdy. Yeah! My kinda guy. We're still rehearsing, no opening band decided yet, and so Jack Irons says, "Hey, my friend Eddie's in this new band out on Epic." Third band on a bill don't matter much, but once the tour got rolling you could see kids coming out earlier. Pearl Jam were really supernice guys — we had a great time with them. People still go to this day, "Oh, those shows were amazing." But at the time you just think you are hanging out with like-minded music people who enjoy playing.

✳ **IT WAS LIKE OPEN UP FOR THE RED HOTS AND YOU'LL BE HUGE — YOU'LL BE BIGGER THAN US! AND THAT WAS REALLY TRUE ON THE *BLOOD SUGAR* TOUR — THE THREE OPENING BANDS BECAME THE DEFINING BANDS OF THE '90s.** At a certain point we kind of caught up with them. We'd been going fifteen years but they became so much huger than us. We got big with "Under the Bridge" and became popular, but Pearl Jam became the biggest rock band on earth.

✳ *Blood Sugar* put us into the mainstream with help from the Lollapalooza tours — the whole alternative thing was in full swing. Timing and the biz finally caught up to what the Chili Peppers were doing. **IT WAS TIME FOR A CHANGE. KIDS WERE TIRED OF HAIR METAL AND THE GRUNGE THING CAME ALONG, WHICH BECAME THE ROCK VERSION OF KEEPIN' IT REAL.** We were perceived by some as something new, but we were still just doing what we were doing. We wanted Nirvana to play, and they'd said yeah two months earlier, but now they're knocking Michael Jackson off

number one. Now it's Nirvana's world. We were on a bus and Anthony finds out they're gonna cancel, so he calls Kurt, "We love you guys, please play with us" and he said, "Okay." But there was a rub with the Pumpkins — they didn't wanna open for Nirvana. Those shows were amazing. Kurt was always by himself. He didn't really hang out at sound checks — him and Courtney were doing whatever. I never really hung out with him. We played five or six shows, I think maybe we did Rock in Rio and they played or something. First time I met Dave Grohl, too, and we're good friends and have toured with Foo Fighters a lot.

As far as Nirvana goes, I was opposed to the idea of pop-punk in general by that period. I didn't want to like it, even after I heard Kurt's voice and thought it was amazing. On principle I just thought pop-punk was an oxymoron or something, I wasn't open to it. I didn't start liking Nirvana until *In Utero*. I love his guitar playing — it reminds me of Greg Ginn.

I remember watching from the side — a big open-seat arena — they are playing and halfway through the set, the opening of "Teen Spirit." I'd never seen anything like

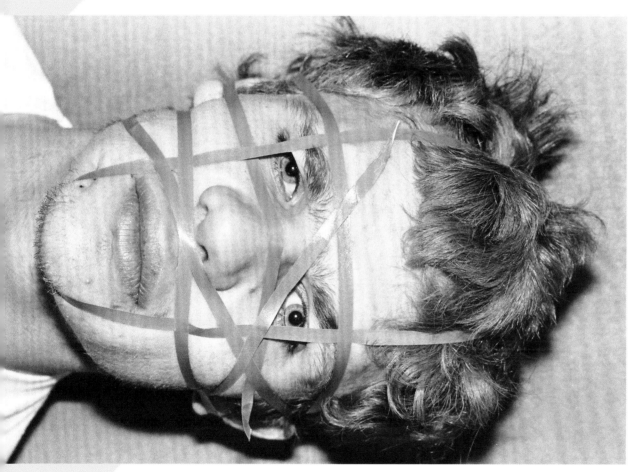

it — unfucking believable. Energy of that song, and the people, and his voice. It was incredible, like I'm looking at my brother going "holy shit!" I'm really happy I was there because you'll never see that again.

A lot of playing that he's done live and on B-sides, I see them being really connected. Masters of style

really. Now I like all their stuff. But at the time they played with us, I didn't care at all. It was more Flea and Anthony that were into what they were doing. I think if I had watched the shows I would have been really excited about it, but I didn't even watch. I just didn't care about someone taking punk and making it popular — even though I know we were a part of that too. **I SO HATED THE IDEA OF PUNK BEING THE COOL THING. I WANTED IT TO ALWAYS BE THIS THING FOR THE SOCIAL OUTCASTS, THE GEEKS, THE NERDS, THE UNPOPULAR OUTSIDERS, THE AWKWARD LONER FREAKS** — and Nirvana totally made it to where high school football jocks now think it's cool. That was the end for me.

I was hypnotized by Kurt's charisma and totally in awe of his talents, especially the song-writing. It was more than a little intimidating.

I remember Cow Palace on New Years Eve '91 when they did the whole amp trashing. It was the apex. "Teen Spirit" was breaking huge on MTV, commercial radio and alternative college radio. — usually they're at odds — now all of Nirvana's stars were lined up, all of 'em blasting out "Teen Spirit" every hour in unison.

183

Apache Rose Peacock

John felt that with *Blood Sugar* we made this amazing album, he was like, "That's it — we hit the pinnacle," and he was going to quit the band.

As we got more successful John began rebelling against everything.

Mother's Milk did pretty well, and by the end we are playing the Greek Theater in Los Angeles — it wasn't punk rock shows anymore. By the time of *Blood Sugar* it's arenas, big places. You could feel the momentum — it was very exciting for me. I dreamed about it when I was in my bedroom. But John just didn't have the same dreams.

Lindy Goetz (manager): Unfortunately John started to fit in by doing drugs — something he clearly couldn't handle — and he hated that he was becoming a star overnight. He hadn't paid any hard-time dues — the rest of the guys had been on the road five or six years already. He stepped into something — people screaming for him — and he just wasn't set up for it.

Anthony was always thinking in terms of protecting the band and our reputation, making sure we were constantly growing in stature. I just can't think in those terms. If I thought that way I don't think I would have the relationship with music that I do. **BUT FOR ALL THE FREEDOMS AND SUCCESS WE'VE HAD, I WOULDN'T HAVE IT WITHOUT ANTHONY. I'D ALWAYS HAVE AN ARTISTIC LIFE, BUT I WOULDN'T BE SET UP THE WAY WE ARE NOW WITHOUT HIS VISION.**

Blood Sugar was a big hit. John got a new girlfriend and just wanted to be with her, listening to Captain Beefheart. Anti-successful music versus music being made for the purpose of selling albums to an extreme. The exact opposite of what Anthony wanted — not that Anthony wanted to be a sellout, but he was always striving for success with our band. Anthony was offended, then John got even more offended in turn, and it just became this downward spiral of mutual animosity.

Anthony's smart with business, and our managers always have a tough relationship with him because he gets on their asses! He's not satisfied with whatever they think is best — he tells them always that they can do better. He constantly lights the fire under their ass. Anthony is on top of that shit. You meet people like that who can be on both sides. Anthony is able to relate to an artist as well as he can relate to someone in business terms. ➤

➤ I've never been able to do that — it's like a special talent Anthony has. I can't connect with anybody except an artist, but he can talk to all kinds of people and get along.

✺ For the first couple of months of the tour John was just isolated doing a lot of drugs with his new girlfriend, and the vibe just got real weird. She was enabling, yeah. Those two would take over the lounge in the back of the bus.

Lindy: JOHN DIDN'T REALLY WANT TO BE PART OF THE TOUR. HE SHOWED UP AND PLAYED AND WENT WITH HIS GIRLFRIEND AND WE WALKED AROUND HIM WITH KID GLOVES — it wasn't comfortable. Whatever it was I don't know.

✺ Anthony wanted to be rejoicing and having the satisfaction of it. We were on the same track with goals for the band and making great music, but Anthony was going for stardom, and I wasn't. I wanted to be able to have a good relationship to art, and me going on tour was a wrong step toward that. I paid a stupid price for it, because by the time I quit I wasn't able anymore to do what I was best at.

Lindy: I've got thirty interviews set up in a day, and everyone had to do eight of them, or whatever, but John didn't wanna do it, wasn't having any of it. In interviews for important media people John's telling them to their faces to go fuck themselves, just like Johnny Rotten in the '70s! We went to Europe with Anthony to do prepress for the next tour and album, and people from the label said John couldn't do it anymore — "Please let him go home, keep him away, he's alienating all the wrong people — those who could help us most."

✺ John and Anthony started going in different directions. We were getting ready to go to Europe

to promote the record. I was like, "I don't wanna go to fucking Europe! I hate doing that shit!" All those interviews and stuff. John said, "Maybe me and Anthony should just go." I was like "Great — I don't wanna do it." So those two went, and John got real unhappy and left. It just kept getting worse and worse.

✺ Anthony wished I would have happily gone along with being hugely popular and running into the arms of the media. Once we got popular I refused to do interviews and

that divided us. Anthony was especially bummed that both Flea and me weren't very excited about it at all. Flea was appreciative, because it was what he wanted, but still, it didn't make him happy.

✺ I really hated the endless touring, but I admit I liked the success — but what a steep price!

✺ **WE GOT BIG, AND IT FREAKED HIM OUT.** The other guys had this gradual rise, and I had played a lot in many different bands and situations already before joining the Chili Peppers, but John had had no real previous band experience.

When Anthony and I were close friends and around each other all the time, the first year and half, there were parts of myself I was denying. In many ways I was a younger, more naive version of him. I wasn't living the way I see fit to be living. Eventually I had to live as me and on my terms.

We weren't that thing he grew up on anymore. He's like, "You guys sold out — you're not the same." This shoot-yourself-in-the-foot roots punk thing was in there too, like, "Wow, we made an amazing record — let's go nowhere from here." Of course we're not the same. If you like *Mother's Milk*, go listen to it because we aren't going to make it again.

I had some serious psychological imbalances at that time. I had this ideal of living life in what I was describing as a holy sanctuary. **THE RED HOT CHILI PEPPERS HAD LOST A LOT OF THE MAGIC FOR ME DURING THE TIME I WAS ON TOUR.** Every time I got home from touring I felt more and more empty — by the time I quit I was a vacuum.

John felt like we were getting too far away from being the band he admired as a kid. He's like, "The Chili Peppers should never play the Forum or a sports arena — this would be so wrong."

John and me got into a fight one night in New York. John just went so anti. Like, when it was time to get loud he'd go all soft — for soft, he'd get loud. Just wanted to do everything to go against what was expected. At one point, we were rocking and he's supposed to do a big solo — I look over and he's hitting his fucking weed pipe behind his amp! I said, **"DUDE, IT'S YOUR SOLO AND YOU'RE TOKIN' UP?!" AND HE'S LIKE PISSED I EVEN SAID ANYTHING. AND HE GOES, "I'LL HIT THAT PIPE AND PLAY THE WICKEDEST FUCKING SOLO YOU EVER HEARD. AND YOU KNOW IT." DAMN, HE WAS RIGHT.**

He would purposely do the opposite, just shy of deliberate sabotage. If it was time to do a solo, he would take the chord out of his guitar. If he was supposed to be playing a rhythm section, he'd play something else — just felt like us three were trying our best, and he just didn't want to be there. Sometimes he wouldn't even sing — he'd squawk and scream into the mic atonally. It wasn't fun.

I really enjoyed playing on that tour. Every night was kind of my little art project onstage. That was the main time we had a chance to be creative. I did some of my favorite guitar playing I've ever done during that tour, but I was more playing games with offsetting things. Soft-loud, fast-slow, the band was loud I played soft. I was doing balance games — the connection between things that are opposed to one another, but I don't think they saw it as connected to what they were doing. But for me it was in a strange way. I was doing a lot more improvising than I was used to, making up new guitar parts, and everything I could to make it a creative experience.

Things were going great. More people were coming to see us, but John was really cutting himself off. I couldn't go, "Hey, John, why are you playing like this? Why are you doing this?"

187

One Hot Minute

🔧 DAVE NAVARRO'S MORE A REACTIVE PLAYER. IN JANE'S, [BASSIST] ERIC [AVERY] COMES UP WITH A LOT. AND THEN IT GOT ADDED ON. INSTEAD OF INITIATING, DAVE WAS REACTING. AND DAVE DOES GREAT WHEN YOU GIVE HIM AN IDEA, BUT WE WEREN'T USED TO THAT — WE WANTED TO ALL JAM AT ONCE. EVERYTHING HAD TO START FROM FLEA. WE HADN'T WRITTEN ANYTHING IN A LONG TIME. WE'RE STILL FEELING EACH OTHER OUT — WHAT'S IT GONNA BE LIKE? A LOT OF THE INITIATING CAME FROM FLEA, BUT IT WAS UNBALANCED. IT WAS A NEW THING FOR THE BAND. SO WE WENT TO HAWAII.

Dave Navarro (RHCP guitarist 1993–98): I had to learn how to bring my style into the Chili Peppers. We were very fluctuating in our timing in Jane's Addiction, but the Chili Peppers are very precise. [Drummer] Stephen [Perkins] and Eric are such a different rhythm section than Flea and Chad. Eric and Stephen are like a combination of Joy Division and Led Zeppelin. And the Chili Peppers are more, like, straight-ahead funk. Bad Brains meets Funkadelic. Different schools, but they appeal to the same people because ultimately they are of the time, of the genre, the era, the soul — two classic rhythm sections of the same city. Similar yet so different.

✳ Flea was leading it more for sure. He was contributing songs and stuff like "River" and some lyrics, I think, singing more. *One Hot Minute* is more a Flea album — as much as you would think it'd be a Dave album because he's the new guy. I'm still very proud of it and I think it holds up very well — just a different baby. We went to Hawaii to get away — we went scuba diving, had our bikes shipped over. Just the four of us. But it wasn't like this fire of writing eight hours a day. No creative spark — a lot fell on Flea's shoulders. From the beginning everyone always had ideas, everyone was always into jamming, but Dave wasn't into it.

Rick Rubin (producer): Dave was not interested in jamming with them so much, where Flea likes to jam more than anyone else in the world. Remember, these were guys who really liked Jane's Addiction, and Dave was probably their favorite guitar player. They didn't think "What is that person's role in that band and how do they function?" They never thought that deep into it.

✳ Picking the best moments out of a jam, that's what Anthony does. He's a genius at it. He'll recognize something and go into a little room, and he's inspired to come up with something. It'll be two days since we last played and we won't remember a part, and he'll go, "Listen, I got this part."

Lindy Goetz (manager): Dave is an amazing guitar player. It is a shame the *One Hot Minute* album was never a huge hit, but I still thought it was the most rocking-est album they ever made. It just didn't have any "Under the Bridges" or "Give It Away Nows" — just fucking rockin' songs. It was a different direction. It had that song "Aeroplane." That was a damn good record — it was still a platinum seller. Obviously not as big as *Blood Sugar*, but we were doing all the dates, selling out shows. We'd built this following from scratch and were able to maintain and expand it

Rick: The Chili Peppers were viewed as being on a downswing because the album only sold under however many millions. After *Blood Sugar*, no one had any realistic expectations and so *One Hot Minute* doing five or six mill — not to be sneezed at — is declared a flop.

Dave: NOT ONLY DO I LOVE THAT RECORD, BUT IT REMAINS THE MOST SUCCESSFUL RECORD I HAVE EVER BEEN A PART OF. I could hear myself growing, evolving as a guitar player. And I couldn't have had a better group of guys to learn dedicated musicianship from. I also learned from them about friendship, brotherhood and just doing it right. I have nothing but fond memories. The Red Hot Chili Peppers have a great work ethic and they're spiritually-minded, healthy fellas. It wasn't until years later that I really missed them. And I remain good friends with them to this day. In some cases, my friendships with them are stronger now than when I was a member of the band.

189

WARPED

RIGHT BEFORE WE WERE SUPPOSED TO PLAY THE STATES ON THE *ONE HOT MINUTE* TOUR, I WAS PLAYING SOFTBALL — THIS LITTLE TEAM I DO ON TUESDAY NIGHTS — TWO NIGHTS BEFORE WE START OUR TOUR. ALL THE GEAR IN DENVER IS ALL SET UP. I WAS PLAYING FIRST BASE AND THE GUY HIT THE BALL DOWN THE LINE, GETS THROWN TO ME AND I REACH OUT AT THE SAME TIME AS THE RUNNER IS COMING, AND *CRACK*. RIGHT AWAY, I KNEW THIS WAS NOT GOOD. I AM NOT GOING TO BE PLAYING THE DRUMS TOMORROW! SO OUR TOUR WAS CANCELLED — IT WAS JUST TOO LATE TO GET ANYONE ELSE. IT WAS ENTERTAINED FOR A MINUTE TO GET JACK IRONS TO COME OUT, BUT IT WAS SO CLOSE. AND THE NEXT DAY I HAD TO PLAY ON THE LETTERMAN SHOW WITH A CAST ON MY ARM — ONE HAND. IT WAS SO HUMILIATING TO BE ON NATIONAL TV PLAYING DRUMS WITH A CAST. WE OBVIOUSLY PLAYED ONE OF OUR MORE MELLOW NUMBERS, I WAS DOING MY DEF LEPPARD IMPERSONATION, BUT IT WAS NOT FUN. I THINK THE DRUMMER FROM LETTERMAN WAS GOING TO PLAY ALONG, BUT IT WAS "MY FRIENDS" WE WERE DOING, AND IT WAS A SLOWER SONG. SO I COULD PULL IT OFF. BUT SURE ENOUGH, I'M ONLY HALFWAY THROUGH THE SONG WITH ONE STICK, AND I BREAK THE STICK! I'M SURE IT IS ON YOUTUBE. BUT ANYWAYS, WE CANCELLED THAT TOUR AND STARTED UP AT THE END OF JANUARY. TOOK SIX WEEKS FOR ME TO HEAL UP. BUT THE TOUR WAS GOOD.

Get Off of My Cloud

C Like you wanna say you opened for the Stones. We got no sound check, don't step on Mick's parquet dance section — he had a little section that was his spot! SHAN'T BE TREADING ON MICK'S DANCE FLOOR! WE JUST WANTED A FUCKING SOUND CHECK. Dave Navarro is swishing around in his garter belts, and we're all in skirts and shit. Buddy Guy played, and we had never really opened for anyone before. The audience was like rich, hip lawyers and the women who love 'em looking at us like "WTF is this? Why are these guys dressed like this?" It sounded horrible and Flea got it to Sir Mick that we didn't get a sound check. Flea had played on his solo album, so Mick fixed it for us. The second night he's all, "Sorry about that, you chaps!"

A An extremely unexciting, underwhelming waste of time from our perspective. We were trying to engage uninterested middle-aged Stones' fans parking their cars, finding their seats — and they only gave us a tiny portion of the stage and the production to work with. We'd come up opening for bands like X who didn't pull that old-school R&R shit. We naively thought the rock world had gotten past that by the mid-'90s.

LOS ANGELES
ROLLING STONES VOODOO LOUNGE
R.H.C.P.

C Louie Mathieu, my tech, is looking at me, "Dude, look over there, Charlie Watts!" Holy shit! Superfucking styled-up sharp dresser, looking the perfect English gentleman, standing in the wings, arms crossed, watching me do my whatever. I'm playing on this green sparkle kit. We finish, and I step off and introduce myself. He didn't really say much, just, "What kind of drums are those? Oh, Pearl. Oh, I had a green sparkle kit in 1964." I liked that. He's an old jazzer — an old-school jazzbo for real! Givin' me the thumbs-up. Three years later, I'm at the Four Seasons in Hawaii and the Stones are there doing a gig for Pepsi. I'm getting my car at the valet, and I spot Charlie. My girlfriend tells me to say hi, and I'm all, "Oh, I don't want to bother him." Charlie's in the middle of the hot sun in Hawaii in this fly fucking dark suit number! So I walk over, "Excuse me Charlie, I'm Chad from the Chili Peppers . . ." "Oh, hey how are you? yeah yeah, 'course I remember you. I'm doing a gig for Pepsi here." I say, "What the fuck are you doing a gig for Pepsi for?" and he goes, "For the fucking bloody money, what do you think?! So dig, you still got that green sparkle kit?" Then his wife came out, and she said she figured I was a musician. "Those are the only people he talks to."

193

Come as You Are

✸ Rio was really fun for all of us. It was like a who's who of L.A. alternative bands of the '90s, playing with Nirvana and Alice in Chains. Courtney Love was there, L7 — all on the same plane at the same time. The great Ian MacKaye was there. I love him. One big crazy group. Eddie Vedder and Anthony kissed backstage. Nirvana played one night — I played once with them.

I KNEW KURT A LITTLE BIT BUT WASN'T CLOSE WITH HIM OR ANYTHING.

✸ They switched instruments and started playing ridiculous pop songs, for like an hour and a half, like an old Replacements' trick, and the crowd didn't know what to think. It was crazy.

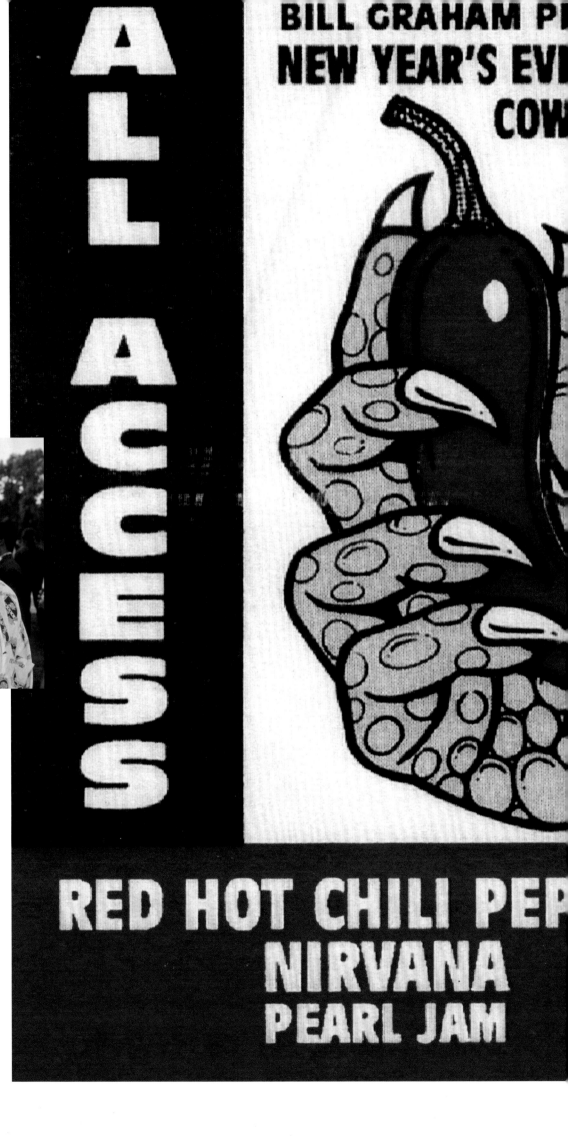

Up from the Skies

A Holy shit, it looks like *Apocalypse Now* out there.

C Jimi Hendrix's sister came to us backstage at 4 p.m., in our little trailer and she said, "I know you guys are finishing the show. Afterward they are going to have a big hologram of Hendrix playing "The Star Spangled Banner," and I know you guys play some of Jimi's songs. It would be a great segue for your last song to go into this hologram thing." Shit, yeah, like we'd done "Fire" before. We hadn't played it in a while. I'm like slapping my knees and air drumming, John isn't plugged in, we haven't played this song in I don't know how long. **LIKE NOW WE'RE GONNA PLAY IT IN FRONT OF 300,000 PEOPLE! FOR LOVE OF HENDRIX, ONE OF OUR SPIRITUAL ANCESTORS? DAMN RIGHT!** So we play the show and Flea comes out buck naked and it was a good gig. And then toward the end — I notice about a mile way in the back what looks like smoke and a little fire, like a hamburger stand had caught fire — that's how small it looked from the stage. Toward the end of our show, a guy comes out and goes, "Hey, can you let the firemen through?" No panic, no weirdness, just let them do their thing and Chili Peppers will come back and play. We stopped five minutes maybe. We come back on and do "Fire." We finish up, get in the cars, drive back to Manhattan and the next day they're talking shit about us all over CNN, about when Woodstock had Jewel, Creed, and Dave Matthews it was all very jolly and nice but when the Chili Peppers came on all fucking hell broke loose! We were accused of inciting the crowd to burn the fucking field down by playing Hendrix's "Fire" — and to prove it they show people throwing chairs into this bonfire. I'm like "Holy shit!" I had no idea, no idea. Flea is up there naked and people are going crazy. That was the end, no more bands, festival over kind of thing. I don't even know if they did the hologram.

197

TIBETAN FREEDOM CONCERT

OLDEN GATE PARK

UNE 15 & 16, 1996

CP ARTIST

The Milarepa Fund

ILL GRAHAM PRESENTS

Funky Monks

✳ Adam Yauch [from the Beastie Boys] had developed a relationship with some Tibetan monks. And he wanted to do something to counter the oppression of the Chinese coming down on them. He wanted to help put on these concerts [1995 Tibetan Freedom Concert in San Francisco]. Coincided at the time with me getting into meditation and a spiritual path, and Anthony, too. It just seemed like a really cool thing — made us want to do it. **IT WAS COOL, BECAUSE JOHN HAD COME BACK FOR ONE OF THEM — HE HAD BEEN GONE A LONG TIME.** That was really exciting.

199

VELVET GLOVE

❋ WE PLAYED IN RED SQUARE — THAT WAS AWESOME! AMAZING! GROWING UP, IN SCHOOL THEY WERE POUNDING IT INTO US THAT RUSSIANS ARE BAD, THEY'RE GONNA TRY AND NUKE US SO WE BETTER DO IT TO THEM FIRST. YOU'RE TRAINED TO BELIEVE THEY'RE ALL EVIL EMPIRE COMMIE SHITHEADS. FOR A KOOKY ROCK BAND FROM HOLLYWOOD TO PLAY NEXT DOOR TO THE KREMLIN — **AND THEY'RE ALL SINGING OUR SONGS** — WAS A TRIP. THINGS WERE CHANGING IN THE WORLD AND HERE'S A CLASSIC EXAMPLE OF HOW MUSIC AT ITS BEST CAN HELP THAT ALONG IN A POSITIVE WAY. I WAS PROUD TO BE A MUSICIAN. SOMETIMES I'M NOT, BUT MOST OF THE TIME.

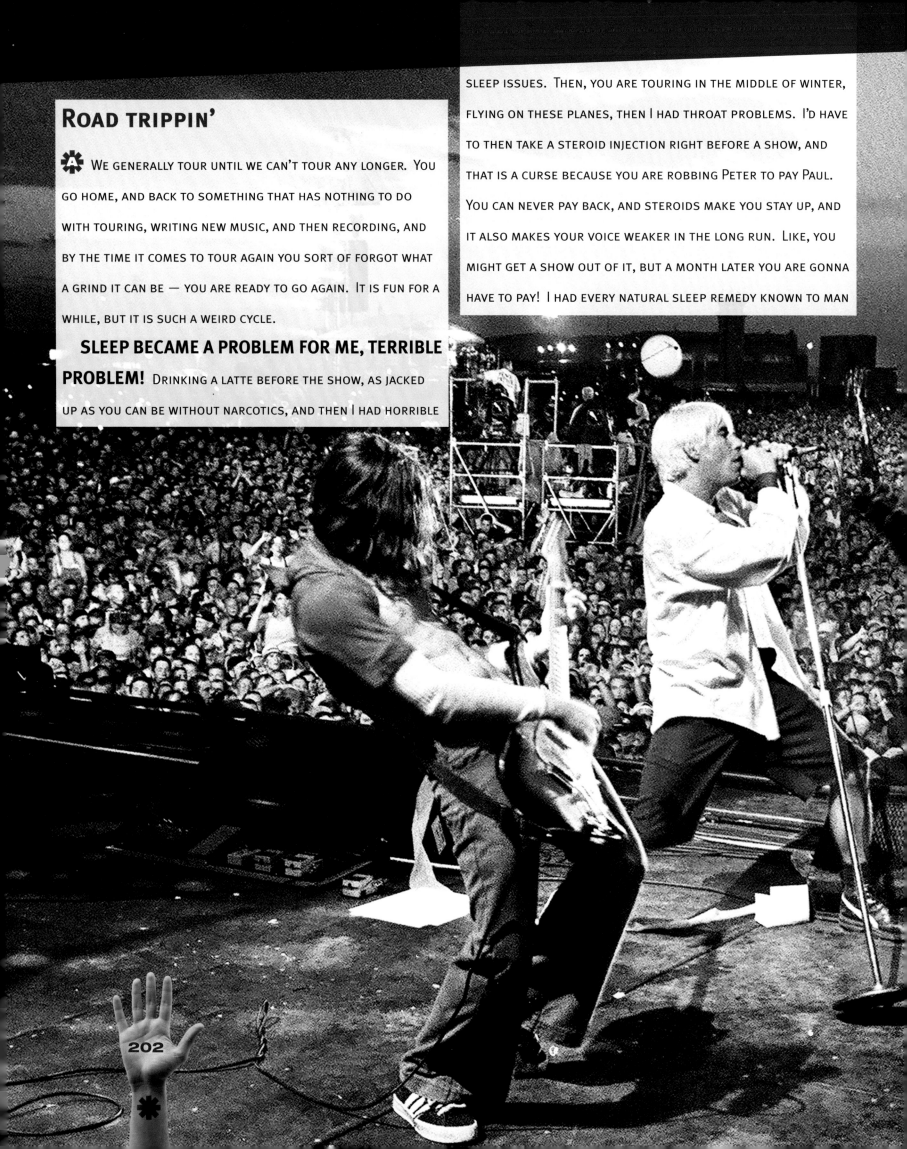

Road trippin'

✳ We generally tour until we can't tour any longer. You go home, and back to something that has nothing to do with touring, writing new music, and then recording, and by the time it comes to tour again you sort of forgot what a grind it can be — you are ready to go again. It is fun for a while, but it is such a weird cycle.

Sleep became a problem for me, terrible problem! Drinking a latte before the show, as jacked up as you can be without narcotics, and then I had horrible sleep issues. Then, you are touring in the middle of winter, flying on these planes, then I had throat problems. I'd have to then take a steroid injection right before a show, and that is a curse because you are robbing Peter to pay Paul. You can never pay back, and steroids make you stay up, and it also makes your voice weaker in the long run. Like, you might get a show out of it, but a month later you are gonna have to pay! I had every natural sleep remedy known to man

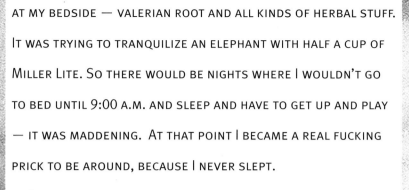

AT MY BEDSIDE — VALERIAN ROOT AND ALL KINDS OF HERBAL STUFF. IT WAS TRYING TO TRANQUILIZE AN ELEPHANT WITH HALF A CUP OF MILLER LITE. SO THERE WOULD BE NIGHTS WHERE I WOULDN'T GO TO BED UNTIL 9:00 A.M. AND SLEEP AND HAVE TO GET UP AND PLAY — IT WAS MADDENING. AT THAT POINT I BECAME A REAL FUCKING PRICK TO BE AROUND, BECAUSE I NEVER SLEPT.

IF YOU ARE SLEEP-DEPRIVED IN YOUR HOME AND YOU HAVE NOTHING TO DO, YOU'LL STILL GO CRAZY. BUT IF YOU HAVE AN IMPORTANT RESPONSIBILITY AND WHATEVER AMOUNT OF THOUSANDS OF PEOPLE HAVE TRAVELED TO COME TO THE SHOW, I HAVE TO BE THERE BECAUSE IT IS THEIR ONE TIME. MAYBE IT IS A TEENAGE GIRL THAT HITCHHIKED FROM TEN CITIES AWAY. **I DON'T WANT TO BE A SELFISH DICK AND NOT GIVE IT EVERYTHING I HAVE. SO THAT KIND OF RESPONSIBILITY AND THE WEIGHT OF "IT IS TIME TO GET INTO THE 'ZONE' FOR THAT PERSON TO EXPERIENCE" — IT WAS REALLY HARD.**

THEN YOU HAVE AN AGENT IN HOLLYWOOD, FROM THE COMFORTS OF HOME, LIKE, "OH, YOU'RE GONNA PLAY MEXICO CITY ON THIS DAY BECAUSE IT IS THE ONLY ONE AVAILABLE" — LOOK AT THE FARMERS ALMANAC AND IT WILL BE OUTSIDE IN 42-DEGREE WEATHER, POURING RAIN. YOU'VE BEEN ON TOUR FOR A YEAR AND HAVEN'T HAD A GOOD SLEEP IN SIX MONTHS, AND FIGHTING OFF SICKNESS AND BEING A JERK, NOW YOU GOTTA GO PLAY IN THE RAIN ON TOP OF A MOUNTAIN IN MEXICO CITY. IT BECOMES A GREATER CHALLENGE. BUT YOU CAN ALWAYS GET TO THAT PLACE LIKE, "HOLY SHIT, THIS IS THE GREATEST OPPORTUNITY I'LL EVER HAVE — I'M TRAVELING THE WORLD WITH MY FRIENDS, PLAYING MUSIC FOR LOVELY HUMAN BEINGS WHO WANT TO DANCE."

204

CALIFORNICATION

C *CALIFORNICATION* WAS AMAZING ON MANY DIFFERENT LEVELS FOR MANY DIFFERENT REASONS. HAVING JOHN BACK WAS A HUGE THING FOR US. IT FELT LIKE A NEW BAND. MANY PEOPLE HAD WRITTEN US OFF — SIX YEARS HAVE GONE BY, NO GUITAR PLAYER, AND WHAT KIND OF SHAPE IS JOHN IN? THERE WAS NO REAL "WOO-HOO! JOHN FRUSCIANTE IS BACK — RECORD SALES ARE GONNA BE HUGE AGAIN!" NO PRESSURE — THIS TIME MORE THAN EVER, WE WEREN'T TRYING TO FOLLOW UP SOME BIG RECORD. WE STILL DO WHAT WE DO, BUT IF YOU START TO SELL 15

MILLION ALBUMS PEOPLE ARE WONDERING WHAT'S NEXT? IT WAS BACK TO JUST WRITING SONGS LIKE FOR *BLOOD SUGAR*. THE FOUR OF US IN A ROOM JUST MAKING A BUNCH OF SONGS QUICK AND EASY. THAT'S HOW GOOD RECORDS ARE MADE. TOUGHEST SONG WAS "CALIFORNICATION." ANTHONY HAD WRITTEN THOSE WORDS LONG BEFORE. USUALLY WE WRITE MUSIC AND MELODIES AND HE WRITES WITH THAT, BUT HE HAD BEEN TRAVELING AND SEEING HOW THE WORLD WAS "CALIFORNICATIONIZED" — WHAT A GLOBAL INFLUENCE HOLLYWOOD HAS ON THE WORLD. WE TRIED TO COME UP WITH MUSIC FOR THAT. IT JUST WASN'T WORKING — NOTHING WAS WORKING UNTIL WE GOT INTO THE STUDIO AND ONE DAY JOHN HAD A PART. IT FELL TOGETHER REALLY QUICK AFTER THAT — BUT THE REST WAS ALL THESE SONGS WE HAD. WE DEMOED IT AT DANIEL LANOIS'S PLACE UP IN OXNARD. WE DID HALF OF THEM, TEN OR ELEVEN SONGS BEFORE WE GOT [PRODUCER] RICK [RUBIN] AGAIN. WE WERE PREPARED THOUGH, VERY PREPARED, AND DID IT REALLY QUICK. THE ALBUM WAS DONE IN MAYBE SIX WEEKS OR TWO MONTHS OR SOMETHING. IT WAS JUST A FUN TIME AND FELT NEW AGAIN. EVERYBODY'S BATTERIES WERE RECHARGED, AND WE WERE EXCITED ABOUT THE MUSIC.

A IT WAS A GREAT CONFLUENCE OF ESSENTIAL EVENTS. IT ALLOWED US TO EXIST AS A BAND AGAIN, AND TO MAKE MUSIC FOR NO OTHER REASON THAN EXPRESSING OUR CREATIVE SPIRIT. IT CREATED A SPACE FOR US TO WORK IN WITHOUT ANY SORT OF EXPECTATION. WE HAD A BALL. WE WERE STILL STRUGGLING WITH PERSONAL DEMONS. I WAS STILL GOING BACK AND FORTH BETWEEN CLEAN AND USING. IT WAS REALLY THE EXPERIENCE OF A LIFETIME MAKING THAT RECORD. WHO KNEW IT WOULD BE THE MOST POPULAR RECORD OF OUR CAREER? THAT'S NOT WHAT WE WERE AIMING FOR. WE HIT A HOT PERIOD WHERE RECORDS WERE STILL SELLING AS THEY WERE IN THE '80S AND '90S, EVEN THOUGH I THINK IT CAME OUT IN '99. "PARALLEL UNIVERSE" WAS A PRIME EXAMPLE OF UNADULTERATED JOY FOR BEING REBORN.

OTHERSIDE

During the *Californication* tour Flea reached the breaking point. We had been on tour and were in Australia, and he was probably feeling how I felt with the broken feet, like totally done. We had a sit-down and decided to reinvent the way we toured — instead of going for months and months and taking a few off, we were going to do three weeks on and ten days off. And obviously, you aren't making the kind of money you would make, because during those ten days you have to pay every single soul who is working for you. On tour that's about seventy people — so ten days zero income but paying seventy people. **THE GOOD NEWS IS, YOU DON'T DIE AND CAN GO ON TO PLAY SHOWS AND SPEAK TO EACH OTHER** — AND HAVE FLEA NOT QUIT. WE DID THE MATH AND THOUGHT THIS WAS BETTER THAN CLOSING UP SHOP AND CALLING IT A DAY.

206

AROUND THE WORLD

We've had a great relationship with Ireland over the years, since the late '80s really. I felt we got into a bear hug with Ireland and never let go. We did a club tour and the potency of appreciation from the fans was so real. I was like, "Holy shit!" — like people aren't just happy anyone showed up, like happy we showed up. They're not just starved humans who haven't had anything good come to their town — they connected with us for real. We went up to Belfast and played. People ask what was the craziest or wildest fans, that's in the top handful. Belfast. You wanna feel a rush out onstage of glee coming off a group of kids? **GO TO BELFAST. THEY'RE MANIACS IN THE BEST POSSIBLE WAY — ABSOLUTELY MENTAL, LIKE THEY USED TO SAY IN MANCHESTER**

Brazil is up there as well, but this Irish thing just kept getting stronger. We are definitely connected to the soul of Ireland. We love them, they love us.

Japan is nutty with the fans and their culture loves all things Western — in Brazil they are just so passionate. Like we had to get bodyguards, people yelling at the hotel, and it was like you are the fucking Beatles. They run after you, pull your hair, throw eggs at your wives, just crazy shit! I had a bodyguard outside of my room! All the time! He's got a

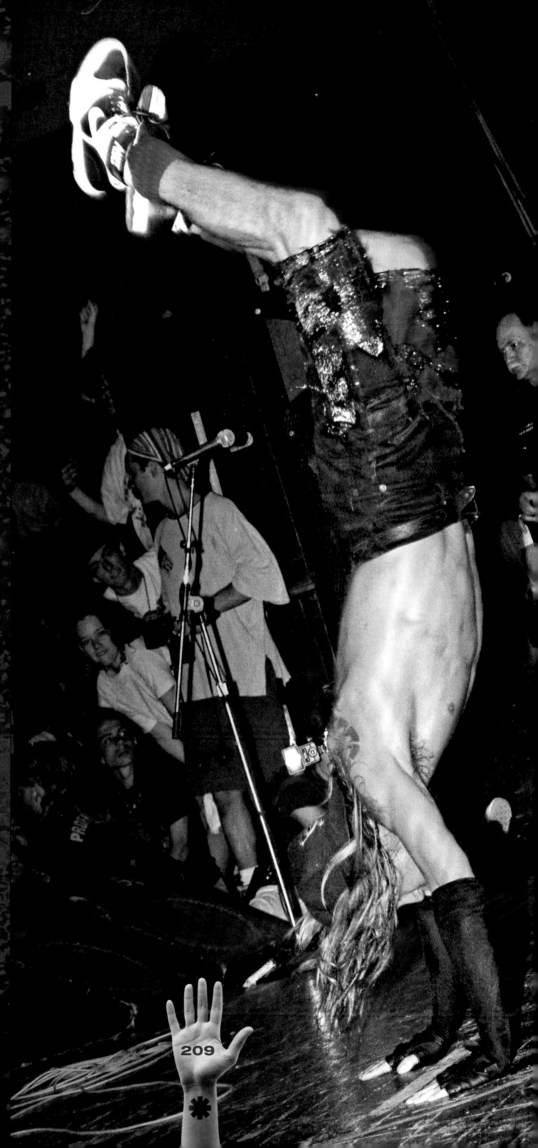

GUN — IT'S FUCKING INSANE. I'M LIKE, "WE'RE JUST A FUCKING ROCK BAND, YOU KNOW?" SO THAT WAS THE FIRST TIME WE PLAYED THOSE HUGE CROWDS.

THE FESTIVALS IN IRELAND WERE HIGHLIGHTS WHEN YOU TALK ABOUT BIG SHOWS AMONG THE ALL-TIME BEST. PROBABLY THE BEST OF THE BEST WAS OPENING FOR U2 AT SLANE CASTLE IN DUBLIN. WE OPENED FOR THEM, AND THEN LATER WE CAME BACK AND HEADLINED. U2 CERTAINLY AREN'T GOING TO OPEN FOR YOU, ESPECIALLY IN DUBLIN, THAT'S FOR SURE!

WE WERE LIKE, "OKAY WE'LL DO IT," AND IT TURNED OUT GREAT BECAUSE THE ENERGY WAS SUCH THAT SOMEHOW NOT BEING THE HEADLINER GAVE US AN EDGE. YOU'RE NOT RESPONSIBLE FOR EVERYTHING THAT NIGHT, LESS PRESSURE, ON THE EDGE OF BEING LIKE THE NONCOMMERCIAL BAND.

THEY TOLD US WE COULDN'T USE THIS RAMP ONSTAGE, AND THEY ACTUALLY TOOK AWAY A TEN-FOOT SEGMENT WHERE THE RAMP WENT WINDING THROUGH THE AUDIENCE. THEY WENT SO FAR AS TO TAKE A CHUNK OUT, SO YOU COULDN'T DEFY THEM. I DON'T KNOW WHAT CAME OVER ME, BUT I ENDED UP LEAPING FROM THE STAGE TO THE RAMP OUT IN THE AUDIENCE AND HAD MY WAY WITH THEIR STAGE PROP — JUST BECAUSE THEY SAID I COULDN'T. I KNEW THERE WOULD BE NO HARM, AND THE AUDIENCE WAS REALLY INTO US AND I KNEW I NEEDED TO GET OUT THERE AND BE WITH THEM.

209

BY THE WAY

✳ MY ORIGINAL CONCEPT FOR *BY THE WAY* WAS TO HAVE A BALANCE BETWEEN REAL KIND OF — I REALLY LIKED THE SONG "THE VELVET GLOVE" A LOT, AND I THOUGHT THERE WERE SOME GOOD AVENUES TO EXPLORE IN TERMS OF DOING SOMETHING LIGHTER. TO REALLY BE EXPLORING THE MELODIC POSSIBILITIES IN WHAT WE DO.

RICK RUBIN (PRODUCER): THE OVERWHELMING SUCCESS OF *CALIFORNICATION* SEEMED TO FUEL JOHN INTO WANTING TO TAKE A BIGGER ROLE — WHICH I THINK REALLY FRUSTRATED FLEA. THE ENERGY CHANGED — JOHN NOW HAD A STRONGER VOICE THAN EVER. THEY JAMMED, SAME AS ALWAYS — IT WAS JUST MORE OF AN INFLEXIBLE "MY WAY IS RIGHT" THING. **FLEA WOULD TELL ME, "THIS IS SO MUCH LESS FUN BECAUSE I FEEL LIKE MY VOICE DOESN'T COUNT AS MUCH." FLEA FELT HIS POWER IN THE BAND WAS BEING DIMINISHED.** I THINK THEY TALKED ABOUT IT AND JOHN REALIZED IT. FOR AT LEAST PART OF THE RECORD THEY GOT IT STRAIGHTENED OUT.

✴ DURING THE MAKING OF *BY THE WAY*, I WAS TAKING SOME TRIPS TO HAWAII AND WOULD BRING TRACKS OF THESE SONGS, AND DRIVE AROUND WRITING LYRICS ON KAUAI, AND IN THE SIERRA MOUNTAINS WITH SNOW AND THESE HUGE REDWOOD TREES, LISTENING TO INSTRUMENTAL MUSIC, LIKE THE SONG "HEY" WHICH IS THIS SORT OF TRIPPY, SLOW AVANT, ALMOST JAZZ-SOUNDING PIECE.

✳ I WAS ALSO LISTENING TO THE DAMNED A LOT AT THAT TIME, AND I WANTED TO DO SIMPLE PUNK ROCK SONGS AS WELL, I WANTED IT TO BE LIKE THE FIRST THREE DAMNED ALBUMS.

✴ BUT AS IT UNFOLDED AND WE GOT INTO THE STUDIO AND WE HAD ALL THIS MUSIC, TENSIONS DOUBLED AND TRIPLED. JOHN HAD A REAL STRONG VISION OF WHAT HE WANTED THE PRODUCTION TO BE LIKE, AND IT WAS A CASE OF TOO MANY PRODUCTION CHEFS COMPLICATING EVERYTHING. THERE WAS NO RIGHT OR WRONG, BECAUSE JOHN HAD A VISION. FLEA HAD A VISION. RICK HAD A VISION.

✳ I WAS REALLY THINKING OF SOME KIND OF CROSS OF HAVING TWO TOTALLY DIFFERENT TYPES OF SONGS — THINGS THAT WERE MORE ENGLISH-SOUNDING — WHICH IS WHAT THE ALBUM ENDED UP BEING ALMOST COMPLETELY — AND HAVING A PUNK THING. I WAS LISTENING TO DISCHARGE A LOT, TOO. I JUST WANTED TO HAVE TWO EXTREMES.

✴ ALL THESE BRILLIANT PEOPLE WERE TRYING TO IMPOSE THEIR WILL ON THE OUTCOME OF THIS MASSIVE AMOUNT OF MUSIC WE'D ACCUMULATED. ALTHOUGH I AM LESS INVOLVED IN THE POSTPRODUCTION MIXING PORTION, I STILL HAVE A VERY CLEAR IDEA OF WHAT I'M HOPING FOR IT TO SOUND LIKE WHEN IT ALL COMES TOGETHER.

✳ RICK WAS REALLY NOT DIGGIN' THE PUNK THINGS WE WERE DOING. HE THOUGHT THE MELODIC THINGS WERE MUCH MORE ORIGINAL AND EXCITING. WE ENDED UP THROWING AWAY ALL THE PUNK THINGS AND FOCUSING ON THE MELODIC THINGS. I WAS SO ZONED IN TO JUST WRITE MUSIC AND STUFF — DEFINITELY A DISCONNECTION STARTED TO HAPPEN BETWEEN ME AND FLEA. IT WAS DIFFICULT, THAT RECORD, FOR FLEA AND MINE'S RELATIONSHIP. I DIDN'T THINK WE SHOULD HAVE ANY FUNK ON THAT ALBUM. WE HAD ALREADY DONE THAT A LOT, BUT AT THE TIME FLEA WANTED TO DO MORE FUNK, AND I WASN'T FEELING IT. I WANTED TO DO A CHILI PEPPERS ALBUM THAT DIDN'T SOUND LIKE THE CHILI PEPPERS.

SOMETHING MORE BASED AROUND WHAT WE COULD DO WITH HARMONY AND CHORDS. THAT'S HOW I AM — I'LL LIKE SOMETHING A LOT FOR ONE PERIOD OF TIME, AND THEN I JUST LOSE MY FEELING FOR IT.

✳ WE RECORDED THE STUFF, TOOK A LITTLE BREAK, AND WENT BACK INTO WRITING. WE REHEARSED AT THIS PLACE CALLED SWINGHOUSE, IN HOLLYWOOD. JOHN WAS GETTING MORE CONFIDENT AND PLAYING A LOT BETTER. HE WAS A DIFFERENT PERSON NOW. JOHN WANTED TO CONTINUE THIS VERY MELODIC BEACH BOYS AND BEATLES THING — HE WAS READING ALL THESE BEATLES BOOKS ABOUT HOW THEY RECORDED, REALLY INTO DOO WOP GROUPS AND HARMONIES AND GETTING INTO THAT. JOHN WOULD BRING IN SOME CHORD STRUCTURE STUFF, YOU KNOW, NOT FINISHED SONGS, BUT HE'D HAVE PARTS. I DIDN'T NOTICE IT AT THE TIME — IT BUMMED FLEA OUT, JOHN DOING ALL THAT. THERE'S ALWAYS BEEN A BIT OF A POWER STRUGGLE BETWEEN THOSE TWO. IT WASN'T A RIFT SO MUCH AS JOHN TAKING THE REINS OF WHAT DIRECTION WE SHOULD BE GOING IN BY COMING IN WITH PREPARED IDEAS. WE ALWAYS LISTEN TO EVERYONE'S IDEAS, AND WE STILL DID THAT, BUT IT CAME MORE TO PRODUCTION AND BACKGROUND VOCALS AND THE LUSHNESS THE RECORD HAS. I WOULD SAY HE WAS PURPOSEFULLY DOING IT. I THINK THAT IS WHAT HE FELT AND HE WANTED TO PURSUE THAT — HE FELT STRONGLY ABOUT THE WAY IT SHOULD SOUND.

✳ THE THING THAT WAS FRUSTRATING FOR ME ABOUT THE CREATION OF *BY THE WAY* HAD NOTHING TO DO WITH THE STYLE OF MUSIC. IT WAS THE LACK OF CAMARADERIE THAT WAS DIFFICULT FOR ME.

✳ FLEA WAS GOING TO QUIT BEFORE THE *BY THE WAY* TOUR. HE REALLY HATED MAKING THE RECORD, AND HE DIDN'T FEEL LIKE HE COULD EXPRESS HIMSELF ANYMORE IN THE CONTEXT OF THE BAND. WHEN THINGS GOT BETTER BETWEEN US AND WE STARTED CONNECTING MORE MUSICALLY, IT WAS A REALLY NICE TIME FOR US. *BY THE WAY* IS OUR MOST POPULAR ALBUM IN ENGLAND. I WAS LISTENING TO ALMOST NOTHING BUT ENGLISH MUSIC IN THAT PERIOD

— POP MUSIC OF THE '60S AND '80S, THINGS LIKE THE SMITHS AND SIOUSXIE AND THE BANSHEES. WE'D NEVER BEEN THAT POPULAR BEFORE IN ENGLAND. THEY SAY THAT ALBUM IS IN ONE OF EVERY THREE ENGLISH HOUSEHOLDS. BUT THAT ALBUM DIDN'T DO AS WELL IN AMERICA, PROBABLY BECAUSE I WAS REALLY TAKING ALL THE AMERICAN INFLUENCE OUT OF IT, ANYTHING BASED AROUND BLUES AT ALL — NO SOUL OR BLUES-BASED STUFF. IT'S ALL VERY ENGLISH AND MINIMAL, EUROPEAN SENSE OF MELODY — A SOLO WAS MORE LIKE A MELODY. NOT MUCH IMPROVISING. WE DIDN'T GO FOR THE HEAVY METAL DYNAMIC AT ALL, THE POWER ROCK, OR THE FUNK.

✳ **THEY HAD TO HAVE A BIG SIT-DOWN BECAUSE FLEA FELT HIS IDEAS WERE BEING DISMISSED. IT WAS VERY DEMOCRATIC — OUR BAND HAS ALWAYS BEEN — AND I THINK HE WAS FEELING JOHN WAS TAKING OVER.** HE DIDN'T LIKE THAT. I DON'T THINK JOHN REALIZED IT, THOUGH. IT DIDN'T FEEL LIKE HE WAS ALL, "WELL, I'M GONNA TAKE OVER." JOHN WANTED THINGS TO SOUND A CERTAIN WAY, AND HE CAN BE VERY DIRECT TO MAKE A POINT. AGAIN, THAT'S MY PLAYING THE DRUMS AND WATCHING THE DYNAMIC. FLEA WAS GOING THROUGH PERSONAL STUFF, AND YOU KNOW, IT WASN'T AS EASY THIS TIME AROUND.

✳ ON THE *BY THE WAY* TOUR I WAS DEFINITELY TO SOME DEGREE GETTING OFF ON THE AUDIENCE INTERACTION. I THINK THERE WERE SOME PROBLEMS FLEA WAS HAVING ON TOUR BECAUSE HE'S ALWAYS REALLY BEEN INTO CONNECTING. HE'S BY NATURE A SHOWMAN, BUT IT WAS ALWAYS OF PRIME IMPORTANCE TO HIM TO STAY CONNECTED AS A BAND, AND I WAS GOING OFF INTO THE WINGS AND BEING BY MYSELF FOR LONG PERIODS OF TIME — REALLY PLAYING TO THE AUDIENCE A LOT OF THE TIME. IT WAS A PHASE I WAS GOING THROUGH, AND FOR WHATEVER REASON I WAS GOING THROUGH DIFFICULT TIMES IN MY PERSONAL LIFE, SO IT MADE ME FEEL GOOD AND FREE TO BE ONSTAGE AND HAVE THAT INTERACTION WITH PEOPLE.

✳ Rick Van Santen, from Goldenvoice Productions, was a friend, lovable good guy, local L.A. concert promoter who'd been really good to the Chili Peppers over the years, as was his boss, Gary Tovar, the original founder before Rick took the company over with Paul Tollett. The company, under Rick's and Paul's direction, had grown from doing small club shows and the Whisky round about the time we were first starting out — now they are the most prolific concert promoter in the country with the most number of shows on the calendar at the same time. Goldenvoice's slow-burn ascent had more or less paralleled ours, and without them there's no way we would have had as big a following in SoCal during the '80s and early '90s. Rick, may he rest in peace, was a major Lakers' fan. Seemed like his purpose in life was to champion music for all to enjoy — what a great legacy to leave behind. We were thrilled and honored to be asked to play the festival he'd conceived.

✳ The first time we played Coachella was amazing, one of the best shows we've ever played. Firing on all cylinders. White Stripes played before us, and it was good. **I REMEMBER JUST FEELING SO ENERGIZED, EVERYTHING WAS WORKING.** Rick, who had been to a lot of our shows, thought that was the best he had ever seen us. We got to play a slightly shorter set, so we didn't have to pace ourselves for the marathon.

WHOLE LOTTA LOVE

The revamped Red Hot Chili Peppers: from left, bassist Flea, guitarist John Frusciante, lead singer Anthony Kiedis and drummer Chad Smith.

Photos by J. ALBERT DIAZ / L.A. Times

Chili Peppers Taste Success at Last

After seven long years, L.A.'s loony punk-funk band finally gains respect for its music as well as its off-stage antics

RICHARD CROMELIN

This was a big day for the Red Hot Chili Peppers, the loony anarchic L.A. band that's worshiped by some and scorned by many. Flea, the group's bass ..., was in lively spirits as he bounced into the back of the limousine in front of his apartment with the ... of a goofy, hyperactive kid

... is great," he said as the limo turned onto nearby ... Boulevard. "It's a novelty to ride in one of these ... own neighborhood. Usually if we do it, it's in New ... or if a promoter gets us picked up at an airport or ... . But to drive down Beverly is a novelty. I ... ride my bike down here."

... enthusiasm last Saturday seemed to brighten the ... his pal Anthony Kiedis, the Chili Peppers' lead ... who had been preoccupied with his right ankle. ... San Francisco show three days earlier, the ... performer did a pole-vault with the mike stand ... a bad landing, tearing his ligaments.

... ury almost ruined the Chili Peppers' big day, but ... en years of hard touring, 18 months after their ... death nearly ended the story, the Chili Peppers ... pinnacle of sorts, and Kiedis was determined to ... best shot.

... 's Milk," released last summer, has become the ... g of the band's four albums, at nearly 400,000. ... p with the reputation for on-stage and off-stage ... the brotherhood of Jimi Hendrix fanatics who ... dress during their shows, was being embraced ... nd played on album-rock radio. And on the last ... of their breakthrough year, they were headlin- ... iggest show yet, at the scaled-down, 6,000-ca- ... g Beach Arena.

... just mean that the Chili Peppers' mixed signals ... coming into focus. The band's blend of punk ... and funk music has drawn a devoted audience ... ergy, slam-dancing kids; the Peps' preoccupa- ... exual organs and activities has given them an ... ouse" reputation as gimmicky exhibitionists, ... verlooked but impressive playing has earned

Founding Chili Peppers Flea and Kiedis cavort in Long Beach: the biggest show of their breakthrough year.

some respect from real music fans.

It's added up to a ball of confusion.

"There's a big misconception about us," said Flea, wearing a beanie in the Lakers' colors of purple and gold. "We have this image of being these nutty, crazy guys that wear socks on their [sex organs] and make funny faces

and jump around. We are very intent on having a good time when we play our music. We're entertainers, we're funny, we like to make the audience laugh and make ourselves laugh.

"But we're very dedicated to the music we play, we've put a lot of hard work and a lot of thought into it, to try not to sound like anybody else and to be ourselves as hard as we can. I think people are starting to realize that we play music and it's real music and it's new music."

John Frusciante, a brash 19-year-old from Chatsworth, knows what the Chili Peppers mean to their audience, because he was a fan of the band before he was hired as its guitarist shortly after his predecessor, Hillel Slovak, died from a drug overdose.

"Their shows were very important to me," Frusciante said earlier in the day when he dropped by Kiedis' apartment. "They expressed a lot of the philosophies that I was feeling in my heart. . . . I think our music comple- ments their lives. . . . All their feelings about sex, or their problems with racism or their problems with just never feeling outside of the rest of the world. I think our music gives those people a path and a feeling there's still hope for the world, or at least hope as individuals."

Kiedis, drinking coffee and packing for the trip to Long Beach, concurred.

"There's millions of people growing up in this world that feel slightly alienated from the mainstream of life. They can't really attach themselves to, say, Mötley Crüe or the Rolling Stones. They just don't feel a part of that style of energy.

"They feel slightly outcast and kind of geeky or different from the rest of the world, and then they hear someone like the Red Hot Chili Peppers who basically represent ultimate honesty and freedom to be whatever it is you are and not be ashamed of it. . . ."

Frusciante placed his straw hat over his dyed-bright- red hair and left for the arena.

"It's a good thing John came along when he did," said Kiedis, who like Slovak used heroin and was shocked into

✳ HYDE PARK WAS A GAS — IT WAS A GREAT SITUATION DURING THE *By the Way* TOUR. A MAGICAL PERIOD. IT WAS FUN WRITING THAT RECORD. I LOVE THOSE SONGS, AND ENGLAND REALLY WENT FOR *By the Way* MORE THAN ANYBODY. **LIKE THERE IS ALWAYS A COUNTRY THAT GOES FOR A CERTAIN RECORD, IT SEEMS. FOR *CALIFORNICATION* IT WAS ITALY — ITALIANS WOULDN'T STOP BUYING THAT RECORD FROM THE SECOND IT WAS RELEASED AND THEY'VE NEVER STOPPED.** ENGLAND WOULDN'T STOP BUYING *By the Way*, AND IN GERMANY IT'S *Stadium Arcadium*.

✳ HYDE PARK WAS FUN, BECAUSE IT'S THREE SHOWS IN A ROW — YOU DON'T HAVE TO TRAVEL! PLUS OUR HOTEL WAS ONLY A FEW BLOCKS AWAY, WITHIN WALKING DISTANCE, AND SO WE GOT TO RELAX AND CHILL, RATHER THAN SCHLEPPING OUT OF SOME AIRPORT, GETTING PICKED UP BY A BUS AND DRIVING ANOTHER TWO HOURS TO SOME OBSCURE HAMLET FOR A FESTIVAL SOMEWHERE IN THE BAVARIAN COUNTRYSIDE. AND THE AUDIENCES WERE WONDERFUL TO US.

✳ HYDE PARK SOLD OUT SUPERFAST, LIKE A DAY. AGAIN THE U.K. WAS "MAD" FOR US LIKE THEY SAY OVER THERE. WE ALSO HAD THE HONOR OF HAVING JAMES BROWN PLAY WITH US — AT HYDE PARK AND ONE OTHER GIG IN MANCHESTER. WHEN I WAS GROWING UP IN MICHIGAN, I LOVED THE ENGLISH BANDS OF THE LATE '60S AND EARLY '70S — THE WHO, CREAM, QUEEN, ZEPPELIN — AND SO TO HAVE JIMMY PAGE COME TO YOUR SHOW AND TELL YOU HOW MUCH HE LOVES YOUR BAND, I ABOUT SHIT! I LOOK OVER FROM THE DRUMS AND IT'S JIMMY PAGE, BRIAN MAY AND ROGER TAYLOR, IAN ANDERSON JUST LIKE ROYALTY STANDING THIRTY FEET FROM ME.

JUPITER MARS

As TIME WENT BY, PARTICULARLY THESE LAST TEN YEARS — ESPECIALLY FOR THE LAST TWO ALBUMS — I WOULD JUST WRITE WHOLE SONGS AT HOME AND BRING THEM IN AND EVERYONE WOULD MAKE UP THEIR PARTS. I'D JUST SKETCH OUT THE FORM OF THE SONG IN TERMS OF SECTIONS AND LENGTH.

WE WENT INTO THE WRITING OF *STADIUM* PRETTY MUCH JUST LIKE WE WERE USED TO DOING — CHECK INTO THE ALLEY IN NORTH HOLLYWOOD AND JUST START JAMMING. IDEAS WOULD FLOW FROM JOHN AND FLEA — THINGS THEY'D BEEN WORKING ON AT HOME, MORE MATERIAL DEVELOPING QUICKER THAN USUAL. WE ALWAYS HAVE THIS HALF-HEARTED, HALF-BAKED DISCUSSION ABOUT, "LET'S DO THE PERFECT ELEVEN-SONG RECORD, À LA THE BEATLES OR NIRVANA. JUST SOMETHING CONCISE — NOT DIFFICULT TO DIGEST. JUST ELEVEN REAL POTENT SONGS."

STADIUM ARCADIUM HAS EVERY ASPECT OF US AND DOESN'T LEAVE ANYTHING OUT. I'D JUST WRITE SOMETHING PRETTY MUCH EVERY DAY AND HAD SO MANY MORE IDEAS MORE THAN WHAT I

BROUGHT IN, SO I'D GO INTO THE STUDIO LIKE "OKAY, I'LL BOUNCE THIS OFF THEM." SOMETIMES THE IDEAS DON'T GO ANYWHERE.

WE BUILT UP A LOT OF MUSIC REALLY QUICKLY AND THREW AWAY TONS OF GREAT STUFF THAT DIDN'T MAKE IT.

VERY QUICKLY WE HAD WELL OVER THIRTY SONG IDEAS AND SO I JUST ZEROED IN ON THE ONES I WAS MOST PASSIONATE ABOUT AND BEGAN WORKING WITH THOSE. THE ONES I STRUGGLE WITH, I NEED MORE TIME TO COME AT THEM AT A DIFFERENT ANGLE UNTIL I MAKE THE CONNECTION. DO MY BEST. SOMETHING WEIRD HAPPENS WHEN YOU DECIDE TO ACCEPT THE CHALLENGE OF WRITING THIRTY OR MORE SONGS — THE WORKLOAD INTENSIFIES, THE HOURS GET LONGER, BECAUSE IT IS NOT JUST THE SONGWRITING, BUT EVERYTHING IS GOING TO TAKE MORE TIME AND ENERGY.

THE ALLEY, WHERE WE DID REHEARSALS BEFORE — THIS OLD BIKER DUDE RUNS THE PLACE SINCE THE '70S — IT'S A VERY COMFORTABLE PLACE FOR US. JUST TWO ROOMS AND NO ONE AROUND. SO

ON *STADIUM* WE FELT REALLY FREE WITH EACH OTHER. I WAS MORE FOCUSED ON BLUES AND ENERGETIC POWER AND THAT ALBUM ENDED UP CONNECTING PEOPLE EVERYWHERE. IT WASN'T LIKE WE THREW AWAY MELODY — WE JUST STARTED BALANCING IT WITH MORE RHYTHMIC INTERACTION. IT WAS MORE WELL-BALANCED THAN ANY OF THE ALBUMS.

I HAD A GREAT TIME, LOVED THE MUSIC. IT WASN'T ONE HUNDRED PERCENT PERFECT — THERE WERE A FEW MISTAKES IN SONG SELECTION, NOTHING TO GET HUNG UP ON. THAT RECORD WAS REALLY BEAUTIFUL FOR ME. I WASN'T CAUGHT UP IN NIT-PICKING DETAILS. THE TOUR WAS FUN. EXPLOSIVE, COOL TIME FOR ME AND THE BAND.

LOTS OF MUSIC WAS COMING REALLY EASY. LOTS OF JAMS. I FELT LIKE IT WAS BACK TO THE OLD WAY, AND WE WENT BACK TO

WE WENT BACK THERE AND CAME UP WITH TWO OR THREE THINGS EVERY DAY. WE LEARNED HOW TO JAM IN MORE OF A SONGWRITING WAY — WE JAM ON SOMETHING THEN TAKE IT TO ANOTHER PART, MORE A SONGWRITING THING THAN JUST TWO CHORDS BACK AND FORTH FOR TWENTY MINUTES. IT WAS FLYING, MAN. WE BANGED AWAY AND KEPT GOING.

EVENTUALLY WE THOUGHT [PRODUCER] RICK [RUBIN] NEEDED TO COME IN. WE HAD THIRTY-FIVE SONG IDEAS. HE WAS JUST REALLY EXCITED LIKE, "THIS SHIT SOUNDS GREAT" SO WE WERE GOING TO GO BACK IN AND DO THAT. AND THEN A MONTH BEFORE, THE STUDIO CLOSED DOWN — A MONTH BEFORE WE WERE SUPPOSED TO GO BACK IN. SO WE KEPT GOING BACK TO THE ALLEY, BACK TO THE MANSION IN LAUREL CANYON. ➤

217

➤ It felt good to be in there. Got a guy to record us who did Brian Wilson's *Smile* — Mark Linett. We wanted it old-school with everything in the same room.

✳ By the time of *Stadium* I was recording everything on mini disc, so anytime anything of importance was played I recorded it. So every day I'd go home and listen to jams and takes of songs and stuff. Sometimes you play something awesome in a jam that could be a really good song, where in the past it would have just gone by the wayside. This way I could make a song out of it. I was starting to also write whole songs and bring them in instead of pieces and things. It just made everything go a lot faster and made us generate a lot more, more quickly. **SO WE ENDED UP WRITING ABOUT THREE TIMES MORE MUSIC THAN WE USUALLY WOULD.**

✳ It's important for Anthony to sing when we are playing, like tempo-wise what feels good, and it dictates a lot of the time the right feel of the song. For me as a drummer every song has a different groove and tempo, and a lot of time that is dictated by the vocals. I always refer to Anthony, like "Is this a good tempo or feeling?" It is important that he is in there singing to develop the phrasing, and even if it isn't finished, at least he's singing something.

✳ There's also the issue of songs that maybe one or two people fall completely in love with and maybe one or two people who are like, out of forty-five ideas, that is not my favorite one. There's a little bit of heartbreak to look in the eyes — of say, John — and realize he is not as in love with

a piece of music as I am. And that kind of raised the anxiety level. What should have been a glorious process that we reveled in the joy of — because it's year twenty-three of our existence — our biggest problem is we are writing too much music! We got caught up in the smaller picture of mixes, tones, overdubs and sounds. It was kind of sad because the creative gifts that were flowing, we lost sight of that a little bit. We had a very bizarre sit-down. We decided we were going to do a double album, no question.

✳ **WE WANTED IT TO BE A TRIPLE ALBUM! I'M SURE THE RECORD COMPANY LOVED THAT IDEA.**

✳ First we wanted to do three albums, then one out every six months — all these ideas until we settled on a double album. We had many powwows about how to release this amount of music. We thought of releasing it in three separate parts over a year and a half, which actually System of a Down had done — two separate records from the same sessions — and Radiohead had done something similar. How do we best format all this music? One big box set? In the end, we just went for a classic double album. And we still had at least fifteen songs leftover so we had to have the big vote-off. We devised a system where all four of us and Rick would have a votes number system, and we tallied the totals to see which songs would make it. And a good sixteen to eighteen songs were obvious. They were clear front- runners, but there were all these interesting pieces of music that were both loved and not so loved. There are some hidden beauties I think. The songs like "If," "Hey," "Hard to Concentrate" — things that would never in a million years be considered for a single, but are really solid pieces.

218

STADIUM ARCADIUM

A IT SEEMED LIKE THE *STADIUM ARCADIUM* TOUR WAS MAYBE A YEAR AND A HALF, BUT THE FIRST SIX MONTHS OR SO WAS FUN AND SO MUCH MATERIAL TO CHOOSE FROM. IT BECAME KIND OF A RUBIK'S CUBE OF SONGS TO FIGURE OUT WHAT OLD SONGS AND THEN THE TWENTY-FIVE NEW SONGS TO CHOOSE FROM. IT WAS FRESH AND WE WERE PLAYING REALLY WELL I THOUGHT — I THOUGHT WE WERE AT THE TOP OF OUR GAME. EVERYTHING WAS FINE. I MEAN THERE'S HUNGER, CONFUSION, DISSATISFACTION, WHATEVER — THOSE MOMENTS WILL ALLOW RESENTMENT TO FESTER BOTH OLD AND NEW. ALL I KNOW IS THE FIRST SIX MONTHS WE WERE KICKING ASS! PLAYING REALLY GOOD. THE ENERGY WAS PHENOMENAL. AND THEN, IT BECAME MORE DIFFICULT TO MAINTAIN THAT ENTHUSIASM FOR THE NEXT YEAR. FLEA HATES TOURING AT THE END. THAT'S ALL HE EVER REMEMBERS I THINK, BY THE END OF A YEAR AND A HALF OUT THERE. EVERY MOTHERFUCKER HATES TOURING. IT WAS DONE — WE WERE CRISPY PIECES OF BURNT-UP EGOMANIACAL TOAST.

J I'M HAPPIER ONSTAGE WHEN I'M GETTING MORE INSIDE MYSELF. ON *STADIUM* I WAS ABLE TO DO THAT WHILE STAYING CONNECTED TO EVERYONE WHILE DOING IT. A LOT OF IMPROVISATION BETWEEN FLEA AND I, A LOT OF CLOSING MY EYES AND DRIFTING AND SEEING WHERE THE FORCE TOOK ME OR WHATEVER. FOR ME THAT'S THE BEST WE'VE EVER PLAYED TOGETHER IN TERMS OF IMPROVISATION, AND MAKING EACH SHOW A REAL UNIQUE ARTISTIC EVENT. BECAUSE WE WERE DOING SO MUCH IMPROVISING, WE TOTALLY HAD SOME BAD SHOWS, AND GOOD SHOWS. BUT THAT'S THE FORCE YOU ARE WORKING WITH AND YOU APPRECIATE THE BAD SHOWS — EVEN THOUGH IF IT IS BAD AND YOUR FRIENDS ARE THERE, YOU FEEL BAD. BUT WHATEVER, IT IS WORTH IT. MORE OFTEN THAN NOT WE HAD THESE GREAT SHOWS WHERE PEOPLE COULD TELL IT WAS HAPPENING IN THE MOMENT — IT WASN'T PLANNED OUT OR ANYTHING.

A THE FIRST SIX MONTHS WERE EXPLOSIVE FUN. ALSO I STARTED DOING THIS THING — FIRST, I WAS WEARING BALLET SLIPPER THIN SOLES TO GET RID OF SHIN SPLINTS — ON TOUR I'M JUMPING SO MUCH I GET SPLINTS SINCE 1990 — SO THIS KOOKY DOCTOR TOLD ME TO GET RID OF THE SOLES AND THE FEET WILL CORRECT IT. IT WORKED, NO SHIN SPLINTS. BUT I STARTED DOING A HAND STAND OFF OF CHAD'S BASS DRUM, AND FORCED MYSELF INTO THE AIR WHICH YOU CAN ONLY DO IN THE MIDDLE OF THE SHOW, AND I GOT HOOKED ON IT, THROWING MYSELF INTO THE AIR FEET FIRST AND A BACKWARDS SWAN DIVE. AFTER SIX OR EIGHT MONTHS, I REALIZED I WAS HAVING A HARD TIME WALKING. I WENT TO THE DOCTOR, GOT X-RAYS AND HE SAYS, "YOU HAVE TWO BROKEN FEET — STAY OFF THOSE FEET FOR A YEAR." I'M LIKE, "I'M GOING ON TOUR FOR SIX MONTHS." NOT ONLY DO YOU HAVE PAIN, BUT ENERGETICALLY IT IS LIKE POKING A HOLE IN A BALLOON. SO I HAD TO FIGURE OUT A WAY TO FULFILL THIS TOUR, AND I ENDED UP GETTING SURGICAL PADDING PUT ON EVERY NIGHT AND THEN I WOULD ICE MY FEET, BUT I BASICALLY BEAT MY FEET INTO OBLIVION. AND MY LEGS HAVE NEVER RECOVERED. I CAN'T REALLY WALK OR RUN FOR ANY DISTANCE, BECAUSE THE BONE HEALED MISSHAPEN IN MY FOOT. SO IT IS LIKE I'M WALKING ON A KNUCKLE ON THE BOTTOM OF MY FOOT — LIKE A BONE TOUCHES WHATEVER SURFACE I'M ON. I WILL FIGURE OUT A SOLUTION.

C IT GETS BRUTAL. THE PLAYING IS GREAT, BUT THE TRAVELING — I DON'T WANT TO SOUND LIKE A WHINER. I HAVE A FUCKING GREAT JOB AND I LOVE IT. THE THING IS, WE ARE NOT TWENTY-FIVE ANYMORE. WE HAVE FAMILIES, AND YOU GET AWAY FROM HOME A LONG TIME, AND IT CAN BE TOUGH. SO WE WENT AGAIN FOR ANOTHER SIX MONTHS — TOWARD THE END IT WAS ROUGH — AUSTRALIA WAS ROUGH AND ANTHONY WAS HURTING WITH HIS FEET. HE COULDN'T DO HIS THING AND IT BUMMED HIM OUT.

FLEA WAS GETTING SICK. IT WAS JUST THE EXCITEMENT WENT OUT THE WINDOW. IT KIND OF TURNED INTO A "JOB" A LITTLE BIT. I COULD SEE JOHN WASN'T ENJOYING IT THAT MUCH, PLAYING GREAT AND ALL BUT WE ADDED [GUITARIST] JOSH [KLINGHOFFER] TO PLAY WITH US.

✳ JOHN BECAME DISILLUSIONED WITH HAVING TO PLAY SONGS OVER AND OVER AND OVER AGAIN. GRANTED WE DO OUR BEST TO CREATE AN OPPORTUNITY FOR IMPROVISATION EVERY SINGLE NIGHT. THE FIRST THREE TO FIVE MINUTES OF A SHOW IS JUST

IN THE THEATER OR CLUB. AS TIME WENT BY AND WE GREW ACCUSTOMED TO ARENAS, OUR MUSIC STARTED BECOMING MORE APPROPRIATE FOR PLAYING THOSE KIND OF VENUES. WE DID A SHOW AT THE TROUBADOUR BEFORE GOING OUT FOR *STADIUM*, AND I WAS SHOCKED TO HEAR THAT OUR MUSIC DIDN'T SOUND SUITABLE AT A CLUB AT ALL! IT WAS TOO POWERFUL AND LOUD FOR SUCH A SMALL SPACE. I REALIZED OUR WHOLE STYLE FOR PLAYING IN THE BAND — OUR WHOLE STYLE OF SONGWRITING — HAD GRADUALLY TRANSFORMED TO BEING SOMETHING SUITED TO A REALLY LARGE VENUE.

✳ TO THE AUDIENCE, IT IS AN IMPORTANT SONG FOR THEM TO HEAR LIVE, WE GET THAT, AND WE TRY TO FIND THE LOVE AND SPIRIT OF THAT SONG EVERY SINGLE NIGHT — AND BY GEORGE WE DO, EVERY SINGLE TIME. BUT THEN THERE'S THAT NIGHT, WHERE YOU ARE NOT FLOWING OR FEELING IT, AND

A JAM — THAT BECAME OUR SIGNATURE SHOW STARTER. THEN, OTHER SONGS DEVELOP WITH JAM SESSIONS, BUT, YOU ARE STILL PLAYING "GIVE IT AWAY" ONE MORE TIME, AND AT A CERTAIN POINT, I THINK JOHN WAS HAVING A HARD TIME FIGURING OUT HOW TO MAKE THE MOST OF THAT.

✳ WHEN I STARTED, I THOUGHT OF US AS A BAND THAT PLAYS CLUBS, SO I WOULD WRITE MUSIC THAT WOULD SOUND RIGHT

YOU'RE PLAYING WHAT YOU FEEL IS A SHITTY PERFORMANCE. YOU ARE PISSED, LIKE WHY DO I HAVE TO DO THIS ONE MORE TIME? AND THEN MELTDOWNS OCCUR, WE ALL HAVE THEM — EVERY ONE OF US HAVE HAD MOMENTS WHERE IT SEEMED LIKE IT WASN'T THE BEST IDEA TO BE DOING THIS ANYMORE.

222

Green Heaven

A AL GORE SAID HE NEEDED US TO PLAY A SONG OR TWO AT WEMBLEY STADIUM FOR EARTH DAY WITH TWENTY OTHER BANDS. OUR HANDLERS WERE SO HYPED ON THE WHOLE AL GORE DEAL. THEY REALLY PUSHED US INTO IT, AND WE WERE REALLY INTO THE CAUSE. ONLY PROB WAS WE HAD A SHOW IN DENMARK, AND IT WAS THE END OF THE TOUR. IT WAS DECIDED WE WOULD PLAY PARIS AT MIDNIGHT, FLY TO LONDON, SLEEP, GET UP AND PLAY EARTH DAY, PACK UP AGAIN AND FLY TO DENMARK TO PLAY ANOTHER OUTDOOR FESTIVAL.

F **THREE SHOWS IN LESS THAN TWENTY-FOUR HOURS AT THE END OF A YEAR AND A HALF. MAN, WE WERE TOTALLY THRASHED, FALLING TO PIECES.**

A ADD TO THAT I GOT WALLOPED WITH A SINUS INFECTION FROM ALL THE FLYING. GETTING IN A PLANE FOR ME WAS LIKE LIGHTING A STICK OF DYNAMITE IN MY HEAD.

C WE WERE FORTUNATE TO HAVE PEOPLE WANTING TO SEE US PLAY. THEY LOVE OUR MUSIC — 200 PEOPLE OR 200,000, WE'RE STILL GOING TO PLAY OUR HARDEST AND WE PRIDE OURSELVES IN PERFORMING WELL. IT CAN FREAK YOU OUT A LITTLE BIT, BUT AT NIGHT OUTDOORS YOU CAN'T REALLY SEE PAST THE FIRST 100 YARDS. SO YOU JUST DO YOUR THING.

F SO WE DO THE SHOW IN PARIS, FLY TO LONDON, GOT SOME BULLSHIT SLEEP THEN WE GET TO WEMBLEY WITH NO SOUND CHECK, AND BASICALLY PLAYED TWO SONGS. IT REALLY SHOULDN'T HAVE HAPPENED — IT WAS TERRIBLE, EMBARRASSING.

A WEMBLEY SUCKED, WE WERE EMBARRASSING — TELEVISED AND ALL. DENMARK WAS FREEZING COLD AND RAIN. THOUSANDS OF AMPED-UP KIDS EVERYWHERE ALL READY TO ROCK THE FUCK OUT WITH US, BUT I COULD BARELY STAND, LET ALONE PLAY FOR TWO HOURS. BUT I FOUND THAT WEIRD LITTLE SPOT WHERE I WAS LIKE, EVERYTHING IS GOING TO BE OKAY AND I'LL DO MY BEST. HAD A REALLY FUN TWO HOURS IN A PONCHO DANCING AROUND, NOT GIVING A FUCK BECAUSE IT WAS THE LAST TIME WE WOULD PLAY FOR A LONG TIME.

MELLOWSHIP SLINKY IN B MAJOR

A I'VE NEVER IN MY LIFE FELT LIKE A SELLOUT BEHIND MAKING MUSIC THAT WE MADE AS THE RED HOT CHILI PEPPERS. I'VE NEVER EVER GONE TO PRACTICE OR A RECORDING SESSION OR ANYTHING, FEELING ANYTHING LESS THAN PERFECTLY INSPIRED BY THE DIVINE NATURE OF ART AND MAKING MUSIC WITH MY FRIENDS. NEVER CROSSED MY MIND TO DO ANYTHING COMMERCIALLY FOR THE SAKE OF COMMERCIAL. I LOVE BEING COMMERCIALLY SUCCESSFUL — I THINK IT'S BITCHIN' AND IT HAS BEEN VERY EXCITING. SELLING LOTS OF RECORDS IS EXCITING, BUT I DON'T CONFUSE THE TWO. **I FEEL LIKE WHEN WE GO INTO THAT ROOM AND START PLAYING, ALL THE PITFALLS STAY OUTSIDE, AND WE JUST DO WHAT WE DO.** WE MAKE THE BEST SONGS WE CAN MAKE, AND I SING THE BEST I CAN, AND FLEA COMES UP WITH THE COOLEST BASS LINE HE CAN, AND FORTUNATELY THE WORLD HAS EMBRACED THAT AS SOMETHING THEY WANNA LISTEN TO AND SUPPORT. SINCE ABOUT 1989, I'VE NEVER HAD TO WORRY ABOUT PAYING A BILL — EVERY BILL I'VE INCURRED SINCE THAT DAY HAS BEEN PAID AS A RESULT OF DOING WHAT I LOVE. SO, WHAT A MASSIVE BLESSING — AND I DON'T FEEL LIKE WE EVER ONCE SOLD OUT. WE MADE SOME BAD CHOICES AND SOME STUPID DECISIONS MAYBE TO LET SOMEONE USE OUR MUSIC FOR SOMETHING THAT TURNED OUT TO BE NOT WORTHY, BUT WHEN IT CAME TO WRITING AND RECORDING, I DON'T FEEL THERE HAS EVER BEEN A SINGLE SELLOUT MOMENT.

Parallel Universe

⬡ I LIKE WINNING — IF WE ARE IN A COMPETITION I DEFINITELY LIKE WINNING. BUT I DON'T TAKE THESE GRAMMY AWARDS VERY SERIOUSLY.

⬡ YOU GET THOSE AWARDS IF YOU SELL A LOT OF RECORDS. IT DOESN'T HAVE MUCH TO DO WITH MUSICAL QUALITY — IF YOUR BAND SELLS 2,000 COPIES, IT DOESN'T MATTER HOW GOOD YOUR RECORD IS, YOU WON'T WIN A GRAMMY. IT'S ALL BASED ON MAJOR LABELS. THEY CERTAINLY WOULDN'T HAND THEM OUT TO AN INDIE LABEL.

⬡ **GRAMMY AWARDS AREN'T THAT IMPORTANT TO ME. I DON'T THINK THEY ARE TRUE INDICATORS OF HOW WELL YOU DID AT WRITING MUSIC. THE SHOCK OF WINNING DOESN'T RESONATE FOR VERY LONG.** THE REAL GRAMMY HAPPENS AT A MUCH DIFFERENT POINT IN TIME. THE REAL GRAMMY HAPPENS WHEN YOU WRITE A GOOD SONG. THE DAY JOHN COMES INTO THE STUDIO AND HE'S BEEN UP UNTIL 5 A.M. FUCKING AROUND WITH THESE CHORDS THAT HE'S TRYING TO GET JUST RIGHT. HE COMES IN, AND I'M ALL, "I KNOW WHAT GOES WITH THAT" AND THEN YOU PUT THEM TOGETHER AND IT'S LIKE, "OH SHIT, THAT'S THE REAL DEAL, A REAL SONG" — THAT'S THE GRAMMY. THAT'S WHEN GOD IS IN THE ROOM GOING, "GOOD JOB, LADS. I'M GLAD YOU FOUND THAT PIECE OF MUSIC I'VE BEEN WAITING FOR SOMEONE TO FIND." I'M PRETTY SURE GOD DOESN'T ATTEND THE GRAMMYS, BUT HE ATTENDS THAT MOMENT WHERE A SONG IS BORN.

⬡ SIX GRAMMYS? MAYBE THEY JUST FELT LIKE, "OH THEY'VE BEEN AROUND LONG ENOUGH, THEY STILL MAKE GOOD MUSIC SO LET'S THROW SOME ALBUM OF THE YEAR AWARDS AT THEM," OR WHATEVER. I MEAN IT IS NICE.

⬡ I WAS EXCITED WE WON THAT GRAMMY FOR *STADIUM*, JUST THAT FUN FEELING OF "ARE WE GONNA WIN OR NOT? OH, WE WON!" IT IS FUN, BUT I NEVER KEPT THE AWARDS. SURE IT MAKES YOU FEEL GOOD THAT PEOPLE LIKE WHAT YOU ARE DOING BUT IT DOESN'T ACCOUNT FOR ANYTHING TO ME. IT DOESN'T REALLY HAVE ANY MEANING OR VALUE TO ME — IT IS JUST A SILLY THING THAT COMES WITH BEING IN A POPULAR BAND. THE MUSIC I LIKE IS TOTALLY IGNORED BY THOSE THINGS. IT IS AS MUCH BASED ON HOW PEOPLE LOOK OR HOW THEY SELL THEMSELVES, HOW FUNNY THEY ARE IN INTERVIEWS. IT IS BASED ON A LOT BESIDES MAKING GOOD MUSIC, ESPECIALLY YOUR ABILITY AND DESIRE TO SELL YOURSELF. YOU'LL NEVER, NEVER GET ACKNOWLEDGED FOR BEING A MUSICAL ARTIST, JUST FOR BEING A MUSICAL ARTIST, BY THAT WORLD. YOU GET ACKNOWLEDGED BY PLAYING THEIR GAME THEIR WAY, AND I DON'T THINK IT IS A HEALTHY LIFESTYLE FOR ARTISTS. IT IS A TESTAMENT TO WHAT I'M SAYING, THAT NO ONE WHO EVER DOES WELL IN THAT BUSINESS HAS ANY LONGEVITY IN TERMS OF EXPLORING NEW THINGS WITH ART. MORE AND MORE, THEIR MUSIC BREAKS LESS GROUND, AND DOES LESS AND LESS NEW THINGS. IT BECOMES A SHALLOW VERSION OF WHAT THEY ONCE DID AND THE SETUP OF THE BUSINESS LENDS ITSELF TO THAT. WHEN SOMEONE FEELS REALLY FULFILLED BY SOMETHING LIKE A GRAMMY, I THINK THEY ARE IN A REALLY CLOSED-OFF PLACE FROM WHAT'S REALLY IMPORTANT.

DOT

231

Walkin' on Down the Road

A When John came and said, "I feel like doing something else now," I really was overcome with a wave of gratitude for the years and months and days and hours of the creative collaboration that I have had with John — the lifetime of him in this band. Normally if someone is going to quit, like Flea sometimes feels like doing, I'm like, "Hey motherfucker, don't quit we have a good thing going." But when John wanted to quit I was like, "How am I going to fight that?" I don't even feel like fighting it — he just wants to, god bless him. **I AM LUCKY TO HAVE HAD SUCH A BOUNTIFUL CREATIVE EXPERIENCE WITH ANOTHER HUMAN BEING, AND THAT IS NOT SOMETHING I TAKE FOR GRANTED.**

This guy, and myself, Flea and Chad, when we get together, this chemistry is just insane and productive, and the neatest thing I've ever done as an artist. I wanted to be clear that there was not a sour feeling or "why is this guy deciding to do something else" kind of thing. It really is a great feeling of thankfulness that we got to make all the songs that we did.

233

WE BELIEVE

F WE'RE A BAND THAT HAS GOTTEN BETTER AND BETTER OVER A LONG PERIOD OF TIME AND BECOME MORE IMPORTANT AS TIME HAS GONE BY. THERE ARE PERIODS OF EXPLOSIVE CREATIVENESS IN OUR BAND AND PERIODS AND MOMENTS WHEN I THINK WE'RE REALLY IMPORTANT. I CONSIDER US TO BE ONE OF THE MOST IMPORTANT BANDS TO COME OUT OF L.A.

C I THINK ANTHONY IS A LITTLE ANXIOUS TO GET BACK TO WORK — FLEA TOO. WHEN WE PLAYED THAT BENEFIT THING WITH RON WOOD [THE FIFTH ANNUAL MUSICARES MAP FUND BENEFIT CONCERT HONORING ANTHONY IN MAY, 2009], WE WERE REHEARSING AND FLEA STARTS PLAYING A LITTLE SOMETHING ON THE PIANO. IMMEDIATELY ANTHONY AND I ARE LIKE, "OH, THAT WOULD BE A GOOD BRIDGE PART!" WE JUST FALL RIGHT BACK INTO IT WITHOUT EVEN TRYING. ANTHONY'S LIKE, "JUST YOU TUNING UP YOUR DRUMS GIVES ME THAT FEELING." AND I REMEMBER WE SAT WITH RONNIE WOOD AND HE WAS LIKE, "IT FEELS LIKE HOME, RIGHT?" "YEAH RON, IT FEELS LIKE HOME." SO I KNOW WE'VE GOT MORE MUSIC TO MAKE.

A THE STORY IS — MAYBE IT IS LIKE ACT ONE AND TWO, HARD TO SAY. IT'S SOMETHING THAT TURNED OUT TO HAVE A HISTORY. **EVERY TIME THE FINAL CURTAIN HAS EVER BEEN SUGGESTED FOR THE RED HOT CHILI PEPPERS IT TURNS OUT A FAKE-OUT.** I HAVE NO IDEA. THERE'S NO PREDICTING HOW MANY MORE YEARS, OR RECORDS, OR TOURS, OR SONGS OR INCARNATIONS THIS THING IS GOING TO EXPERIENCE. THERE'S A LOT OF DOT-DOT-DOTS.

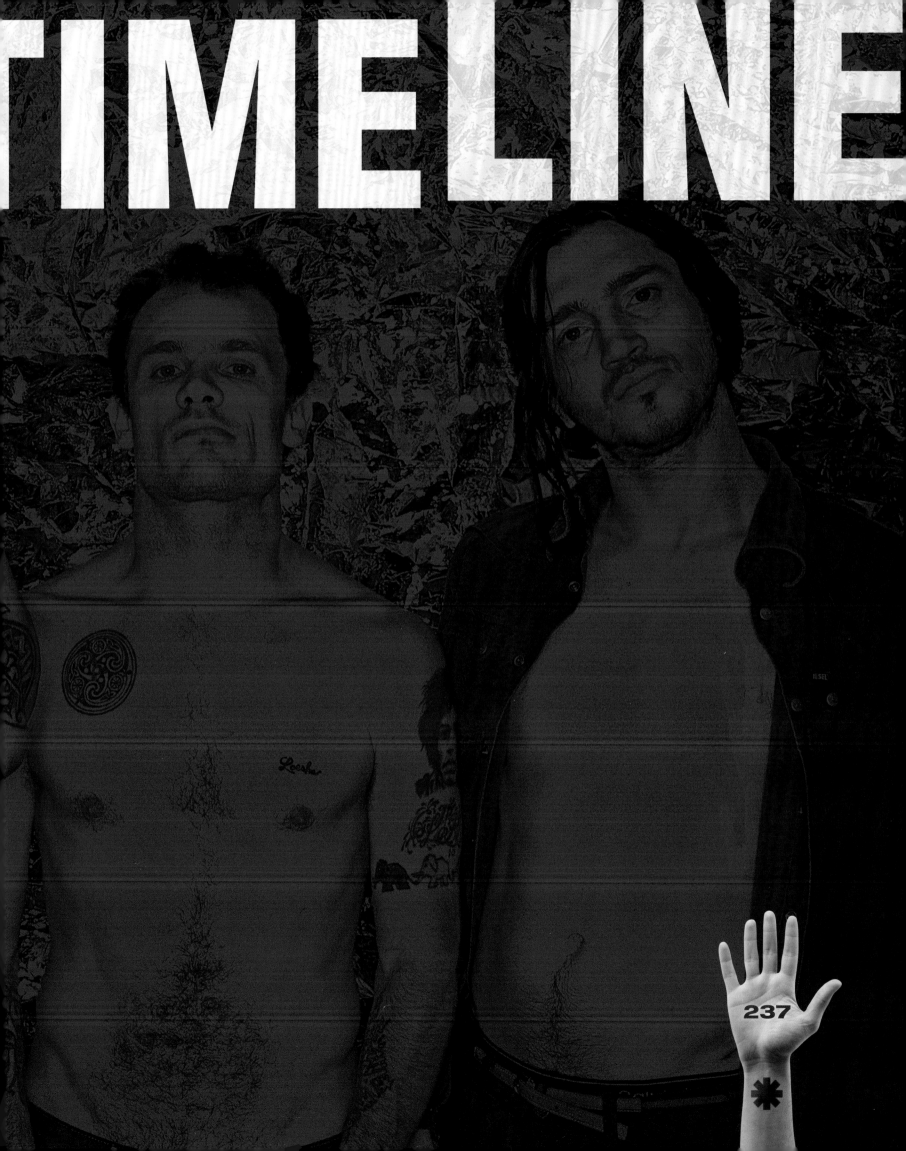

237

NOVEMBER 1983

Manager Lindy Goetz gets the band a seven-album deal with EMI

DECEMBER 1983

Hillel Slovak and Jack Irons leave to join What Is This?; guitarist Jack Sherman and drummer Cliff Martinez join RHCP

JANUARY 6, 1983

Singer Anthony Kiedis, bassist Flea, guitarist Hillel Slovak, and drummer Jack Irons play as the Flow at the Rhythm Lounge

MARCH 25, 1983

Official name change from the Flow to Red Hot Chili Peppers

AUGUST 16, 1985

Freaky Styley released

JANUARY 1985

Hillel Slovak quits What Is This? to rejoin RHCP

OCTOBER, 1985

RHCP starts six-month U.S. tour

1983

1980s

1985

1984

1986

AUGUST 10, 1984

The Red Hot Chili Peppers is released

OCTOBER 1984

RHCP plays 60 shows in 64 days; Jack Sherman is fired after tour ends

JANUARY 1986

Jack Irons quits What Is This? and rejoins RHCP in the summer

238

OCTOBER 1987
RHCP STARTS TWO-MONTH TOUR WITH FAITH NO MORE AS THE OPENING ACT

SEPTEMBER 9, 1989
YEAR-LONG NATIONAL TOUR TO PROMOTE *MOTHER'S MILK* BEGINS

SEPTEMBER 29, 1987
The Uplift Mofo Party Plan IS RELEASED AND GOES TO NUMBER 148 ON *Billboard*'s HOT 200

MARCH 5, 1987
RHCP WIN BEST BAND IN A READER POLL AT *L.A. Weekly*'s MUSIC AWARDS

AUGUST 1989
MOTHER'S MILK IS RELEASED.

1987

1989

1988

AUGUST 1988
FORMER DEAD KENNEDYS DRUMMER D. H. PELIGRO AND FUNKADELIC GUITARIST DeWAYNE "BLACKBYRD" McKNIGHT BRIEFLY JOIN RHCP; BOTH LET GO IN NOVEMBER

JUNE 25, 1988
HILLEL SLOVAK DIES; JACK IRONS LEAVES RHCP

MAY 1988
Abbey Road EP IS RELEASED

NOVEMBER 1988
GUITARIST JOHN FRUSCIANTE JOINS RHCP

DECEMBER 1988
DRUMMER CHAD SMITH JOINS RHCP

SEPTEMBER 24, 1991
Blood Sugar Sex Magik IS RELEASED

OCTOBER 1991
U.S. TOUR FOR *BLOOD SUGAR SEX MAGIK* BEGINS WITH SUPPORTING ACTS PEARL JAM AND SMASHING PUMPKINS FOR THE FIRST LEG; THEN CONTINUES WITH NIRVANA AND PJ HARVEY

JANUARY–FEBRUARY 1993
RHCP PLAY THE HOLLYWOOD ROCK FESTIVAL IN RIO AND SÃO PAULO WITH NIRVANA, ALICE IN CHAINS AND L7

SEPTEMBER 1993
JANE'S ADDICTION GUITARIST DAVE NAVARRO JOINS RHCP

SEPTEMBER 1993
GUITARIST JESSE TOBIAS FROM MOTHER TONGUE REPLACES ARIK MARSHALL; TOBIAS LEAVES THE BAND ABOUT A MONTH LATER

1991

1993

1990s

1990

1992

1994

APRIL 1990
Mother's Milk BECOMES RHCP'S FIRST GOLD RECORD

1990
RHCP LEAVE EMI AND SIGN WITH WARNER BROS. FLEA APPEARS IN GUS VAN SANT'S *My Own Private Idaho*

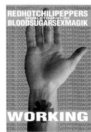

FEBRUARY 1992
Blood Sugar Sex Magik TOUR CONTINUES TO EUROPE

MAY 7, 1992
JOHN FRUSCIANTE QUITS RHCP IN JAPAN; REST OF THE TOUR IS CANCELLED

FEBRUARY 1992
"GIVE IT AWAY" WINS 1992 GRAMMY FOR BEST HARD ROCK PERFORMANCE WITH VOCAL

JULY–SEPTEMBER 1992
GUITARIST ARIK MARSHALL PLAYS THE LOLLAPALOOZA 2 TOUR WITH RHCP

AUGUST 14, 1994
RHCP PLAYS THE 25TH ANNIVERSARY OF WOODSTOCK

JULY 1994
Plasma RELEASED

NOVEMBER 1994
Out in L.A., A COMPILATION OF OUTTAKES, EARLY DEMOS, B-SIDES, RARITIES AND REMIXES, IS RELEASED

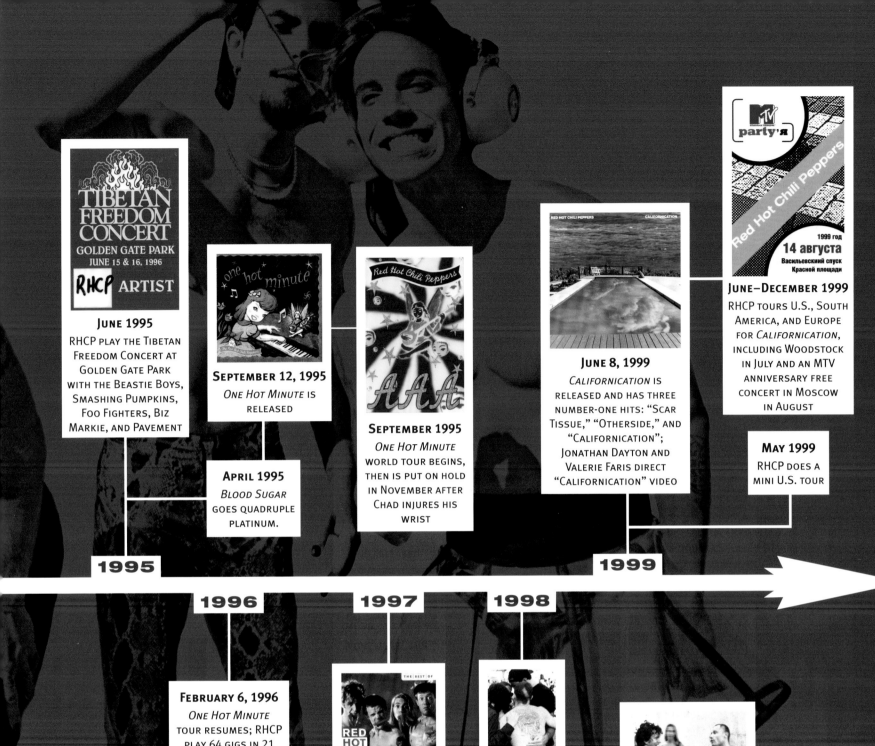

JUNE 1995

RHCP play the Tibetan Freedom Concert at Golden Gate Park with the Beastie Boys, Smashing Pumpkins, Foo Fighters, Biz Markie, and Pavement

SEPTEMBER 12, 1995

One Hot Minute is released

APRIL 1995

Blood Sugar goes quadruple platinum.

SEPTEMBER 1995

One Hot Minute world tour begins, then is put on hold in November after Chad injures his wrist

JUNE 8, 1999

Californication is released and has three number-one hits: "Scar Tissue," "Otherside," and "Californication"; Jonathan Dayton and Valerie Faris direct "Californication" video

JUNE–DECEMBER 1999

RHCP tours U.S., South America, and Europe for *Californication*, including Woodstock in July and an MTV anniversary free concert in Moscow in August

MAY 1999

RHCP does a mini U.S. tour

1995

1996

1997

1998

1999

FEBRUARY 6, 1996

One Hot Minute tour resumes; RHCP play 64 gigs in 21 countries

NOVEMBER 1997

The Best of the Red Hot Chili Peppers is released

APRIL 1998

Dave Navarro is fired; John Frusciante rejoins RHCP

JUNE–SEPTEMBER 1998

RHCP tour U.S.

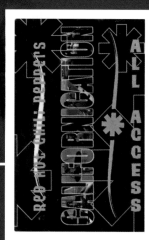

JANUARY 2000

RHCP WIN FAVORITE ALTERNATIVE ARTIST AT THE AMERICAN MUSIC AWARDS

JANUARY–NOVEMBER 2000

CALIFORNICATION TOUR CONTINUES IN JAPAN, AUSTRALIA, AND NEW ZEALAND, THEN RETURNS TO THE U.S., WHERE OPENING ACTS INCLUDE THE FOO FIGHTERS, BICYCLE THIEF, BLONDE REDHEAD, STONE TEMPLE PILOTS, AND FISHBONE

JULY 9, 2002

BY THE WAY IS RELEASED.

JULY–DECEMBER 2002

RHCP TOUR THE U.S., EUROPE, KOREA, JAPAN, SOUTH AMERICA, CENTRAL AMERICA, MEXICO, AUSTRALIA, NEW ZEALAND, PHILIPPINES, THAILAND, AND SINGAPORE FOR *BY THE WAY*

JUNE–OCTOBER 2004

RHCP TOUR U.S., JAPAN, AND EUROPE

OCTOBER 2004

RHCP PLAY NEIL YOUNG'S ANNUAL BRIDGE SCHOOL BENEFIT, WITH BEN HARPER, EDDIE VEDDER, SONIC YOUTH, TEGAN & SARA, SIR PAUL MCCARTNEY, TONY BENNETT, AND LOS LONELY BOYS

AUGUST 2004

LIVE IN HYDE PARK IS RELEASED

JUNE 19–20, 2004

RHCP PLAY HYDE PARK CONCERTS

2000 **2002** **2004**

2000s

2001 **2003** **2005**

JANUARY 2001

RHCP PLAYS ROCK IN RIO 3; LINEUP INCLUDES GUNS N' ROSES, NEIL YOUNG, OASIS, AND R.E.M.

APRIL 12, 2001

RHCP RECEIVE THE ARTIST CONTRIBUTION AWARD AT ESPN'S SECOND ANNUAL ACTION SPORTS & MUSIC AWARDS

AUGUST 2001

RHCP OPEN FOR U2 AT SLANE CASTLE

DECEMBER 2001

RHCP'S FIRST CONCERT DVD, *OFF THE MAP*, DIRECTED BY DICK RUDE, IS RELEASED

JANUARY–OCTOBER 2003

BY THE WAY TOUR CONTINUES IN EUROPE AND BACK TO THE U.S., WHERE OPENING ACTS INCLUDE THE MARS VOLTA, QUEENS OF THE STONE AGE, SNOOP DOGG, FLAMING LIPS, AND MIKE WATT

APRIL 2003

RHCP PLAY THE COACHELLA FESTIVAL

FEB. 11, 2005

RHCP PLAY THE MUSICARE'S TRIBUTE TO THE BEACH BOYS

JULY 2, 2005

RHCP PLAYS A FREE SHOW FOR LAS VEGAS' CENTENNIAL CELEBRATION

AUGUST 2003

RHCP HEADLINE SLANE CASTLE

NOVEMBER 21, 2006
RHCP WIN THE AMERICAN MUSIC AWARDS' FAVORITE POP/ROCK BAND/DUO/ GROUP AND FAVORITE ALTERNATIVE ARTIST

MAY 9, 2006
STADIUM ARCADIUM IS RELEASED

MAY–DECEMBER 2006
WORLD TOUR FOR *STADIUM ARCADIUM*

JUNE 14, 2008
CHAD PERFORMS AT THE LONDON INTERNATIONAL MUSIC SHOW

SEPTEMBER 27, 2008
FLEA PERFORMS AT THE FOURTH ANNUAL HULLABALLOO TO BENEFIT THE SILVERLAKE CONSERVATORY OF MUSIC, ALONG WITH THE LOS ANGELES PHILHARMONIC STRING BASS QUARTET

AUGUST 8–9, 2008
ANTHONY HOSTS THE NEW AMERICAN MUSIC UNION FESTIVAL AND BOOKS THE LINEUP, WHICH INCLUDES BOB DYLAN, GNARLS BARKLEY, AND THE ROOTS

JANUARY 29, 2010
RHCP, WITH GUITARIST JOSH KLINGHOFFER, PLAY AT MUSICARE'S 20TH ANNUAL PERSON OF THE YEAR EVENT HONORING NEIL YOUNG

SEPTEMBER 4, 2008
JOHN, FLEA, JOSH KLINGHOFFER, AND STELLA MOZGAWA PERFORM AT THE ROCK 4 CHANGE BENEFIT.

2006

2007

2008

2009

2010

JANUARY–AUGUST 2007
STADIUM ARCADIUM TOUR CONTINUES IN THE U.S., WITH GNARLS BARKLEY OPENING, THEN CONTINUES TO MEXICO, JAPAN, AUSTRALIA, NEW ZEALAND, AND EUROPE

FEBRUARY 2007
STADIUM ARCADIUM WINS GRAMMYS FOR BEST ROCK ALBUM AND BEST ROCK PERFORMANCE BY A DUO OR GROUP WITH VOCAL FOR "DANI CALIFORNIA"; RHCP PERFORMS "SNOW ((HEY OH))"

MAY 5, 2007
RHCP PLAYS WITH EDDIE VEDDER, CHARLIE HADEN, AND THE DITTY BOPS AT A BENEFIT FOR THE SILVERLAKE CONSERVATORY, FOUNDED BY FLEA AND KEITH BARRY IN 2001

JANUARY 20, 2009
JOHN RELEASES *THE EMPYREAN*

JULY 2009
JOHN LEAVES RHCP

JULY 7, 2007
RHCP PLAY LIVE EARTH AT WEMBLEY STADIUM

MAY 8, 2009
ANTHONY, FLEA, CHAD, AND GUITARIST JOSH KLINGHOFFER, ALONG WITH RON WOOD, IGGY POP, THE MARS VOLTA, IVAN NEVILLE, BOB FORREST AND ELIJAH FORREST, PLAY AT THE FIFTH ANNUAL MUSICARES MAP FUND BENEFIT CONCERT HONORING ANTHONY

243

RCHP DISCOGRAPHY

STADIUM ARCADIUM

DISC 1: JUPITER
01 DANI CALIFORNIA
02 SNOW (HEY OH)
03 CHARLIE
04 STADIUM ARCADIUM
05 HUMP DE BUMP
06 SHE'S ONLY 18
07 SLOW CHEETAH
08 TORTURE ME
09 STRIP MY MIND
10 ESPECIALLY IN MICHIGAN
11 WARLOCKS
12 C'MON GIRL
13 WET SAND
14 HEY

DISC 2: MARS
01 DESECRATION SMILE
02 TELL ME BABY
03 HARD TO CONCENTRATE
04 21ST CENTURY
05 SHE LOOKS TO ME
06 READYMADE
07 IF
08 MAKE YOU FEEL BETTER
09 ANIMAL BAR
10 SO MUCH I
11 STORM IN A TEACUP
12 WE BELIEVE
13 TURN IT AGAIN
14 DEATH OF A MARTIAN

LABEL: WARNER BROTHER RECORDS
RELEASE DATE: MAY 9, 2006
PRODUCER: RICK RUBIN
RECORDED AT THE MANSION IN LAUREL CANYON, AKADEMIE MATHEMATIQUE OF PHILOSOPHICAL RESEARCH, THE CENTER FOR THE CULTIVATION OF THE INVISIBLE AND LITTLE KICKER SOUND
ALL SONGS BY ANTHONY KIEDIS, FLEA, JOHN FRUSCIANTE AND CHAD SMITH.

BY THE WAY

01 BY THE WAY
02 UNIVERSALLY SPEAKING
03 THIS IS THE PLACE
04 DOSED
05 DON'T FORGET ME
06 THE ZEPHYR SONG
07 CAN'T STOP
08 I COULD DIE FOR YOU
09 MIDNIGHT
10 THROW AWAY YOUR TELEVISION
11 CABRON
12 TEAR
13 ON MERCURY
14 MINOR THING
15 WARM TAPE
16 VENICE QUEEN

LABEL: WARNER BROTHER RECORDS
RELEASE DATE: JULY 9, 2002
PRODUCER: RICK RUBIN
RECORDED AT CELLO STUDIOS AND CHATEAU MARMONT; STRINGS RECORDED AT WARNER BROTHERS STUDIOS
ALL SONGS BY ANTHONY KIEDIS, FLEA, JOHN FRUSCIANTE AND CHAD SMITH.

CALIFORNICATION

01 AROUND THE WORLD
02 PARALLEL UNIVERSE
03 SCAR TISSUE
04 OTHERSIDE
05 GET ON TOP
06 CALIFORNICATION
07 EASILY
08 PORCELAIN
09 EMIT REMMUS
10 I LIKE DIRT
11 THIS VELVET GLOVE
12 SAVIOR
13 PURPLE STAIN
14 RIGHT ON TIME
15 ROAD TRIPPIN'

LABEL: WARNER BROS.
RELEASE DATE: JUNE 8, 1999
PRODUCER: RICK RUBIN
RECORDED AT CELLO STUDIOS
ALL SONGS BY ANTHONY KIEDIS, FLEA, JOHN FRUSCIANTE AND CHAD SMITH

ONE HOT MINUTE

01 WARPED
02 AEROPLANE
03 DEEP KICK
04 MY FRIENDS
05 COFFEE SHOP
06 PEA
07 ONE BIG MOB
08 WALKABOUT
09 TEARJERKER
10 ONE HOT MINUTE
11 FALLING INTO GRACE
12 SHALLOW BE THY GAME
13 TRANSCENDING

LABEL: WARNER BROS.
RELEASE DATE: SEPTEMBER 12, 1995
PRODUCER: RICK RUBIN
ALL SONGS WRITTEN BY ANTHONY KIEDIS, FLEA, DAVE NAVARRO AND CHAD SMITH

BLOOD SUGAR SEX MAGIK

01 THE POWER OF EQUALITY
02 IF YOU HAVE TO ASK
03 BREAKING THE GIRL
04 FUNKY MONKS
05 SUCK MY KISS
06 I COULD HAVE LIED
07 MELLOWSHIP SLINKY IN B MAJOR
08 THE RIGHTEOUS AND THE WICKED
09 GIVE IT AWAY
10 BLOOD SUGAR SEX MAGIK
11 UNDER THE BRIDGE
12 NAKED IN THE RAIN
13 APACHE ROSE PEACOCK
14 THE GREETING SONG
15 MY LOVELY MAN
16 SIR PSYCHO SEXY
17 THEY'RE RED HOT ♥

LABEL: WARNER BROS.
RELEASE DATE: SEPTEMBER 24, 1991
PRODUCER: RICK RUBIN
ENGINEER: BRENDAN O'BRIEN

RECORDED AT THE MANSION IN LAUREL CANYON
ALL SONGS WRITTEN BY ANTHONY KIEDIS, FLEA, JOHN FRUSCIANTE AND CHAD SMITH (EXCEPT ♥ BY ROBERT JOHNSON)
ALL PHOTOS BY GUS VAN ZANT
DEDICATED TO MIKE WATT

MOTHER'S MILK

01 GOOD TIME BOYS
02 HIGHER GROUND ♦
03 SUBWAY TO VENUS
04 MAGIC JOHNSON
05 NOBODY WEIRD LIKE ME
06 KNOCK ME DOWN
07 TASTE THE PAIN
08 STONE COLD BUSH
09 FIRE ♣
10 PRETTY LITTLE DITTY
11 PUNK ROCK CLASSIC
12 SEXY MEXICAN MAID ♥
13 JOHNNY, KICK A HOLE IN THE SKY

LABEL: EMI
RELEASE DATE: AUGUST 1989
PRODUCER: MICHAEL BEINHORN
ALL SONGS WRITTEN BY ANTHONY KIEDIS, FLEA, JOHN FRUSCIANTE AND CHAD SMITH (EXCEPT ♥ BY FRUSCIANTE, KIEDIS, FLEA AND D. H. PELIGRO; ♦ BY STEVIE WONDER; AND ♣ BY JIMI HENDRIX)

THE UPLIFT MOFO PARTY PLAN

01 FIGHT LIKE A BRAVE
02 FUNKY CRIME
03 ME AND MY FRIENDS
04 BACKWOODS
05 SKINNY SWEATY MAN
06 BEHIND THE SUN
07 SUBTERRANEAN HOMESICK BLUES ♦
08 SPECIAL SECRET SONG INSIDE
09 NO CHUMP LOVE SUCKER
10 WALKIN' ON DOWN THE ROAD ♦
11 LOVE TRILOGY
12 ORGANIC ANTI-BEAT BOX BAND

LABEL: EMI
RELEASE DATE: SEPTEMBER 29, 1987
PRODUCER: MICHAEL BEINHORN
ALL SONGS WRITTEN BY ANTHONY KIEDIS, FLEA, HILLEL SLOVAK AND JACK IRONS (EXCEPT ♥ MICHAEL BEINHORN, KIEDIS, FLEA, SLOVAK AND IRONS; ♦ FLEA, IRONS, KIEDIS, SLOVACK AND CLIFF MARTINEZ; AND ♦ BY BOB DYLAN)

FREAKY STYLEY

01 JUNGLE MAN
02 HOLLYWOOD ♥
03 AMERICAN GHOST DANCE
04 IF YOU WANT ME TO STAY ♦
05 NEVERMIND ♦
06 FREAKY STYLEY
07 BLACKEYED BLONDE
08 THE BROTHERS CUP
09 BATTLE SHIP
10 LOVIN' AND TOUCHIN'
11 CATHOLIC SCHOOL GIRLS RULE ♦

12 SEX RAP ♦
13 THIRTY DIRTY BIRDS
14 YERTLE THE TURTLE

LABEL: EMI
RELEASE DATE: AUGUST 16, 1985
PRODUCER: GEORGE CLINTON
RECORDED AT UNITED SOUND STUDIOS
ALL SONGS BY ANTHONY KIEDIS, FLEA, HILLEL SLOVAK AND CLIFF MARTINEZ (EXCEPT ♥ BY THE METERS; ♦ BY FLEA, KIEDIS, SLOVACK AND JACK IRONS; ♦ BY FLEA, KIEDIS AND MARTINEZ; ♦ SYLVESTER STEWART)

THE RED HOT CHILI PEPPERS

01 TRUE MEN DON'T KILL COYOTES
02 BABY APPEAL ♥
03 BUCKLE DOWN
04 GET UP AND JUMP ♥
05 WHY DON'T YOU LOVE ME ♦
06 GREEN HEAVEN
07 MOMMY WHERE'S DADDY
08 OUT IN L.A. ♥
09 POLICE HELICOPTER ♥
10 YOU ALWAYS SING THE SAME ♥
11 GRAND PAPPY DU PLENTY ♦

LABEL: EMI
RELEASE DATE: AUGUST 10, 1984
PRODUCER: ANDY GILL
ALL SONGS BY ANTHONY KIEDIS, FLEA, JACK SHERMAN AND CLIFF MARTINEZ (EXCEPT ♥ BY KIEDIS, FLEA, HILLEL SLOVAK AND JACK IRONS; ♦ BY FLEA, ANDY GILL, KIEDIS, MARTINEZ AND SHERMAN; AND ♦ BY HANK WILLIAMS

REMASTERS, COMPILATIONS, EPs AND LIVE ALBUMS

LIVE IN HYDE PARK

DISC 1
01 INTRO
02 CAN'T STOP
03 AROUND THE WORLD
04 SCAR TISSUE
05 BY THE WAY
06 FORTUNE FADED
07 I FEEL LOVE
08 OTHERSIDE
09 EASILY
10 UNIVERSALLY SPEAKING
11 GET ON TOP
12 BRANDY
13 DON'T FORGET ME
14 ROLLING SLY STONE

DISC 2
01 THROW AWAY YOUR TELEVISION
02 LEVERAGE OF SPACE
03 PURPLE STAIN
04 THE ZEPHYR SONG
05 CALIFORNICATION
06 RIGHT ON TIME
07 PARALLEL UNIVERSE
08 DRUM HOMAGE MEDLEY
09 UNDER THE BRIDGE
10 BLACK CROSS
11 FLEA'S TRUMPET TREATED BY JOHN
12 GIVE IT AWAY

LABEL: WEA INTERNATIONAL
RELEASE DATE: AUGUST 3, 2004

Live at Slane Castle

01 By the Way
02 Scar Tissue
03 Around the World
04 Universally Speaking
05 Parallel Universe
06 The Zephyr Song
07 Throw Away Your Television
08 Havana Affair
09 Midnight
10 Purple Stain
11 Don't Forget Me
12 Right on Time
13 Can't Stop
14 Venice Queen
15 Give it Away
16 Californication
17 Under the Bridge
18 The Power of Equality

Label: Warner Bros.
Release date: November 18, 2003

Mother's Milk
(Remastered Version)

01 Good Time Boys
02 Higher Ground
03 Subway to Venus
04 Magic Johnson
05 Nobody Weird Like Me
06 Knock Me Down
07 Taste the Pain
08 Stone Cold Bush
09 Fire
10 Pretty Little Ditty
11 Punk Rock Classic
12 Sexy Mexican Maid
13 Johnny, Kick a Hole in the Sky
14 Song That Made Us What
  We Are Today (demo version)
15 Knock Me Down
  (original long version)
16 Sexy Mexican Maid
  (original long version)
17 Salute to Kareem
  (demo w/guitar track)
18 Castles Made of Sand (live)
19 Crosstown Traffic (live)

Label: EMI
Release Date: 2003

The Uplift Mofo Party Plan
(Remastered Version)

01 Fight Like a Brave
02 Funky Crime
03 Me and My Friends
04 Backwoods
05 Skinny Sweaty Man
06 Behind the Sun
07 Subterranean Homesick Blues
08 Special Secret Song Inside
09 No Chump Love Sucker
10 Walkin' on Down the Road

11 Love Trilogy
12 Organic Anti-Beat Box Band
13 Behind the Sun
  (instrumental demo)
14 Me & My Friends
  (instrumental demo)

Label: EMI
Release date: 2003

Red Hot Chili Peppers
Greatest Hits

01 Under the Bridge
02 Give It Away
03 Californication
04 Scar Tissue
05 Soul to Squeeze
06 Otherside
07 Suck My Kiss
08 By the Way
09 Parallel Universe
10 Breaking the Girl
11 My Friends
12 Higher Ground
13 Universally Speaking
14 Road Trippin'
15 Fortune Faded
16 Save the Population

Label: Warner Bros.
Release date: November 18, 2003

Under the Covers: Essential
Red Hot Chili Peppers

01 They're Red Hot
02 Fire
03 Subterranean Homesick Blues
04 Higher Ground
05 If You Want Me to Stay
06 Why Don't You Love Me?
07 Tiny Dancer (live)
08 Castles Made of Sand (live)
09 Dr. Funkenstein (live)
10 Hollywood
11 Search and Destroy
12 Higher Ground (daddy-o mix)
13 Hollywood (extended dance mix)

Label: Capitol
Release date: March 1998

Off the Map (live)

01 Around the World
02 Give It Away
03 Usually Just a T Shirt #3
04 Scar Tissue
05 Suck My Kiss
06 If You Have to Ask
07 Subterranean Homesick Blues
08 Otherside
09 Blackeyed Blonde
10 Pea

11 Blood Sugar Sex Magik
12 Easily
13 What is Soul?
14 Fire
15 Californication
16 Right on Time
17 Under the Bridge
18 Me and My Friends

Label: WEA/Warner
Release date: December 18, 2001

The Best of the
Red Hot Chili Peppers

01 Behind the Sun
02 Johnny, Kick a Hole in the Sky
03 Me and My Friends
04 Fire
05 True Men Don't Kill Coyotes
06 Higher Ground
07 Knock Me Down
08 Fight Like a Brave
09 Taste the Pain
10 If You Want Me to Stay

Label: EMI
Release date: November 4, 1997

Out in L.A.

01 Higher Ground (12" vocal mix)
02 Hollywood (Africa)
  (extended dance mix)
03 If You Want Me to Stay
  (pink mustang mix)
04 Behind the Sun
  (Ben Grosse remix)
05 Castles Made of Sand (live)
06 Special Secret Song Inside (live)
07 F.U. (live)
08 Get Up and Jump (demo version)
09 Out in L.A. (demo version)
10 Green Heaven (demo version)
11 Police Helicopter (demo version)
12 Nevermind (demo version)
13 Sex Rap (demo version)
14 Blues for Meister
15 You Always Sing the Same
  (demo version)
16 Stranded (demo version)
17 Flea Fly (demo version)
18 What It Is (aka Nina's Song)
  (demo version)
19 Deck the Halls

Label: EMI
Release date: November 1, 1994

Plasma

Disc 1

01 The Power of Equality
02 If You Have to Ask
03 Breaking the Girl
04 Funky Monks
05 Suck My Kiss

06 I Could Have Lied
07 Mellowship Slinky in B Major
08 The Righteous and the Wicked
09 Give It Away
10 Blood Sugar Sex Magik
11 Under the Bridge
12 Naked in the Rain
13 Apache Rose Peacock
14 The Greeting Song
15 My Lovely Man
16 Sir Psycho Sexy
17 They're Red Hot

Disc 2

01 Give It Away (in progress)
02 If You Have to Ask (radio mix)
03 Nobody Weird Like Me (live)
04 Sikiamikanico
05 Breaking the Girl (radio edit)
06 Fela's Cock
07 If You Have to Ask (Friday night
  fever blister mix)
08 Soul 2 Squeeze

Label: Alex
Release date: June 27, 1994

What Hits!?

01 Higher Ground
02 Fight Like a Brave
03 Behind the Sun
04 Me and My Friends
05 Backwoods
06 True Men Don't Kill Coyotes
07 Fire
08 Get Up and Jump
09 Knock Me Down
10 Under the Bridge
11 Show Me Your Soul
12 If You Want Me to Stay
13 Hollywood
14 Jungle Man
15 The Brothers Cup
16 Taste the Pain
17 Catholic School Girls Rule
18 Johnny, Kick a Hole in the Sky

Label: Capitol
Release date: September 29, 1992

The Abbey Road EP

01 Fire
02 Backwoods
03 Catholic School Girls Rule
04 Hollywood
05 True Men Don't Kill Coyotes

Label: EMI
Release date: May 1988

WWW.REDHOTCHILIPEPPERS.COM

PHOTOGRAPHY CREDITS

MEET THE RED HOT CHILI PEPPERS 2

V: COURTESY OF THE AUTHOR; 2–3: KRISTIAN DOWLING/GETTY IMAGES; 4–5: TONY WOOLLISCROFT; 6: GODEFROIT MUSIC/LFI; 7: COURTESY OF *L.A. WEEKLY*, PHOTOGRAPH © 2002 GEOFF MOORE/ICON INTERNATIONAL; 8: COURTESY OF THE AUTHOR; 9: TONY WOOLLISCROFT; 10–11: TONY WOOLLISCROFT; 12–13: TONY WOOLLISCROFT

MUSICAL CHAIRS: THE MAKING OF THE BAND 15

14–15: MICHAEL HALSBAND/LANDOV; 18: ANN SUMMA; 19: EDWARD COLVER; 20: NELS ISRAELSON; 21, TOP: IVY NEY; 21, MIDDLE: FABRICE DROUET; 21, BOTTOM LEFT: COURTESY OF THE AUTHOR; 21, BOTTOM RIGHT: NELS ISRAELSON; 23: DAVID HERMON; 25: JOY SCHELLER/LFI; 26–27: TONY WOOLLISCROFT; 28, TOP: GARY LEONARD; 28, RIGHT SIDE: EDWARD COLVER; 29: DAVID HERMON; 30: BRUCE WEBER; 30, INSET: COURTESY OF THE AUTHOR; 31, TOP: ARMANDO GALLO; 31, MIDDLE: TONY WOOLLISCROFT: 31, BOTTOM: SUZAN/AA/RETNA; 32: ANTHONY ST. JAMES/RETNA; 33: ROBERT MATHEU/RETNA; 34–35: EDWARD COLVER; 37: CHRIS CLUNN; 38–39: EDWARD COLVER; 40: NELS ISRAELSON; 41, TOP: NELS ISRAELSON; 41, MIDDLE: COURTESY OF THE AUTHOR; 41, BOTTOM: WILLIAM HAMES 42–43: MICHAEL HALSBAND/LANDOV; 46–47: MICHAEL INSUASTE; 48: TONY WOOLLISCROFT; 49: LISA JOHNSON; 50: JUSTIN BORUKI/RETNA; 52–53: JAMES CUMPSTY; 54–55: NELS ISRAELSON; 56: TONY WOOLLISCROFT; 57: © HARRY F. DALRYMPLE & YUKI SAKURAI; 59: TONY WOOLLISCROFT; 61: FRANK FORCINO/LFI; 62: TONY WOOLLISCROFT; 64: CHRIS CUFFARO/JBG PHOTO; 66: © CATHERINE MCGANN PHOTOGRAPHY; 67: KEVIN ESTRADA/RETNA; 68: CHRIS CUFFARO/JBG PHOTO; 69: TONY WOOLLISCROFT; 70–71: SUNSHINE/RETNA

HEART AND SOUL: FLEA AND ANTHONY 72

72–73: KEVIN ESTRADA/RETNA; 74–75: COURTESY OF THE AUTHOR; 76–77: MICHAEL INSUASTE; 78: NELS ISRAELSON; 79: EDWARD COLVER; 80: TONY WOOLLISCROFT; 81: KEVIN MAZUR/GETTY; 83, TOP AND BOTTOM: COURTESY OF THE AUTHOR; 83, MIDDLE: EDWARD COLVER; 85: COURTESY OF THE AUTHOR; 86: GARY LEONARD; 87: LYNDA BURDICK; 88: EDWARD COLVER; 89: TONY WOOLLISCROTT; 90: LYNDA BURDICK; 91: IVY NEY; 92–93, LYNDA BURDICK; 94–95 TONY WOOLLISCROFT; 96: GARY LEONARD; 97: DAVID HERMON; 98: © THE ANDY WARHOL FOUNDATION/CORBIS; 99: © THE ANDY WARHOL FOUNDATION/CORBIS; 100: ANN SUMMA; 101: COURTESY OF RUBEN MACBLUE

REFLECTIONS AND RUMINATIONS: ANTHONY CHAD FLEA JOHN 103

102–103: STEPHEN STICKLER; 104–105: JACKIE BUTLER; 106: MB CHARLES/RETNA; 107, TOP: SUNSHINE/RETNA; 107, MIDDLE: COURTESY OF THE AUTHOR; 107, BOTTOM: GARY LEONARD; 108: ANN SUMMA; 109: ANN SUMMA; 110: PHOTOGRAPH BY OPHELIA WYNNE, CAMERA PRESS LONDON; 111: TONY WOOLLISCROFT; 113: JAMES CUMPSTY; 114: BRUCE WEBER; 114–115, INSETS: TONY WOOLLISCROFT; 116: DAVID HERMON; 117: CLAY PATRICK MCBRIDE; 118: TONY WOOLLISCROFT; 119: TONY WOOLLISCROFT; 120: FOTOS INTERNATIONAL/GETTY IMAGES; 121: GODEFROIT MUSIC/LFI; 122–123: TONY WOOLLISCROFT; 124: NELS ISRAELSON; 126: PAMELA LITTKY/RETNA; 127: PAMELA LITTKY/RETNA; 128: FRANK MICELOTTA/GETTY; 129: CHRIS CLUNN; 130–131: GARY MALERBA/CORBIS; 132: JAY BLAKESBERG/RETNA; 133: JAY BLAKESBERG/RETNA 134: COURTESY OF THE AUTHOR; 135: COURTESY OF THE AUTHOR; 137: SUSAN MERRELL

THE CREATIVE PROCESS: IN THE STUDIO AND ON THE ROAD 139

138–139: EBET ROBERTS; 140: MICHEAL SCHREIBER; 141: FRANK MICELOTTA/GETTY; 142: LYNDA BURDICK; 143: DAVID HERMON; 144: DAVID HERMON; 145: NELS ISRAELSON; 146: NELS ISRAELSON; 148: EDWARD COLVER; 149: ANN SUMMA; 150–151: CLIFF MARTINEZ; 152: COURTESY OF THE AUTHOR; 154: LYNDA BURDICK; 155: DAVID HERMON; 156–157: EDWARD COLVER; 159: LISA JOHNSON; 160: NELS ISRAELSON; 161: DAVID HERMON; 162: FABRICE DROUET; 163: SANTE D'ORAZIO; 164: WILLIAM HAMES; 166–167: CHRIS CLUNN; 168: JAY BLAKESBERG/RETNA; 169: LISA JOHNSON; 171, ALL: JEFF KRAVITZ/GETTY; 173: COURTESY OF THE AUTHOR; 174–175: SUNSHINE/RETNA; 176: GUY OSEARY; 177–178: ARMANDO GALLO; 178–179: HENRY DILTZ/CORBIS; 182: COURTESY OF THE AUTHOR; 183: EDWARD COLVER; 184: TONY WOOLLISCROFT: 186: MICHAEL INSUASTE; 188: JEFF KATZ; 190–191: TONY WOOLLISCROFT; 192: TONY WOOLLISCROFT; 194: KEVIN MAZUR/GETTY; 195: JACKIE BUTLER; 196: MARC MORRISON/RETNA; 197: TONY WOOLLISCROFT; 198: EBET ROBERTS; 199: COURTESY OF THE AUTHOR; 200–201: IVAN NIKITIN/GETTY; 202–203: TONY WOOLLISCROFT; 204: ROBERT MATHEU/RETNA; 205: ARMANDO GALLO; 206–207: JOE TRAVER/GETTY; 208: MICHAEL INSUASTE; 209: MICHAEL INSUASTE; 210: STEPHEN STICKLER; 212: STEVE STARR/CORBIS; 213: *L.A. TIMES*; 214: WILLIAM HAMES; 215: SANTE D'ORAZIO; 216–217: TONY WOOLLISCROFT; 219: JAMES CUMPSTY; 220: JACKIE BUTLER; 222: COURTESY OF THE AUTHOR; 223: CHRIS CUFFARO/JBG PHOTO; 224–225: TONY WOOLLISCROFT; 226–227: KEVIN ESTRADA/RETNA; 228: MICHAEL INSUASTE

THE DOT DOT DOTS . . . 231

230–231: JACKIE BUTLER; 232: MICHAEL INSUASTE; 233: ANTHONY ST. JAMES/RETNA; 234: TONY WOOLLISCROFT; 235: TONY WOOLLISCROFT; 236–237: PHOTOGRAPH BY MARK O'FLAHERTY, CAMERA PRESS LONDON

TIMELINE 237

1980s

238–239: BACKGROUND PHOTOGRAPH: EBET ROBERTS

JANUARY 6, 1983: LYNDA BURDICK
DECEMBER 1983: GARY LEONARD
OCTOBER 1984: LYNDA BURDICK
JANUARY 1985: WILLIAM HAMES
JANUARY 1986: SUNSHINE / RETNA
JUNE 25, 1988: CHRIS CLUNN
NOVEMBER 1988: LISA JOHNSON
DECEMBER 1988: TONY WOOLLISCROFT
SEPTEMBER 9, 1989: TONY WOOLLISCROFT

1990s

240–241: BACKGROUND PHOTOGRAPH: STEVE DOUBLE/RETNA
JULY–SEPTEMBER 1992: CATHERINE MCGANN/GETTY
SEPTEMBER 1993: JEFF KATZ PHOTOGRAPHY
APRIL 1998: TONY WOOLLISCROFT
JUNE–SEPTEMBER 1998: TONY WOOLLISCROFT

2000s

242–243: BACKGROUND PHOTOGRAPH: SANDRA JOHNSON/RETNA
AUGUST 2001: TONY WOOLLISCROFT
OCTOBER 2004: ANTHONY PIDGEON/RETNA
SEPTEMBER 27, 2008: MAX SMITH/RETNA
MAY 5, 2007: STACY KRANITZ/CORBIS

DISCOGRAPHY 244

LIVE IN HYDE PARK © 2004, WARNER BROS. RECORDS INC.
LIVE AT SLANE CASTLE © 2003, WARNER BROS. RECORDS INC.
GREATEST HITS © 2003, WARNER BROS. RECORDS INC.
OFF THE MAP (LIVE) © 2001, WARNER BROS. RECORDS INC.
THE PLASMA SHAFT © 1994, WARNER BROS. RECORDS INC.
STADIUM ARCADIUM © 2006, WARNER BROS. RECORDS INC.
BY THE WAY © 2002, WARNER BROS. RECORDS INC.
CALIFORNICATION © 1999, WARNER BROS. RECORDS INC.
ONE HOT MINUTE © 1995, WARNER BROS. RECORDS INC.
BLOOD SUGAR SEX MAGIK © 1991, WARNER BROS. RECORDS INC.

ALBUM ARTWORK COURTESY OF CAPITOL RECORDS, LLC:
THE UPLIFT MOFO PARTY PLAN
FREAKY STYLEY
THE RED HOT CHILI PEPPERS

PHOTO RESEARCH AND EDITING BY LISA CORSON

INDEX

HARPERCOLLINS BOOKS MAY BE PURCHASED FOR EDUCATIONAL, BUSINESS, OR SALES PROMOTIONAL USE. FOR INFORMATION, PLEASE WRITE: SPECIAL MARKETS DEPARTMENT, HARPERCOLLINS PUBLISHERS, 10 EAST 53RD STREET, NEW YORK, NY 10022.

FIRST EDITION

LIBRARY OF CONGRESS CATALOGING-IN-PUBLICATION DATA HAS BEEN APPLIED FOR.

ISBN 978-0-06-135191-4

10 11 12 13 14   ID4/RRD   10 9 8 7 6 5 4 3 2

PRINTED AND BOUND BY BUTLER TANNER AND DENNIS LTD, FROME AND LONDON.

DESIGN BY JOHN CURRY/SMARTPILL
www.smartpillmedia.com